The Presidency of
THOMAS
JEFFERSON

AMERICAN PRESIDENCY SERIES

Donald R. McCoy, Clifford S. Griffin, Homer E. Socolofsky
General Editors

George Washington, Forrest McDonald
John Adams, Ralph Adams Brown
Thomas Jefferson, Forrest McDonald
James Madison, Robert Allen Rutland
John Quincy Adams, Mary W. M. Hargreaves
Andrew Jackson, Donald B. Cole
Martin Van Buren, Major L. Wilson
William Henry Harrison & John Tyler, Norma Lois Peterson
James K. Polk, Paul H. Bergeron
Zachary Taylor & Millard Fillmore, Elbert B. Smith
Franklin Pierce, Larry Gara
James Buchanan, Elbert B. Smith
Abraham Lincoln, Phillip Shaw Paludan
Andrew Johnson, Albert Castel
Rutherford B. Hayes, Ari Hoogenboom
James A. Garfield & Chester A. Arthur, Justus D. Doenecke
Grover Cleveland, Richard E. Welch, Jr.
Benjamin Harrison, Homer B. Socolofsky & Allan B. Spetter
William McKinley, Lewis L. Gould
Theodore Roosevelt, Lewis L. Gould
William Howard Taft, Paolo E. Coletta
Woodrow Wilson, Kendrick A. Clements
Warren G. Harding, Eugene P. Trani & David L. Wilson
Herbert C. Hoover, Martin L. Fausold
Harry S. Truman, Donald R. McCoy
Dwight D. Eisenhower, Chester J. Pach, Jr., & Elmo Richardson
John F. Kennedy, James N. Giglio
Lyndon B. Johnson, Vaughn Davis Bornet
James Earl Carter, Jr., Burton I. Kaufman

The Presidency of
THOMAS
JEFFERSON

by
Forrest McDonald

UNIVERSITY PRESS OF KANSAS

© 1976 by the University Press of Kansas

Published by the University Press of Kansas (Lawrence, Kansas 66049),
which was organized by the Kansas Board of Regents and is
operated and funded by Emporia State Univesity, Fort Hays State
University, Kansas State University, Pittsburg State University,
the University of Kansas, and Wichita State University

Library of Congress Cataloging in Publication Data

McDonald, Forrest.
The Presidency of Thomas Jefferson.

(American Presidency series)
Bibliography: p.
Includes index
1. United States—Politics and government—1801–1809.
      I. Title   II. Series.
E331.M32   320.9′73′046   76-803
      ISBN 0-7006-0147-3

Printed in the United States of America

10 9 8 7

Editors' Preface

The aim of the American Presidency Series is to present historians and the general reading public with interesting, scholarly assessments of the various presidential administrations. These interpretive surveys are intended to cover the broad ground between biographies, specialized monographs, and journalistic accounts. As such, each will be a comprehensive, synthetic work which will draw upon the best in pertinent secondary literature, yet leave room for the author's own analysis and interpretation.

Each volume in the series will deal with a separate presidential administration and will present the data essential to understanding the administration under consideration. Particularly, each book will treat the then current problems facing the United States and its people and how the president and his associates felt about, thought about, and worked to cope with these problems. Attention will be given to how the office developed and operated during the president's tenure. Equally important will be consideration of the vital relationships between the president, his staff, the executive officers, Congress, foreign representatives, the judiciary, state officials, the public, political parties, the press, and influential private citizens. The series will also be concerned with how this unique American institution—the presidency—was viewed by the presidents, and with what results.

All this will be set, insofar as possible, in the context not only of contemporary politics but also of economics, international relations, law, morals, public administration, religion, and thought. Such a broad approach is necessary to understanding, for a presidential administration is more than the elected and appointed officers composing it, since its work so often reflects the major problems, anxieties, and glories of the nation. In short, the authors in the series will strive to recount and evaluate the record of each administration and to identify its distinctiveness and relationships to the past, its own time, and the future.

Donald R. McCoy
Clifford S. Griffin
Homer E. Socolofsky

v

Preface

Of all the presidents of the United States, none save Washington and Lincoln have inspired half so much historical writing as Thomas Jefferson. Books and articles by the score have dealt with the Sage of Monticello in one or another of his myriad aspects—Virginian, statesman, philosopher, scientist, farmer, architect, rationalist, theologian, slaveholder, apostle of liberty, author of the Declaration of Independence. His most intimate letters have been published and analysed and published again; pedants have used his offhand utterances as the basis for ponderous tomes; there have been treatises on his health, his psyche, his sex life, and the history of his reputation. One could, in fact, spend years reading the literature on Jefferson and never come close to exhausting the supply.

But there is a curious thing about this huge volume of writing: precious little of it is concerned with Jefferson as president, though that was the most important (as well as the most dramatic) phase of his long public career. It is almost as if there were a conspiracy of silence on the matter. Only two historians, Henry Adams and Dumas Malone, have essayed major works on Jefferson's presidency, and both those works are veritable lawyers' briefs, one for the prosecution and the other for the defense. Indeed, any literate person with access to a good library could read virtually every line even tangentially related to the subject in a month or so.

There are, I believe, two main reasons why historians have steered clear of Jefferson's presidency. The first is the towering figure of Henry Adams. Adams had independent means and a genteel background, and he lived and worked in a slower-paced world than our own; and all that, as well as his superlative mind, contributed to making possible his monumental, nine-volume *History of the United States during the Administrations of Thomas Jefferson and James Madison*. Moreover, Adams's skill as a literary craftsman has rarely been excelled by anyone writing in the English language, and certainly by no American historian. Any historian who ventures into territory where Henry Adams trod does so with either trepidation or foolhardy courage—lest one offend not only Clio, the muse of History, but also Calliope, the muse of Epic Poetry.

The other reason derives from Jefferson's peculiar niche in the hagiology of America's Founding Fathers. To all but the handful who still idolize Alexander Hamilton or John Adams, Jefferson is holier than holy, and the Hamiltonians and Adamsites have long since abandoned the effort to point out what they regard as weaknesses, inconsistencies, and blunders in Jefferson's presidency. To everyone else, though Jefferson is sacrosanct, his canonization derives from his being the patron saint of one or another of a bewildering variety of ideological positions. Statists and libertarians, nationalists and states' righters, conservatives and radicals—all claim his blessing; but if and when they look into the eight years during which Jefferson wore the splendid lonely mantle of presidential power, such "Jeffersonians" learn quickly that their hero was himself not what they could properly regard as a Jeffersonian. Accordingly, they shun the presidency and return to rummaging through Jefferson's voluminous and eclectic correspondence, where they can find comforting support for the ideology of their choice.

My own approach to Jefferson has been along rather different lines. Though the man fascinates me as he has fascinated others, I, unlike most historians, am more interested in what he did than in what, as a matter of abstract intellectuality, he said and thought— except insofar as his words and ideas reflect the broad social matrix on which he and his followers erected all their ideological thinking. And there is another thing. Throughout most of my adult life I have lived and taught in northern urban centers, have been concerned with subjects relating to economics and fiscal policy, and have directed the larger part of my researches toward the 1780s and 1790s. My orientation, in other words, has been what might loosely be styled Hamiltonian. For the past few years, however, I have been increasingly interested in ethnicity and other aspects of the cultural anthropology of early, rural, and especially southern American life. As a part of that interest, I have been attracted to the Jeffersonians, and among other things I conducted, for ten or twelve academic quarters, a seminar on that subject at Wayne State University. Then, eighteen months ago, I moved away from northern urban climes to a small farm in the deep South. Here, in

Jefferson's phrase, I have been laboring in the earth, and I have been observing at close range the kind of rural folk who were the original backbone of the Jeffersonian party—in all their meanness and grandness, their bigotry and openness, their clannishness and hospitality.

One other element went into my decision to have a go at Jefferson's presidency, and that was a gradual realization that the eighteenth-century tradition of agrarian oppositionism, far from being the tangential phenomenon that historians have generally treated it as having been, was absolutely central to the ideology of Jeffersonian Republicanism. Years ago Professor Thomas P. Govan, in that uncanny way he has of making an offhand remark that penetrates to the very heart of a complex matter, said to me that very nearly everything in Jeffersonian Republicanism was to be found in Bolingbroke. He referred to Henry St. John, First Viscount Bolingbroke, the English Tory who in the 1720s and 1730s led the Opposition to Sir Robert Walpole and the English Financial Revolution—the British predecessor of the Hamiltonian fiscal revolution in America. At that time I had no ready way of looking into the suggestion, for virtually no one (but Govan) knew much of anything about Bolingbroke except that he was involved in various treasonable plots to overthrow the Hanoverians. Then, in 1968, Isaac Kramnick published a brilliant pioneering work called *Bolingbroke and His Circle*, which elucidated Bolingbroke's thinking and made Professor Govan's remark comprehensible. Meanwhile Bernard Bailyn and his students have shed light upon the influence in America of some of Bolingbroke's predecessors, notably John Trenchard and Thomas Gordon; Trevor Colbourn has rediscovered the Anglo-Saxon myth and its influence upon both Bolingbroke and Jefferson; and one of my own students, Rodger D. Parker, has recently completed an exhaustive dissertation on Bolingbroke and the whole range of Oppositionists who preceded and followed him and carried his ideas to America. To anyone steeped in the propaganda, the political tracts, and the rhetoric of the Jeffersonian Republicans in the 1790s and afterward—as I have been for a long time—the connections are overwhelmingly clear.

Thus fortified with a different (and I believe sound) perspective, I have become emboldened to venture this work on Jefferson's presidency. As to trespassing upon Henry Adams's turf, I can only pay my sincere homage to the man and his work, and be on with the task.

In this undertaking I have incurred considerable debts of gratitude. Librarians at several institutions were most helpful; I should particularly like to thank the library personnel at the Alderman Library of the University of Virginia, James Servies of the University of West Florida, and the American Council of Learned Societies, whose financial assistance made travel to various repositories possible. Professors Thomas P. Govan, William G. McLoughlin, Grady McWhiney, John S. Pancake, Donald R. McCoy, Clifford S. Griffin, and Homer Socolofsky generously read all or parts of the manuscript and gave me the benefit of their expertise and keen critical judgment. Mrs. Virginia Seaver, in editing the manuscript, not only brought her high standards and talents to bear, but was also, as usual, a joy to work with. I hesitate to mention the person who was most helpful of all—Ellen Shapiro McDonald, my wife, partner, research assistant, typist, business manager, and general factotum—for to acknowledge her help is to suggest that I could have done the work without her, only with more difficulty; and that is not the way things are. Rather, though it may be true that no man is indispensable, there is an indispensable woman.

Forrest McDonald

Walton County, Florida
October 1975

Contents

1

★★★★★

THE FAITHFUL AND
THE CRISIS OF FAITH

By most objective criteria, the Americans of 1800 had abundant cause to be proud, confident, even smug. As yet, it is true, they had produced few painters, fewer poets, and no composers, had built no cathedrals, could scarcely be reckoned as a military power. But these were measures of quality and achievement in the Old World, and in terms of the more materialistic and quantified standards that would prevail in the aborning nineteenth century, the United States had already accomplished mightily and was on its way to greatness. It had firmly established a government system, based upon popular consent and written law, whose jurisdiction spread over an area of 888,000 square miles. Its population had doubled in the scant twenty-four years that the nation had existed, from around two and a half million people to more than five. The country was prosperous and was rapidly growing wealthy; the value of its imports and exports had nearly quintupled in the eleven years since the founding of the national government under the Constitution. And the bounty was widely shared: more Americans owned land than Europeans did, though there were thirty Europeans for every American, and more Americans had a real voice in their government.

And yet a sense of decadence had plagued the land for five years and more. From the pulpit rang cries of despair and doom; dishonesty as well as panic had invaded the marketplace; liars and libelers made a travesty of freedom of the press; violence, hysteria,

1

and paranoia infested the public councils. Those Americans who called themselves Federalists felt betrayed by an ungrateful people for whom they had labored long and well, and feared that the horrors of Jacobinism and anarchy were hourly imminent. Those who called themselves Republicans felt betrayed by the twin evils of money and monarchy, and feared that liberty was about to breathe its last. Many who embraced neither political sect, whether from apathy or disgust, nonetheless shared the general feeling that the nation was in an advanced state of moral rot.

What the Federalists thought was actually of little consequence, for they were soon to expire, in what Thomas Jefferson called the Revolution of 1800. Almost miraculously, with their demise—though not because of it—despair suddenly gave way to euphoria. The new optimism, like the pervasive gloom and the defeat of Federalism that preceded it, stemmed from an interplay of social, religious, ideological, and economic forces and institutions, and from certain ingrained American characteristics. If one would understand the Jeffersonian revolution—how it happened and how it affected the nation's destiny—one must seek first to understand those forces, institutions, and characteristics.

One of the tenets of Republicanism in America was that, contrary to the teachings of Montesquieu and other theorists, republican government was best adapted to large territories, since in an area as vast as the United States the very diversity of the people would prevent an accumulation of power inimical to liberty. If the principle was sound, the Americans were truly blessed, for their culture was nothing if not plural. At first blush that generalization might appear strong, or indeed entirely unfounded. Overwhelmingly, Americans were farmers or traders of British extraction and the Protestant faith; and even in politics, as Jefferson said in his inaugural address, "we are all republicans, we are all federalists." But the mother country itself was scarcely homogeneous, despite the amalgamation that financial and governmental power had brought to Great Britain in the eighteenth century; it comprised a host of different Celtic peoples—the Irish, the Welsh, the Cornish, and three distinct varieties of Scots—as well as Englishmen who differed from one another from north to south and east to west. Americans had proved slow to cast off the cultural baggage that they or their ancestors had brought with them; and a generation of independence, though building some sense of nationhood, had erased neither their original ethnic traits nor the intense localism that complemented and nourished those traits. As to differences in political principles, Jefferson was right in regarding them as largely superficial; yet they were substantive enough to lead many men to fight, and some to kill, one another.

European travelers to the United States repeatedly recorded evidence of the diversity, though they were not always aware of what they were seeing because they were looking for qualities that made Americans one people. Typically, a traveler set out to write a general description of the Americans for a European audience; but he no sooner completed an account than, upon visiting another part of the country, he found that revision was in order. A historical tour over the same terrain will be more revealing, for advance notice of the differences heightens their visibility.

We may begin as a traveler would, in the cities. To be sure, that is to start with the atypical, for the United States was overwhelmingly rural: nineteen Americans in twenty lived on farms or in villages of fewer than 2,500 inhabitants. Philadelphia, with nearly 70,000 souls, and New York, with 60,000, were as large as any English-speaking cities outside London, but the next-ranked American cities were far smaller, Baltimore being third with 26,000, Boston fourth with 25,000, and Charleston fifth with 20,000. Only seven others had more than 5,000, and only another dozen had more than 2,500.

Yet the cities had life styles of their own, and that—together with the influence and wealth they commanded, the frequency of communication between them, and the web of commercial networks they constituted—made them a subculture distinct from the rest of the nation. In part the difference lay in physical circumstances. Proximity of people to one another was the most obvious and important of these, but there was also the high quality of life, at least in comparison with European cities or most American farms. Though lighting, sanitation, fire-fighting, and police services were crude or nonexistent, and though Thomas Jefferson and many other country dwellers refused to set foot in any city during the "sickly months" of July and August except on urgent business, American cities were relatively clean, attractive, orderly, and safe. Some of them also offered theater, music, learned and scientific societies, and museums as well as the bustle and opportunity of commercial activity.

But there was another, a more subtle, quality that set the cities apart, namely their system of social organization. In keeping with

3

a tradition that dated back to William the Conquerer, American cities derived their legal and political existence from charters of incorporation. Every urban place of consequence except Boston, which continued to be governed by the town-meeting system, owed its formal existence to an act of a farmer-dominated state legislature. In the English tradition, only designated persons or classes—merchants, traders, master craftsmen, and sometimes their professional adjuncts—were members of the corporate body. All others who might reside in the city (the "mobs" whom Jefferson regarded as contributing "so much to the support of pure government, as sores do to the strength of the human body") were socially and politically nonexistent. State legislatures in the United States, influenced as they were by republican principles and bills of rights, had granted charters that were less rigidly restrictive, but in their social substance American cities were not drastically different from the English model. That is to say, they were ruled by small, hierarchically ordered groups, with merchants, traders, lawyers, and "gentlemen" at the apex and tradesmen, shopkeepers, master craftsmen, and sometimes their journeymen at the base. This group normally constituted around a quarter of a city's population. All the other inhabitants—including apprentices, unskilled workers, sailors, servants, slaves, and rabble—were entitled to show deference toward their betters, and to do almost nothing else. In a manner of speaking, the upper class was the only class; urban affairs were a matter of private, not public, concern.

Yet society was open and fluid. Any man who became moderately wealthy by playing the commercial game honestly and according to the rules, as hundreds in every city did every year, was readily admitted into its ranks; he who played dishonestly or lost his fortune, as many also did, was as readily dropped. Furthermore, though local loyalties and rivalries between urban centers were extremely intense, individual members of society who moved from one city to another found themselves accepted and in familiar circumstances almost at once. As a result, it was in the cities, not on the remote frontier, that traditional ethnic and religious differences were most rapidly eroded, and where aristocratic family connections were least likely to be perpetuated.

This democratic oligarchy of the talented and the lucky was in process of becoming far more democratic, for the basis of urban society was being greatly expanded through institutional innovations. Since 1793, when the wars of the French Revolution began in earnest, American commerce had been booming on a phenomenal scale—partly because inflation in Europe had increased the value of American staples, partly because American shippers had been allowed to act as neutral carriers of the goods of belligerents. The boom brought floods of newcomers pouring into the cities from abroad as well as from neighboring towns and farms, with the result that traditional restraints were breaking down. What was more important, it created more and bigger opportunities for profit than members of the commercial elite could capitalize upon within the framework of their existing institutions and ways of doing business.[1]

In response, they made three sets of adjustments whose long-range consequences were enormous. The first was to embrace group or associational activities—principally in the form of joint-stock companies but also including corporations—which facilitated the pooling of capital or the spreading of risks necessary for profiting from large-scale ventures or for providing hazardous but vital services. This had been done before, but only, as a rule, on a small or temporary scale. The second was to create banks, which enabled merchants to enlarge their operating capitals by monetizing their expectations of future profits. The number of banks in the United States grew from three at the time of the adoption of the Constitution to twenty-nine when Jefferson was inaugurated, and would increase fourfold again during Jefferson's presidency. The third was to condescend to go political. The great international merchants, who were overwhelmingly Federalist in 1787–1788 and were still so throughout most of Washington's first term, had begun by 1793 to perceive that state political power could facilitate their associational and banking activities; and they broke from the Federalist ranks and courted the urban multitudes as well as farmer-politicians in order to gain that power. Rather, some of them did. The "merchant-Republicans" of New York City, then the Mifflinites of Pennsylvania, then the Smith faction in Baltimore, and then counterparts in other cities departed in that manner from the company of their more conservative peers. Into the bargain they made it possible for the "agrarian" Thomas Jefferson to become president of the United States.

But that, as far as the character of life in the cities was concerned, was not the most significant product of their efforts. More so were the effects of their opportunistic activities upon urban social forms and norms. Relying on group forms of business enterprise—and especially the extreme profitability of so doing—considerably undermined the traditional reliance upon individual or family ac-

5

tivity, and also broadened the base of society by allowing small investors to participate in grand undertakings. Banking proved extremely advantageous, but it also democratized and depersonalized credit by making credit dependent upon collateral rather than upon reputation or personal and family connections. Going political helped to maximize opportunity and helped to make the rich richer; but it also entailed indulging in a resort to democratic rhetoric, and thus split the ranks of the elite and simultaneously taught the lower orders of men to forget their place.

The more conservative of the merchants saw the new activities in just such terms, and were willing to foresake opportunity and profit rather than change their accustomed ways. The more daring were the wave of the future.

The rest of the nation consisted of farms and rural towns, but it was far from uniform: it comprised five broad, regional subcultures that differed from one another as greatly as the cities differed from the country. In declining order of economic importance, though not of political influence, they were the Middle Atlantic region, the lower South, New England, the upper South, and the West.

The inhabitants of the middle region—where Scotch-Irishmen raised livestock and almost everybody else raised wheat—were prosperous, industrious, ethnically and religiously diverse, and by and large the most sophisticated of nonurban Americans. No single ethnic or religious group made up more than a third of the population in New York, New Jersey, Pennsylvania, and Delaware, though perhaps half the people were Calvinists of one sort or another, mainly Scotch-Irish Presbyterians and transplanted New England Congregationalists. But Englishmen, Welshmen, Germans, Dutchmen, Scandinavians, and blacks were all numerous, and their religious orientations ranged from Anglican and Quaker to Moravian and Dutch Reformed.

Conditions of life in the area were conducive to frequent contact between the members of this polyglot population, and that was the key to its relative sophistication. Communication between the country towns and New York and Philadelphia, carried on in the normal course of trade, was made easy by the abundance of navigable waterways and passable roads. The merchants and storekeepers who conducted this trade were also carriers of information and ideas from the outside world; and a host of newspapers, published in the larger towns as well as in the cities, circulated throughout the region. Perhaps most important, political activity (especially in Pennsylvania and New York) was intensely partisan, highly organized, and oriented toward national and international as well as local concerns. All these things homogenized and democratized the area, making it at once less provincial and more self-consciously American than any other part of the United States.

But there was a disruptive force in the society, one that threatened at all times to return the area to the turbulence it had known on the eve of the Revolution and in the early days of the Republic. This was the habit of indulging in ethnic politics, a practice particularly common among the Scotch-Irish. A coalition of Scotch-Irish with Yankees had radicalized Pennsylvania during the Revolution, and Ulstermen in New York had formed the backbone of the Clintonian party, which wrested power from the manor-lord aristocracy. Such coalitions came and went, but whenever the Scotch-Irish formed a part of them, instability was almost sure to follow, for the Scotch-Irish were eminently gifted in all the political arts save the most important—that of the ability to compromise. The Ulsterman's instinct on gaining power, first and always, was to destroy his enemies.

Far to the south lay the second regional subculture, that of the slave-manned rice plantations in the low country of South Carolina and Georgia. The rice planters were proud, highly cultured, and rich beyond belief, at least by American standards. They were also socially the most self-confident of Americans, despite being outnumbered by their slaves by a ratio of six to one. Children of this aristocracy grew up believing that all land and every soul for a day's ride in any direction belonged to their families or their kin, and learning that a seat in the legislature more or less went with the lands. In their teens they went to London to study and afterwards toured the Continent, discovering that the world consisted of interesting people who were less blessed than themselves. As adults they lived in splendor, reckoned slaves as the only genuine wealth, regarded women as having certain rights (for instance, women could own slaves and land), and believed their social order to be immutable and immortal.

Except for the possibility, usually remote, of slave uprisings, there was only one discordant note in their lives, and that emanated from the same source as it did in the Middle States, namely the Scotch-Irish. The South Carolina back country was overrun with Ulstermen; and though the interior of Georgia—which stretched all the way to the Mississippi River—was dominated by Indians, it was also teeming with Scotch-Irishmen and with Yankees as well. The

7

rice planters in Georgia had long since ceased to dominate the state's government, and the state's politicians were as uncouth a band of brigands as ever graced a statehouse. Planter-politicians in South Carolina still controlled state government (and prevented the development of autonomous local government) by virtue of a legislative apportionment system that disregarded the distribution of the voting population, but they also had a longer-range method for coping with the Scotch-Irish. That method wants some notice, for it was of considerable importance in the Jeffersonian era and would be of even great moment in the future.

In a word, the method was to assimilate the back-country men, to absorb them into the aristocracy. The South Carolina nabobs, unlike the tobacco planters of Virginia, made little pretense of being English country gentlemen who stood above sordid commerce: they were unabashedly and opportunistically commercial, and their society was open and fluid in much the same way that urban society was. As long as the Scotch-Irish continued to be primarily cattle herders and hog raisers, as most of them were, they could form no part of the planters' scheme of things except as suppliers of food. But increasing numbers of them, since the invention of the gin in 1793, had gone into the planting of short-staple cotton, with ever-growing gangs of slaves. Cotton exported from the United States, mainly from Charleston, had increased from 200,000 pounds in 1791 to 18 million by 1800, and would quadruple again before Jefferson's presidency ended. All but a few bales of this was grown on the uplands of the Carolinas and Georgia by herdsmen-turned-planters. True to the rules of the game as they played it, the South Carolina rice planters admitted the new-rich cotton planters into their ranks as equals, even as they had admitted the French Huguenots many years earlier. But the Scotch-Irish were a different people entirely from the Huguenots. They were also far more numerous, and to attempt to assimilate them was to invite a radical transformation of the society. When people named Calhoun and Cheves moved in with people named Rutledge and Pinckney, nothing would ever be the same again.

New England was a world apart: culturally, ethnically, and in religion the Yankees were the most nearly homogeneous of Americans. To be sure, there were a few enclaves of Scotch-Irish on the Merrimack River; Rhode Island was an exception to every generalization; and the inhabitants of the old Plymouth Colony (who had originally come largely from the Celtic or the southern and western parts of England) were not yet entirely reconciled to being part of

Massachusetts, after more than a century. But otherwise New England was overwhelmingly populated by people who had originated in England (mainly East Anglia and the Home Counties) and who professed the Congregationalist religion. Society was hierarchical, deferential, and remarkably stable, despite a certain tension between those persons who regarded themselves as gentlemen and those who (fortunately for the area's survival) had debased themselves by "going into trade."

Moreover, after thirty years of economic dislocation and decline, the area was prosperous once again. Producers of traditional export commodities—lumber in the north, fish and whale products from the sea, horses in the south, and wheat and tobacco in the Connecticut valley—were genuinely thriving for the first time since the early 1760s, rum was as profitable as it had ever been, and household manufacturers of textiles were beginning to turn out considerable surpluses. Public creditors, who had almost been wiped out by the financial dislocations that followed the War for Independence, had been rescued by Alexander Hamilton's fiscal program, and had profitably invested their surplus liquid capitals in diverse banking, insurance, and other service enterprises. Most tellingly of all, the merchants and traders and sea captains of the area, having floundered like so many lack-wits for a decade after independence, had regained their vitality in the 1790s, discovered the China trade, opened new markets in South America, cashed in on the wartime bonanza of carrying neutral goods, and otherwise brought money and profitable employment flowing into the region.

Yet three clouds darkened the New Englanders' horizons. One was a sense of impending doom based upon the fear—well founded, as it turned out—that southerners and westerners were about to take over the government of the country and run it according to their own alien lights. The other two were internal and more complex. Through the interaction of a stern religion and a harsh environment, the Yankees had learned to thrive in adversity, but they had never learned to live comfortably with success. If things got too good for too long, they began to suspect that the devil was at work, and they grew restless in the extreme. When that happened, vast numbers of them became caught up in crazes to purge society of evil, to reform it from within. Equally large numbers determined to get out, to emulate their Puritan forebears and flee to the wilderness, where they could retain their own purity and offer a beacon to sinful mankind. By 1800, sufficient prosperity plagued the region to set both manias hard to work.

Back to the South—the other, older, upper, tobacco-growing South. A quarter-century earlier, temporary concatenations of circumstances had brought Yankees and tobacco planters together politically, and the independence of the United States came as a result. But the two societies were natural antagonists, and they soon drifted apart. One was slave, the other free; one was Anglican, the other Puritan; one was prodigal, the other frugal. And deep as these differences were, they were superficial in comparison to what underlay them. Seven Yankees in ten, personally or through their forebears, had come from the southeastern half of the island that housed England and Scotland, that part which had been successively ruled by ancient Anglians, Romans, Saxons, and Normans—and in the seventeenth century had supported the Puritan Commonwealth. Seven Virginians in ten, personally or through their forebears, had come from the northwestern half of the island, where Celtic and Scandinavian peoples, though regularly subjugating one another, had never yielded to Latin or Germanic conquerers—and in the seventeenth century had been Royalists. In sum, the differences between New England and the tobacco region, between Massachusetts and Virginia, between John Adams and Thomas Jefferson, had roots that extended back two thousand years, maybe longer.[2]

A great deal more will be said about the denizens of the tobacco belt; they are, after all, the central characters in this story. For now, a few facts, figures, and conditions must be mentioned. The tobacco country extended from North Carolina to Maryland and from the seaboard to central Kentucky and Tennessee. Most of the weed was grown on large slave-manned plantations. The work of tobacco culture, being fussy but not requiring much physical strength, could be done by women and children. For those reasons, and because living conditions were healthy, large slave families were encouraged and developed on the plantations. Adult males, who would otherwise have been an excess labor force, worked in lumbering or were taught a variety of crafts so as to make the plantations more nearly self-sufficient. Planters tended to view slaves solicitously, almost as members of an extended family with a common sire, which in fact they not uncommonly were.

But the tobacco business had been in the doldrums for the better part of four decades now, and planters habitually blamed everyone but themselves. Before the Revolution they had overproduced and devastated their lands so as to produce even more, and they attributed the resulting depression in world market prices to the British monopoly established by the Navigation Acts. They got a fresh start during the war by repudiating some £2 million sterling of debts they owed British merchants, though they (a) lived in continuous fear that through the federal courts or a treaty with Great Britain they might yet have to pay, and (b) sank promptly back into debt again after the war. During the 1780s they blamed their woes on Robert Morris, Philadelphia merchant prince and erstwhile Financier of the Revolution, and during the 1790s they saw Alexander Hamilton as the cause of their plight. Never did they realize that curtailed production and careful management was the answer to what ailed them, and never did they cut back appreciably on their lavish way of living. Instead, they stalled off or defrauded their creditors in whatever ways seemed most feasible, being able to do so in good conscience, as members of the gentry class, on the ground that their merchant-creditors were grubby swindlers and social inferiors. Meanwhile, almost without exception, they gambled in western land speculation, in the hope that a bonanza strike would make them rich for all time.

That hope was inherently forlorn, for most of the prospective settlers of western lands were Scotch-Irish, who squatted, poached, or defaulted more commonly than they actually bought land and paid for it. The Scotch-Irish, descendants of Lowland Scots who had settled in northern Ireland in the early seventeenth century, had poured out of Ulster to America in the eighteenth. By 1800 they and kinsmen who had come directly from the Lowlands numbered perhaps a fifth of the white American population; from Pennsylvania southward they, along with such other Celtic peoples as the Highlanders, the Welsh, the Irish, and the Cornish, constituted nearly half the population; and in the back country of that vast area the Scotch-Irish alone were in the majority. In and west of the Appalachians and south of the Ohio River there were few whites except Ulstermen.

For centuries before and after their great migration most of the Scotch-Irish (and most other Scots as well) had been primarily herdsmen, only secondarily farmers. As such, they were accustomed to grazing their animals free on the lands of others, by virtue of common pasturage rights in the Old World and of open-range rights in the New (not until Jefferson had been dead a quarter of a century would Virginia pass its first law permitting planters to fence entire plantations against the cattle and swine of the drovers). On such land as they did acquire, by squatting or by purchase from speculators or the federal government, they grew corn for feeding their stock and distilling into whiskey. Because they lived in squalor and had little visible property—their wealth was on the hoof, foraging the woods—travelers and historians alike have mistakenly thought them extremely poor or have regarded them as struggling subsistence farmers. But each year, in late summer, they rounded up a portion of their stock and drove the animals long distances, by the tens of thousands, to markets in New York, Philadelphia, Baltimore, Charleston, and the plantations along the way.[3]

Because the menfolk required their women to work hard and have prodigious numbers of children, while they did little, most of the year, save hunt, fish, get drunk, and fight, they were often regarded by outsiders as being shiftless and lazy, just as many Indians were regarded. They were disputatious, nosy, shrewd, unlettered, superstitious, clever with words, and at once clannish and hospitable. They enforced morality through social disapproval and ridicule, rather than through developing an internalized sense of guilt. They distrusted all things English, and they were by English standards outlandish—which is precisely how Romans had described their ancestors fifteen hundred years earlier.

One more thing: in 1800 they supported Thomas Jefferson, almost to a man.

Socially and politically, then, the United States was a cauldron of sectional and cultural conflicts. Possibly because of preoccupation with such secular concerns, possibly because the economic boom of the 1790s made the Americans even more eager than usual to seize the main chance, religion in the new nation had gone into a cataclysmic decline. Or so, at any rate, did professional divines view the state of the Union. In actuality the matter was rather more complex.

As to the reality of the decline, there could be no doubt. In the beginning, Americans had been devoutly religious; and despite a reaction against the witchcraft craze, on one extreme, and the growth of skepticism in the wake of Newtonianism and the new spirit of rationalism, on the other, they had remained so until the time of the Revolution. In New England, the Great Awakening of the 1740s and 1750s had factionalized as well as rekindled the faith, though most people remained Calvinists theologically and, except in Rhode Island, Congregationalism continued to be established by law—which is to say that Congregational churches were supported by taxes, from which certain dissenting sects were exempt. Pennsylvania and New Jersey, where Quakers were numerous and were politically and socially dominant until the eve of the Revolution, had harbored a wide variety of Protestant sects without discrimination, and Maryland had allowed Roman Catholics all common rights except participation in government; but otherwise, the Anglican Church was at least partially established by law in every colony from New York to Georgia and generally enjoyed some measure of popular support. But after 1776 the religious order began to come apart.

The first step in the decline that was widely visible by 1800 was the breakdown of the establishments. In New England, Congregationalism retained its legal standing—the churches were not totally disestablished in Connecticut until 1818 and in Massachusetts until the 1830s—but it rapidly lost its substantive hold on the people. The Baptists spread their influence in northeastern Connecticut and southeastern Massachusetts; Arminianism (the doctrine that everybody was at least potentially eligible for salvation and capable of making a free choice in the matter, contrary to the Calvinist belief in a predestined elect) gained a considerable following among the common people; and the intellectual leaders of the sect drifted toward a rationalistic theology, bordering on deism, that would soon evolve into Unitarianism. Elsewhere, the Anglican establishment simply fell apart, whether from acts of disestablishment (as in Virginia and Maryland) or from an interplay of incompetence and Toryism on the part of ministers, apathy on the part of parishioners, and a general discrediting of the church that attended the divorce from England.

Into the breach came three dissenting faiths which were destined to be America's foremost sects for some time—the Presbyterian, Baptist, and Methodist—but they scarcely came in with a rush. The Presbyterians had great numbers of adherents, at least nominally, since theirs was the official church of Scotland and since the United States contained so many persons of Scottish descent. One feature of the church's polity, however, a source of strength in the old country, was fatal in the new. Presbyterians required their ministers to have a college education, and with their members scattered along a frontier that extended nearly a thousand miles, it was simply impossible to train enough ministers to service every congregation. Methodists and Baptists had institutional devices—especially circuit riders and a tradition of a lay ministry—which would solve that problem, but so far they had been unable to capitalize upon them. After a sensational start in the 1780s, the Methodist Church lost members during the next decade, despite the increase in population, falling from 67,643 in 1794 to 61,351 in 1800.

Baptists were increasing somewhat in southeastern New England and were breaking even in their other stronghold, the piedmont area of the tobacco belt, but they were not keeping pace with the expansion of the population.[4]

More important than declining membership was the waning of regular religious practice in most places and its virtual disappearance in others. Foreign travelers and divines of every sect commented on the phenomenon. The Frenchman La Rochefoucauld-Liancourt observed that "few nations are less addicted to religious practice than the Virginians." Isaac Weld, a British traveler, remarked in 1796 that in Virginia "between the mountains and the sea, the people have scarcely any sense of religion, and in the country parts the churches are all falling into decay." A Georgia Presbyterian minister, echoing a sentiment felt among ministers everywhere, wrote that he was "greatly distressed" at the "languishing state of religion in this country"; Devereux Jarratt, an evangelical Anglican minister who traveled widely in the United States, recorded that "religion is at a low ebb" among the Presbyterians. "The baptists, I suppose, are equally declining," he added, and "the Methodists are splitting and falling to pieces."[5]

The shrinking band of the faithful readily diagnosed the nature of the evil. Some of them saw the "contagious influence of vice" spreading because the growth of materialism made it inevitable. "By adopting and acting upon the principles & maxims of this world," wrote the Presbyterian minister David Rice, repeating a diagnosis pronounced by Lyman Beecher and William Ellery Channing, "Christians & ministers contribute more to the spread of infidelity & impiety than all the infidel writers of Europe and America." New Englanders tended to view the rampant "intemperance, profanity, gambling, and licentiousness" as resulting from the work of the devil's conscious or unconscious agents—such as the "arch infidel" Thomas Paine, whose deistic tract *The Age of Reason* was as widely circulated as it was attacked, and the "Bavarian Illuminati," an imaginary secret conspiracy against the Republic that Jedidiah Morse dreamed up and warned the people against. In truth, deists were growing bolder, publishing, and gaining followers in New England and the middle states. In the South, though deism made some inroads (Jefferson himself was essentially a deist), fear of an infidel conspiracy was less common than a nostalgic diagnosis: almost universally, southern Protestant ministers believed that "their people had originally (or at some period not far removed) been pious and were currently backsliders."[6]

14

Ministers of the dissenting faiths had their own simple, home-spun theological explanation for the backsliding. Contrary to the Newtonian and deistic notion of a God who had created the universe as a perfect machine and then stepped back to let it work, their God minutely supervised everything to the falling of a sparrow. He loved mankind, but they had displeased Him, so He had allowed them to sink into irreligion and wickedness so they would know the futility and absence of fellowship that followed being separated from the Almighty. If they would admit and repent of their sins and pray for forgiveness, He in His infinite mercy would forgive them and reinvest society with vital piety. Unfortunately for such ministers, most people persisted in their indifference to both divine mercy and Christian fellowship.

Throughout the South and West in the late 1790s, congregation after congregation adopted resolutions of fasting and prayer in order to please God and hasten the day of revival, but it did not come. In the absence of a sign, no small number of the faithful consoled themselves with an old notion, based upon an interpretation of Holy Scripture: that falling away from God would be followed by the temporal reign of an Antichrist, which was the unmistakable omen of the imminent Second Coming of Christ.

One instrument of deliverance, typical of many others, appeared in the person of an itinerant Scotch-Irish Presbyterian minister, born in Pennsylvania and named James McGready. A huge man with piercing eyes and great oratorical gifts, McGready might have moved audiences with almost any message, but he chose to revive the old evangel that eternal damnation was in store for every individual who did not, through an act of personal volition, immediately repent of his sins, pray for forgiveness, and open his heart to the divine gift of rebirth. In a dozen or more crossroads towns in North Carolina, McGready sparked a number of local revivals, and he also gained five disciples, young converts to his evangelistic zeal who, as preachers, were almost as talented as he was: William McGee, Barton W. Stone, William Hodge, Samuel McAdow, and John Rankin. But in 1796 the time was not yet ripe, and North Carolina was not the place for him; so he and his five converts left the state. They headed for Kentucky, then the most barren of religious wastelands.

For three years, then four, they preached their gospel—repent, believe, and be reborn—and though they had ups and downs, they set off a series of miniature revivals that foretokened the Great Revival to come. They especially directed their appeal toward the young, whom conventional ministers had regularly ignored, even though persons under sixteen constituted more than 55 percent of Kentucky's population. Whether in response to their bald emotionalism or simply because the climate was becoming conducive, by 1800 listeners and even the ministers themselves were increasingly being "seized with the Holy Spirit," falling into catatonic states, "talking in tongues," or being smitten with seizures indistinguishable from epilepsy. These were interpreted as genuine manifestations of the work of God, and word of the miracles spread through the countryside. In August of 1800 the first of the great interdenominational "camp meetings" was called to convene at Gasper River, where sinners were invited to come and listen to three days and nights of round-the-clock preaching. Several hundred showed up, and after about twenty-four hours of mounting tension, an explosion erupted. As McGready described it: "The divine flame spread through the whole multitude. Presently . . . sinners [were] lying powerless in ever part of the house, praying and crying for mercy."[7] And that was just the beginning: the revival blazed throughout Kentucky and into Tennessee, gaining power with every passing month. In August of 1801, at Cane Ridge, Kentucky, an estimated 25,000 people—nearly an eighth of the entire population of Kentucky, and probably three times as many as had taken part in the presidential election in the state a year earlier—showed up to be saved at the greatest camp meeting of them all. Meanwhile the revival had spread as no wildfire ever spread, awakening religious zeal in the back country from New York to Georgia.

Conservative and established ministers, along with most deists and other rationalists, deplored the emotionalism of the Great Revival and belittled its accomplishments, charging that its effects on the converts were neither deep nor lasting. They were quite wrong, for the effects of the revival were indelible. The theological message it left imprinted upon the southern soul was a melange of earlier theology, but it was essentially one of individual responsibility for salvation. Only God, through Jesus Christ, could grant salvation, but every individual had a choice of remaining in sin or repenting his wickedness and opening his heart to the Holy Spirit. Salvation was therefore through faith and divine grace, not through the blasphemous notion that by good works man could save himself. But good works, after a fashion, were also necessary: for the entirely nonsupernatural reason that society, in those areas where revivalism took its strongest hold, was governed by the shame principle rather than the guilt principle—by fear of ridicule from one's fellows rather than by an internal or extrahuman moral force—it was important that one behave piously, though not necessarily charitably, so as to demonstrate one's salvation to one's peers. Behaviorally, then, the requirement for the saved was essentially negative: do not sin, or at least do not engage in visible sin, and feel free to punish those who do, as God Himself does. Every manner of evil as reckoned by humanistic standards, including slavery, could be accommodated within the framework of that cosmology.

There were, in addition, economic and political overtones to such a theology. In economics, it was acceptable to acquire a temporal command of a portion of God's green earth and work it honestly, or even to buy land and sell it at a profit. If one grew affluent in that manner, that was also acceptable; but to live in the pursuit of abstract, man-defined notions of paper "wealth"—as the adherents of Hamiltonian Federalism were clearly doing—was a virtually unforgiveable sin. As to government, it was necessarily imperfect, being the creature of mere sinful man, and it should therefore be kept at a minimum. In the remote eventuality that government should temporarily come under the control of the saved, the best thing they could do would be to emasculate it, to render it incapable of offering new temptations to mankind in the future.

State by state, county by county, congregation by congregation, revival country was also Jefferson country.

It should not be surprising that those who were saved through revivalism were also supporters of Jeffersonian Republicanism, for the theology of the one was psychologically akin to the ideology of the other. In part, to be sure, religious dissenters supported Jefferson because of his well-known championship of the cause of religious liberty. New England Baptists, for instance, having fought long and vainly for disestablishment, virtually idolized Jefferson. South and west of New England, however, establishment had long since ceased to be a live issue, and in much of that area Jefferson's religious views, to the extent that they were fully known, were if anything a political handicap. Rather, it was the compatibility of outlooks that made it possible for southern and western revivalists simultaneously to embrace evangelical Arminianism in religion and Republican ideology in politics.

Anglo-Americans, like the English themselves, were by and large nonideological people, but in 1800 the country was divided into two fiercely antagonistic ideological camps. In a loose, general sort of way, and with allowance for a number of exceptions, it can

17

be said that the rival ideologies derived from contrasting views of the nature of man. The first view, that associated with the Hamiltonian Federalists, was premised upon the belief that man, while capable of noble and even altruistic behavior, could never entirely escape the influence of his inborn baser passions—especially ambition and avarice, the love of power and the love of money. The second, that espoused by the Jeffersonian Republicans, held that man was born with a tabula rasa, with virtually boundless capacity for becoming good or evil, depending upon the wholesomeness of the environment in which he grew. From the premise of the first it followed that government should recognize the evil drives of men as individuals, but check them and even harness them in such a way that they would work for the general good of society as a whole. From the premise of the second it followed that government should work to rid society of as many evils as possible—including, to a very large extent, the worst of evils, government itself. The one was positive, the other negative; the one sought to do good, the other to eradicate evil.

But the ideological division was more specifically focused than that. The High Federalists believed in and had fashioned a governmental system modeled upon the one that began to emerge in England after the Glorious Revolution of 1688 and was brought to maturity under the leadership of Sir Robert Walpole during the 1720s and 1730s. In part the system worked on the basis of what has often, simple-mindedly, been regarded as the essence of Hamiltonianism: tying the interests of the wealthy to those of the national government or, more accurately, inducing people of all ranks to act in the general interest by making it profitable for them to do so. But the genius of Hamilton's system ran much deeper. He erected a complex set of interrelated institutions, based upon the monetization of the public debt, which made it virtually impossible for anyone to pursue power and wealth successfully except through the framework of those institutions, and which simultaneously delimited and dictated the possible courses of government activity, so that government had no choice but to function in the public interest as Hamilton saw it. For instance, servicing the public debt, on which the whole superstructure rested, required a regular source of revenue that was necessarily derived largely from duties on imports from Great Britain. For that reason the United States could not go to war with Britain except at the risk of national bankruptcy, but could fight Revolutionary France or France's ally Spain, which were owners of territories that the United States avidly desired. Hamilton regarded this as the proper American foreign policy, at least for a time; and should circumstances change, he was perfectly capable of redefining the rules and rerigging the institutions so as to dictate another policy. In domestic affairs, a wide range of implications of his system was equally inescapable.

The Jeffersonian Republicans regarded this scheme of things as utterly wicked, even as the English Opposition had regarded Walpole's system. Indeed, though the Jeffersonians borrowed some of their ideas from James Harrington and other seventeenth-century writers and some from John Locke, their ideology was borrowed *in toto* from such Oppositionists as Charles Davenant, John Trenchard, Thomas Gordon, James Burgh, and most especially Henry St. John, First Viscount Bolingbroke. As a well-rounded system, it is all to be found in the pages of the *Craftsman*, an Oppositionist journal that Bolingbroke published from 1726 to 1737. The Republicans adjusted the ideology to fit the circumstances, to fit the United States Constitution and the "ministry" of Alexander Hamilton rather than the British constitution and the ministry of Robert Walpole; but that was all, and astonishingly little adjustment was necessary.

The Bolingbroke-Oppositionist *cum* Jeffersonian Republican ideology ran as follows.[8] Corruption was everywhere, it was true; but given a proper environment, that need not be the way of things. Mankind could be rejuvenated through education and self-discipline, but that was possible only in the context of a life style that exalted living on, owning, and working the land. Only the land could give people the independence and unhurried existence that were prerequisite to self-improvement.

In some Edenic past, "the people"—which both Bolingbroke and Jefferson understood to mean the gentry and the solid yeomanry, and not to include aristocrats, money jobbers, priests, or the scum in the cities—had enjoyed the proper atmosphere, and therefore had been happy. Relationships were based upon agriculture and its "handmaiden" commerce, upon ownership of land, honest labor in the earth, craftsmanship in the cities, and free trade between individuals. All men revered God, respected their fellows, deferred to their betters, and knew their place. Because they were secure in their sense of place, they were also secure in their identities and their sense of values; and manly virtue, honor, and public spirit governed their conduct.

Then a serpent invaded the garden. To Bolingbroke, the evil started with the Glorious Revolution, which begat two bastard offspring: the Financial Revolution and the system of government by ministry, rather than the system of separation of powers that had been embodied in the ancient English constitution. To Jefferson, things were slightly more complex. America had been spared the corruption that had poisoned England until the accession of George III, and when it began to infest America, the spirit of 1776 had saved the day. Yet the American Revolution, because of the Hamiltonians, was ultimately undermined in just the way the English revolution had been: both were waged to check executive power, and both ended in the worst form of executive tyranny, ministerial government. The instrument of corruption in both instances was money—not "real" money, gold and silver, but artificial money in the form of public debt, bank notes, stocks, and other kinds of paper —the acquisition of which had nothing to do with either land or labor. Government ministers assiduously encouraged people to traffic in such paper, and with that stimulus the pursuit of easy wealth proved irresistible. A frenzy for gambling, stock-jobbing, and paper shuffling permeated the highest councils of state and spread among the people themselves. Manly virtue gave way to effeminacy and vice; public spirit succumbed to extravagance, venality, and corruption.

Jefferson never tired of telling a story which, to him, epitomized what had gone wrong. Early in Washington's first administration, Jefferson recalled, he had been engaged in a friendly discussion of political principles with Hamilton and Vice-President Adams. Jefferson had maintained that an agrarian republic was most conducive to human happiness. Adams disagreed and, to Jefferson's horror, said that monarchy was better, that if the British government were purged of corruption it would be the best system ever devised. Hamilton, to the astonishment of both his listeners, declared that if the British system were purged of corruption it would not work: it was, he said, the most perfect system of government as it stood, for corruption was the most suitable engine of effective government.

In the matter of foreign relations, Republicans opposed the corrupt new order on two interrelated sets of grounds, with the same logic and often the same language that the Oppositionists had used earlier. One was that it entangled the nation with foreign powers, making independent, self-determined action impossible. Not only had Hamilton's system prevented the United States from siding with Revolutionary France against Britain in the early 1790s—which the Republicans believed to be the moral course, as well as the one most advantageous to the country—but it continually subjected America to alien influences because foreigners owned a large percentage of the public debt and the stock of the Bank of the United States. This involvement, in turn, gave rise to the second set of grounds for objection: foreign entanglements necessitated standing armies and navies, the support of which added to an already oppressive tax burden. The gentry and yeomanry, the Republicans believed, had been carrying more than their share of the tax load, even when taxes had been mainly in the form of import duties; and when excise taxes were levied specifically to support the military during the quasi war with France in 1798, the new burden fell almost exclusively on the landed. Taxes to support standing armies and navies were doubly galling because a professional military corps, as a class distinct from the people, was a threat to liberty in its own right, and it could also be unleashed to collect taxes by force, thus making the people pay for their own oppression. (English Oppositionists had been afraid of standing armies, but not of navies, for they had regarded a strong naval establishment as necessary for the protection of British commerce. The American Republicans' fear of standing armies was largely abstract, since they believed that the traditional American reliance on militias would prevent the rise of dangerous armies; but their hostility to navies was immediate and strong, for navies seemed most likely to involve the United States in fighting, and besides, navies cost a lot of money for upkeep even when they were not actively employed.)

Given all that, a revolution in the form of a return to first principles was called for. The several branches of government must be put back into constitutional balance, the moneychangers must be ousted from the temples, the gentry and yeomanry must be restored to supremacy, commerce must be returned to its subordinate role as agriculture's handmaiden, and the values of the agrarian way of life must be cherished anew. In the undertaking, the Republicans had reason for hope—as, in reality, Bolingbroke and his circle had not —for it could all be done within the framework of the Constitution. The Constitution made it possible for the Republicans to gain control of the national government, and should they prove able to do so, only two major tasks needed to be done. The first was to purge government of extreme, irreconcilable monarchists. Jefferson believed that this could be done quickly and easily, for he thought that all but a handful of the people in government were men of sound and honorable principles. The second was to pay off the public debt as rapidly as possible, since that was the wellspring of the whole system of corruption. This would not be easy; but with good management, honest administration, and rigid economy, Jefferson believed that it could be accomplished within sixteen years.

That was the Republicans' ideology and the essence of their program: restore the separation of powers through the voluntary restraint of virtuous officials, cast out the monarchists and the money men, repeal the most oppressive of taxes, slash expenses, pay off the public debt, and thus restore America to the pristine simplicity of an Arcadian past.

It is to be observed that nothing has been said of strict construction of the Constitution and the extreme states'-rights doctrine of interposition, with which Jefferson was associated in his argument against the constitutionality of the Bank in 1791 and in his authorship of the Kentucky Resolutions against the Alien and Sedition Acts in 1798 and 1799. The fact is that only a handful of people knew of those documents or knew that Jefferson had written them; they were not a part of his public identity. Moreover, they were arguments that had been coined in the first instance as matters of political expediency—as means of heading off what Jefferson regarded as dangerous activity by the Federalists—and he never thought of them as sacred principles of constitutional government.

It is also to be observed that nothing has been said of the federal judiciary or of territorial expansion, two matters that consumed much of the energy and attention of the Jeffersonians when they came to power. The judiciary was of merely tangential consequence in the Jeffersonians' thinking; it became important to them only when it loomed as an unexpected stumbling block. Territorial expansion was an integral part of their program, but only implicitly: it went without saying that the nation should expand as the opportunity arose, to make room for generations of farmers yet unborn.

There was one more area in which those of the Jeffersonian persuasion had cause for concern, and that had to do with the institution of human slavery. The Republicans were the party of slavery: in 1800 Jefferson would receive more than 85 percent of the electoral votes cast by states in which slavery was an important socioeconomic fact of life, and nearly three-quarters of his electoral votes (53 of 73) would come from other slaveholders. By all accounts Jefferson himself agonized a great deal over the conflict between his professed belief in human liberty and his ownership of slaves, but his attitude was not shared by most of his supporters, and agony or no, he retained his slaves and lived in splendor off their labors.

But owning slaves was not, in 1800, so comfortable a circumstance as it once had been. Black rebels on the West Indian island of Hispaniola had risen against their French and Spanish masters, butchered those who were unable to flee, found inspired leadership in the person of Toussaint L'Ouverture, and emerged as a de facto republic. The British, after futilely and foolishly attempting to seize the island, had reverted to supporting the blacks as a means of striking a blow against France. The American Federalists, partly on the moral ground of opposition to slavery and partly on the practical ground that it was profitable business, also supported the rebels by opening trade with them, supplying them with the foodstuffs and lumber products they needed for survival. That was too much for southern Republicans to abide. It was one thing for God to put frontier preachers on trial, or for the monarchical money power to pervert the gentry ethic; such matters had a certain abstract quality about them, and might be coped with; but to abet slaves in revolt was to transcend the very boundaries of civilization. Southern state governments clamped tight restrictions on trade with the West Indies so as to keep the news from Haiti from reaching and inciting their own blacks, but an air of fear continued to pervade the atmosphere.

There was more, of course, to the slaveholders' mentality than just that. In order to understand their mentality it is necessary to observe that there were in America three distinct kinds of plantations, which varied from one another in their forms of social organization and therefore in their bases of authority. Broadly speaking, American plantations specialized in producing one of three crops —rice, cotton, or tobacco. On the rice plantations the labor was back-breaking, the mortality rate among field hands was high, and authority rested upon naked force, upon control of the gun and the whip. Slaves, or field hands anyway, were reckoned not as humans but as capital investment, just as animals and tools and land were reckoned. On the cotton plantations, three special conditions resulted in a somewhat different social order: much of the work could be done by women and children, most of the plantations were on the frontier, and the masters had, for the most part, grown up as slaveless farmers or livestock raisers and had not forgotten their earlier ways. As a result, masters and whole families of slaves lived together in some intimacy; the masters worked hard alongside their slaves, and established their authority through brutal, one-on-one displays of strength and will, tempered by kindness toward the obedient.

23

The characteristic response of both rice and cotton planters, when faced with adversity, was whatever form of violence seemed most appropriate. When Indians stood in their way, they killed. When a peer behaved offensively, they challenged the offender to a duel. When inferiors did so, they responded with a caning or a horsewhipping. When nations did so, they were ready for war. Their style, in contrast to that of various other Americans, was epitomized in their attitudes toward the mob violence that erupted in city after city between 1799 and 1801. Mobs ran amock in Phila-delphia in 1799, and President Adams fled to the sanctuary of his farm in Braintree, Massachusetts. Mobs crowded the halls of Con-gress in Washington again two years later, and Virginians im-mediately proposed laws that would severely punish such unruly behavior. Senator William Jackson of Georgia, a cotton planter and an incorruptible Republican, refused to have any part of either pusillanimous course. He faced the mob squarely, pointed a brace of pistols in their direction, and informed them to begone, lest he shoot them dead—"dead, sirs, dead"—and they departed.

And yet the cotton and rice planters' society was wide open to any who had the stomach, the toughness, the audacity, and the luck to enter it successfully. Cotton planters were growing unconscion-ably wealthy, and rice planters were already so, but the ranks of both were swelling. Rice planting, to be sure, was less easy to enter because the capital investment was high and the supply of suitable swamp land was limited, whereas cotton planting cost little at the start and the area for its expansion seemed virtually infinite. There were but two barriers: the prime cotton lands in the vast state of Georgia were occupied by Indians, and the area's natural ports on the Gulf of Mexico were held by Spain. So far the federal govern-ment had interfered with efforts to remove either barrier—which made a change in government seem all the more necessary.

The social order in tobacco country was another matter entirely. On the tobacco plantations, as indicated, the work was tedious but not hard, slaves were encouraged to have families, and society was organized as more or less a cross between the English village-and-manor system and a patriarch-dominated extended family. No new slaves had been imported into the area for more than three decades. Thus authority over the blacks rested not on force but upon habit, upon the fact that every slave was acculturated into the system from birth, knew his place in it, and really could imagine no other scheme of things. Relations among whites rested on not dissimilar foundations. Possibly half of Virginia's 100,000 adult white males

24

were eligible to vote, and half the eligible sometimes did vote, but power was totally monopolized by the 300 or 400 broadly extended, many-branched, and much-intermarried families who constituted the gentry. No others ran for any of the few offices that were popularly elected. The ordinary yeoman knew his place and did not dare challenge the established gentlemen, and the expense of electioneering was beyond his means anyway. Moreover, the gentry itself was closed: no one reached the seats of power unless his family had been prominent for two or three generations. So, life in the tobacco country was a pyramid of oligarchies—the plantation, the county, the House of Burgesses—at each level of which the power of the gentry was virtually absolute.

The tobacco planters fancied themselves as cultivated, paternalistic country gentlemen, and normally they managed to live up to that image of themselves. When hard pressed, to be sure, they could resort to fraud, but almost never to force; and usually they relied upon reasonable discussion or, that failing, upon fraud's next of kin, politics. They were extremely gifted in the political arts, and indeed they were well trained for statesmanship—as is attested by their producing Washington, Jefferson, Madison, Henry, Marshall, and a legion of other towering figures in a single generation. From the experience of running their plantations and participating in county government, they gained a wide range of practical skills in managing other people. The best of them also read deeply in the classics and mastered the extant works of every political and constitutional theorist and historian since ancient times. They all liked to think of themselves as public-spirited, as disinterested servants of the people—which was true enough, if it is understood that by "the people" they meant the gentry and the yeomanry and that really, at least in times of adversity, they meant only the members of their own social class.

The adverse condition that beset them most just now, however, apart from the possibility of slave insurrection, was one that did not lend itself to management in any of their accustomed means: they had an excess of slave mouths to feed and a shortage of income to do it with. The older generation of tobacco planters—Jefferson's generation—was thereby stimulated to discover what their consciences had already hinted to them, namely that slavery was evil and must be abolished. Fearing their blacks as much as they loved them, however—with a fear soon to be heightened by Gabriel's Conspiracy in Richmond—they dared not emancipate them into their own midst, and so for a whole generation they played at

25

schemes of manumission and recolonization to Africa. The younger generation, more tough-mindedly, perceived that if they could not raise tobacco profitably and did not have a long-enough growing season to raise cotton at all, they could raise people for sale at a handsome profit in the rapidly expanding cotton belt. Only two things were necessary to make that possible. One was to see to the continued expansion of cotton culture, which would involve joining cotton planters and land speculators in ridding Georgia of Indians and Spaniards. The other was to see to the abolition of the importation of slaves from Africa or the West Indies, which would become constitutionally permissible in 1808.

Thus the interests of the various kinds of slaveholders were compatible, even if their life styles were different. Moreover, virtually all slaveholders shared the habit of command and the psyche that went with it. Their whole way of life rested upon personal relationships in which they paid appropriate deference to their peers and gave orders to all others. Because external authority by definition threatened their personal and local domains, they resisted it with passionate intensity; and they embraced the doctrine of states' rights with far greater ardor than did their more cosmopolitan leader Jefferson. Finally, they surpassed him in hostility to the monetized, commercialized, democratized, and, above all, depersonalized world that was being born through the midwifery of Walpole and Hamilton and their ilk. For in that world they could not cope.

The Republicans gained control of the national government, after twelve years of Federalist domination, in a bitterly contested election that began in April of 1800 and was not completed until February of 1801. Their triumph was not a popular mandate for the implementation of the Republican ideology, nor was it a popular mandate for anything else. The presidential electors were, for the most part, chosen by the state legislatures, who also chose all the members of the United States Senate. The decision was in the hands of no more than a thousand men, and for practical purposes it turned on the activities of two or three dozen factional leaders. The supporters of Thomas Jefferson proved to be more skillful as political manipulators and masters of intrigue than were the supporters of President John Adams—they had already proved, in capturing majorities in most legislatures, they they were better organized and more artful in arousing the voters—and that was the key to their success.

Nonetheless, their program had a broad basis of popular support, for it was peculiarly suited to the genius of the American people, and it appealed to their prejudices and interests as well. Moreover, there was no doubt that the Republicans had the talent, the energy, and the determination to carry the program into execution. But there was a question, a very large one. Republican theory was wondrous potent as an ideology of opposition. It remained to be seen whether it was a sound basis for administration.

2

★★★★★

THE REPUBLICAN TACK:
AT HOME, 1801–1803

Thomas Jefferson referred to the ascent of his party as the Revolution of 1800—a claim that scholars have almost uniformly regarded as exaggerated. Indeed, political scientists long maintained that the significance of the event lay in demonstrating that popular governments could be stable, since a major change in administrations was effected without the shedding of blood; and historians have tended to view the change as one of principles and tone but not of substance. In fact, however, Jefferson's statement is inaccurate only in regard to its dating: the Republicans won the votes necessary to gaining control of the presidency and the Congress in 1800, but because of the leisurely ways of the age, it was a year and a half, sometimes two and a half years, before much of anything could happen. Leisurely or not, a great deal did happen. There was no Reign of Terror, and nobody was guillotined; nothing that was done was spectacular, and little of it was dramatic; yet in that short space of time the American government made a more profound turn toward what a majority of its people desired than had almost any other government, ancient or modern.

To appreciate what the Jeffersonians accomplished, one must look more closely at who they were, understand in particular what they aimed to do, and observe how they went about their task. In general terms, they were the groups already described: most Americans of Celtic descent, most evangelical Protestants, virtually all

29

republican ideologues in the tradition of Bolingbroke, and most southern slaveholders. But they were also specific human beings, many of them extremely gifted and dedicated, and they had formed a superb organization for the attainment of their ends. First and foremost, of course, there was Jefferson himself, a man at once greater, simpler, and yet more complexly human than the mere "apostle of liberty" or "spokesman for democracy" that his adulators have relegated him to being. Next were his lieutenants and veritable alter egos, James Madison and Albert Gallatin. Then came his leaders in Congress, notably Nathaniel Macon, Joseph Nicholson, and John Randolph of Roanoke in the House and William Branch Giles in the Senate; and then such faithful newspaper publishers as William Duane of the Philadelphia *Aurora*, the less faithful but equally important political "bosses" and factional leaders in the Middle Atlantic States, and the legions of Republicans who permeated all levels and ranks of government throughout Jefferson's presidency, unwaveringly following his lead.

It is no easy task just to describe these people, their organization, and their methods of operation. It is even less easy to dissect the motives that impelled them, the admixture of their greed and love of power with their ideals and hopes for mankind. But if these things can be done, the unparalleled success of Thomas Jefferson's first term in office can be readily understood. So can the unmitigated failure of his second term.

Even in his own time, Jefferson was regarded by friends and foes alike as a champion of liberty—whatever that elusive word may mean. Jefferson himself never wrote a systematic treatise on the subject, and he never thought it through as a concept. Its meaning to him can scarcely have been a conventional one, since Jefferson owned several hundred human beings during his lifetime and theirs, never made any serious effort to liberate them, purchased at least eight more while he was president, and once asked his friend Madison to acquire a black person for a visiting French lady who sought to be amused by breeding them—a request which the libertarian Madison cheerfully honored. Nor can liberty as Jefferson conceived of it have had much to do with such legal and constitutional rights—enshrined in English and American law from the seventeenth to the twentieth century—as the writ of habeas corpus, freedom of the press, freedom from unlawful search and seizures, and judicial review of the acts of legislatures and law enforcers. Regarding some of these, Jefferson wrote strong words of support;

but equally often he denounced the abuse of these "rights," and when he exercised executive authority he was capable of running roughshod over them in what he regarded as a higher interest.

All of which is to say that to regard Jefferson as an apostle of abstract liberty, with the connotations that later generations would impart to it, is a distortion of history and a perversion of his vision for mankind. He saw broadly, but only from where he stood; and we can best appreciate him by trying to see from his perspective. He grew up in a woman-dominated household. His father, Peter Jefferson, was a physical giant who carved out a vast estate by overawing and outwitting his peers, speculating in lands, persuading or killing Indians as the case required, marrying well, acquiring slaves, and otherwise living up to the mid-eighteenth-century Virginian's notions of manhood. But then, when his elder son, Thomas, was thirteen, he deserted the adoring son by dying. For the next few years the son—the only whole white male (his brother being a half-wit) in the family—grew up in a most unmasculine atmosphere. Women gave the orders, and slaves carried them out. He read books, practiced the violin, studied poetry, and took long hand-in-hand walks in the woods with a sister whom he devoutly loved and who, like his father, died. He studied under male schoolmarms, then went to the College of William and Mary. There he was exposed to some potent influences for his later development as a theorist of republican government, but more importantly he was exposed to and felt himself lacking in the attributes of the Young Buck Virginian. His distant cousin John Marshall and his early hero Patrick Henry epitomized the type: neither of them ever seemed to study, both wore hunting clothes and dirty shirts and chewed tobacco, both were surrounded by giggling girls who idolized them, both were men's men whom other men flocked around enviously and attentively and in whose company others pretended to be comfortable. All his adult life Jefferson hated them.

After embarrassing himself totally in the pursuit of an appropriate damsel, he married a widow with two children and a large estate, mostly in the form of slaves inherited from her miscegenist father. They adored one another in a short, happy life, but soon she too died. Meanwhile he had written his most revealing document, *A Summary View of the Rights of British America* (1774), his most celebrated document, the Declaration of Independence (1776), and his most extensive treatise on any subject, the *Notes on the State of Virginia* (1781). He had two daughters who survived to maturity, Martha and Maria, whom he held onto passionately and suffocatingly. He also held several high governmental posts, in none of which was he particularly effectual. As governor of Virginia during the Revolution, handicapped by the antiexecutive features of a state constitution that he had helped design, he confronted a British invasion with what many regarded as cowardice. As a legislator in the same state and during the same period, he fought quixotically for reforms—especially the abolition of primogeniture and entail and of the established Anglican Church, which were essentially meaningless, since neither evil had any real substance; and he failed besides, leaving it for others, later, to achieve the enactment of those hollow changes. As American minister to Paris after the Revolution, he tilted at more windmills, spending most of his diplomatic efforts in a four-year tour there trying to undo a tobacco-marketing arrangement which he thought undermined Virginia planters but was actually to their advantage. For another four years, from 1789 to 1793, he was secretary of state under Washington—whom he idolized as a father figure for a time, until it became clear to him that Hamilton was Washington's favorite son—but in that capacity he was inefficacious and out of harmony with the drift of the administration. In 1797 he became vice-president under John Adams, whose policies were totally repugnant to him.

This is scarcely the background, one might suppose, of which presidential greatness is made; but so to think is to regard the man as narrowly as critical libertarians regard him. Until 1801, to be sure, he was in his own terms a failure as a public man, despite his celebration as the author of the Declaration of Independence, but that failure derived from the fact that in public life he had never been in a position to be master of his own responsibilities. For Jefferson, in order to function well, required complete authority that was based upon habit and consent. Far more than the Father of His Country, George Washington, Jefferson in real life was the ultimate paternalist. He took care of people—his daughters, his sons-in-law, his brother, his slaves, his friends, and every manner of helpless, weak, or ill-fitting person he encountered—and managed their lives gently, kindly, tactfully, and totally. All he asked in return was their absolute devotion, and he got it. He was quite inept at dealing with peers, but when he was master of his circumstances he had no peers.

His political philosophy, or rather the mytho-historical conception of the ideal life that served him as a substitute for a philosophy, was entirely consistent with his life as he lived it.[1] Though he read and could quote a staggering variety of philosophers in several languages, he derived his own philosophy from history, agreeing with Bolingbroke that history is "philosophy teaching by examples." He found all history interesting and instructive, but thought British history most important, provided that it was history on "true principles." In Jefferson's time, two quite opposite versions of British history were current. They were called the whig and tory interpretations, though without reference to existing English political parties. (The whig version, for instance, was an integral part of the ideology of Bolingbroke's Tory Opposition.) The whigs were seeking to support Parliament against executive encroachment and the broadening of the royal prerogative; they justified their position by maintaining that it was rooted in ancient custom. Their history told of an idealized Anglo-Saxon "democracy" that had existed before the Normans had undermined it through treachery, not conquest. The Normans, in their view, had saddled the Anglo-Saxons with feudalism and an established church, and the history of England ever after had been the history of legitimate struggles to shake off the "Norman Yoke." The tory historians maintained that Anglo-Saxon society had already been feudalistic, but barbaristically and chaotically so, and that the Normans performed a great service by bringing stability and order to the Anglo-Saxons.

Jefferson ardently embraced the whig version, and saw in it all the guidelines necessary to making America into an earthly paradise. Ancient Anglo-Saxon society, according to the whig historians, exalted just the kind of life in which Jefferson personally found greatest happiness, and the kind he believed most conducive to human happiness in general. Society and such government as existed were organized around farmers, large or small, who held their lands in allodial (or absolutely free) tenure, and around all-powerful fathers—heads of families, narrow or extended. No coercion was necessary for the smooth functioning of that society, relations were governed by consent and by norms universally agreed upon, and every man was free to think and to worship God as he pleased. When disputes arose, they were resolved through established customs and the procedures of the common law, which all men understood and cheerfully accepted. When foreign armies threatened, the heads of families rallied into militia companies and repulsed the invader. True liberty and true democracy, to Jefferson, were no more complex than that.

The problem was that evil and designing men were engaged in a never-ending conspiracy to destroy this Eden, and "eternal vigilance" was the price of preserving it. The Normans had destroyed

33

it in old England, establishing the tyranny of an alien king and landlords, replacing the Saxon militia and allodial tenure with a feudal system of holding land from the king in exchange for military service, and imposing a system of religion by force. In 1215 the Saxons won it back, at least in part, through the Magna Carta, but it continued to be imperiled. In the seventeenth century the whigs' (and Jefferson's) heroes fought the same fight against the Stuarts, and seemed to triumph in the Glorious Revolution. But the English were not vigilant, and through the instrumentality of the Financial Revolution, evil and designing men once again reduced England to tyranny and corruption.

The Americans, Jefferson believed, had the virtue and the social forms necessary for restoring the idealized world of their Anglo-Saxon ancestors, but they had relaxed their vigil and had allowed the Hamiltonian conspiracy to yoke them with corrupt modern English institutions. Jefferson's mission as president—the revolution as he conceived it—was to cast off that yoke, restore what once had been, govern with paternal wisdom, and, through public education, instill the people with the historical knowledge and true principles that would prevent them from losing their liberties ever again.

(It is ironic that more of Jefferson's ancestors were Celtic and Scandinavian than were Anglo-Saxon, as were those of most of his followers. It is ironic, but it does not alter the case, any more than the case is altered by the fact that the tory interpretation of history was far more nearly in accord with what had happened than was the whig interpretation. Such is the force of the myths that men live by.)

The first step in reforming the government was to change its personnel—or, in the metaphor that the new president regularly employed, to assemble a loyal crew for steering the ship of state on a republican tack. Jefferson saw this as a less involved undertaking than did most of his supporters, for he counted only 316 civilian employees of the federal government as being subject to presidential appointment and removal. Subordinates of those employees, who numbered perhaps 700 clerks and assistants, were chosen by the presidential appointees, and the vast majority of the remaining 3,000 or so government jobholders were in the Post Office Department and were appointed by the postmaster general. Within the ranks of those who were chosen by the president, Jefferson contemplated no wholesale ousting of Federalists: he proposed to fire only those who were guilty of malfeasance or incompetence and those whom he regarded as irreconcilable monarchists, namely the devout

Hamiltonians. All other federal employees, he believed, were honest and true to "ancient whig principles" and should be retained in office unless the offices themselves were inimical to the public interest. In sum, Jefferson had no intention of introducing into the national government what would later be called the spoils system, the notion that members of the victorious political party had a right to patronage and jobs simply because they had won an election.[2]

Political sagacity as well as principle underlay this determination. The principle was one to which Jefferson was firmly committed: that offices should be filled on the basis of merit, not influence. The French, whom he greatly admired, had gone a long way toward creating a bureaucracy of merit, whereas the despised British government remained one of slipshod administration based upon corruption and influence. Hamilton, as Jefferson saw things, had followed the British example, and Jefferson was determined to follow the more efficient French. As to politics, Jefferson shrewdly perceived the need to move with caution—he cited Solon's wise observation "that no more good must be attempted than the nation can bear"—lest the country be irreparably torn by total alienation of the Federalists.[3] Moreover, a prudent policy with regard to appointments and removals could increase his political capital, whereas a reckless one could deplete it.

But two complications arose at the outset. The first was that President Adams, after learning that Jefferson had defeated him, busied himself filling every vacant position in government with diehard Federalists—his most significant appointment being that of John Marshall as chief justice. To compound the affront, on February 27, 1801, five days before Adams's term expired, the Federalist-dominated Congress amended the Judiciary Act of 1789, creating in the process a host of new judicial positions. Under the terms of that act, Adams appointed a large number of judges, marshals, and attorneys, continuing to sign commissions of appointment "till 9 o'clock of the night, at 12 o'clock of which he was to go out of office." The other unanticipated problem was that Jefferson's supporters proved to be rather more bloodthirsty than he: large numbers of them believed that government should be entirely purged of Federalists in the interest of Republican purity, and just as many believed, more crassly, that the losers should be fired to make room for those who had backed the right candidate. The first complication sent Jefferson into a towering rage; the second forced him to temper his principled approach.

There were limits to what could be done immediately about

Adams's "midnight appointments." The major new judgeships had been filled through presidential appointment and senatorial confirmation, and since the Constitution vested federal judges with tenure during good behavior, the judiciary seemed destined to remain a bastion of Federalism for a long, long time—or at least until Congress convened in December, when some legislative remedy might be devised. Meanwhile, Jefferson considered all other appointments made after December 12, 1800 (when the result of the South Carolina election, ensuring Adams's defeat, had reached Washington), as both indecent and illegal; and in various ways he attempted to nullify them. The handiest means to that end was to refuse to sign commissions of appointment, which prevented a number of minor appointees from taking office.

Among his adherents, Jefferson's appointments were less vexing than his removal policy, for within reasonable limits he was willing to reward the faithful, which is to say that he would appoint people on political grounds if they were otherwise qualified. For example, Republican leaders in Connecticut and Rhode Island were given collectorships of ports; certain key congressmen who helped make his election possible were given government jobs when they lost their congressional seats; Charles Pinckney, who had helped swing South Carolina away from his Federalist cousin—Adams's running mate, Charles C. Pinckney—was appointed minister to Spain; Robert R. Livingston, leader of one of the major Republican factions in New York, was appointed minister to France; and several choice offices were given to lieutenants of Vice-President Aaron Burr, whose maneuverings had been crucial to Jefferson's election. But party hacks from one end of the country to the other demanded more jobs than were available without making removals on purely political grounds, and they exerted a great deal of pressure upon the president. He yielded in a number of instances, but by and large, he held firm in his moderation: the turnover in federal jobholders was only one-third during his first two years in office, and only one-half during his entire first term. Too, with rare exceptions his appointees were men from established elite backgrounds, mostly the gentry; and more than half were college-educated, though only a tiny fraction of the whole population had attended college.[4] By these means he brought about a radical change in the tone of administration and improved its quality into the bargain.

To a considerable extent, Jefferson's success in bringing his policies into execution was due to his departure from the methods followed by his predecessors in regard to appointments at the highest levels. Washington had sought to find the best available man for every position and had given little if any thought to policies. Adams had retained Washington's cabinet, mainly because public office had proved to be a frightful consumer of reputations and therefore replacements were not easy to find; only gradually and timorously had he fired disloyal or incompetent subordinates and replaced them with men more to his liking. Jefferson, from the start, surrounded himself only with dedicated, loyal Republicans whose principles were the same as his own. To be sure, his appointments to the less important cabinet posts—Henry Dearborn of Maine (Massachusetts) as secretary of war, Robert Smith of the Baltimore Smiths as secretary of the navy, Levi Lincoln of Massachusetts as attorney general, and Gideon Granger of Connecticut as postmaster general—were made with political considerations in mind, and a certain mediocrity was the result. To head the State and Treasury departments, however, Jefferson opted for brilliance as well as for solid principles, and James Madison and Albert Gallatin joined him to form a virtual triumvirate—though always with the understanding that they stood to him as the second and third consuls stood to Napoleon.

Madison's relationship with Jefferson was intensely personal and immensely complex, and perhaps it has never been fully fathomed. Psychologically and intellectually they were complementary. Madison was a secret epileptic, and Jefferson was a compulsive father-to-all-who-needed-him: that formed a part of the relationship. But Madison was cagey, ever-wary, whereas Jefferson was expansive, sometimes even foolishly so when he thought himself totally in command of a situation; and so Madison acted as a check upon Jefferson even as Jefferson acted as imagination and protector for Madison. Jefferson was often inclined to carry a good thing too far, as he did for instance when he once suggested that a bloody revolution every generation was the the best way to remove the oppressively dead hand of the past; Madison gently refrained from telling Jefferson that he was being carried away, not to say silly, and instead merely pointed out some of the practical difficulties that would attend following this otherwise admirable course. Yet Madison, once he came under Jefferson's spell, was incapable of thinking independently. Separately, the one was rash and the other was pedantic; together the two men formed a multitude.

Gallatin's role was less personal, more intellectual. This Swiss-born Pennsylvanian was also more logical than either Jefferson or Madison, and he understood (or seemed to understand) public finance, as neither of them could pretend to do, save to know intuitively that it was a pernicious evil as Hamilton practiced it. As a congressman a few years earlier, while his Republican colleagues had been able to combat the Hamiltonian system only with seventy-year-old Bolingbrokean epithets, Gallatin had bedazzled them all by taking the system apart piece by piece. He had charged, and documented the charge, that Hamilton through carelessness or corruption had unnecessarily padded the national debt by $10 million out of a total of $77 million. Gallatin had also, virtually as a personal invention, brought into being the House Ways and Means Committee as a watchdog over public expenditures. Jefferson and other Republican leaders knew in their bones that dismantling the Hamiltonian system was the foremost of their missions. Only Gallatin could tell them why, in fiscally respectable language, and only Gallatin could tell them how.[5]

Jefferson handled his subordinates masterfully, as he handled most men. As he described cabinet meetings—varnishing the truth only slightly—"there never arose . . . an instance of an unpleasant thought or word between the members" during his entire presidency. To be sure, they "sometimes met under differences of opinion, but scarcely ever failed, by conversing and reasoning, so to modify each other's ideas, as to produce an unanimous result."[6] That was the way of things, too, when department heads met separately with the president (his door was always open to them, and they were frequent dinner guests as well). The atmosphere was relaxed, informal, almost casual, and opinions were voiced freely without fear of incurring the wrath of the chief; yet, such was Jefferson's presence that no one ever forgot who was in charge.

A similar arrangement marked the relations between the executive and legislative branches of government. Jefferson established a rapport with Congress that neither of his predecessors and few if any of his successors could match. He used none of the techniques that are usually associated with "strong" presidents—popular pressure, naked power, bribery, flattery, cajolery, blackmail, or shrewd trading—yet he had but to suggest legislation and it was almost invariably forthcoming.

In no small measure the achievement was based upon the way Jefferson dealt with the congressmen personally. Officially he stood aloof from them, maintaining a wall of absolute separation between the branches. Beginning with his first annual message in December of 1801, he abandoned the traditional practice of appearing in person before Congress, sending written communications, usually quite brief, by a messenger instead. In point of political form, that was a radical break from a ritual that had originated with the English Crown and Parliament and had been followed in both state and national government in the United States. In point of practice, the change reflected Jefferson's realization that he was simply no good at dealing with men in the aggregate: his inaugural address, for instance, was a rhetorical and political gem, but it was delivered in a voice so unprepossessing that few could even hear it, much less be inspired by it. Rather, his touch, to be effective, had to be personal. To that end he feted all the congressmen, in carefully chosen groups, at a rotation of dinner parties, where—in an environment of seemingly casual elegance—he maintained the same kind of comfortable, informal atmosphere that prevailed in cabinet meetings.

Always unwigged, sometimes dressed in frayed homespun and run-down slippers, the president put his guests at their ease with the folksy, open hospitality of a country squire; but the dinner (prepared by a French chef and accompanied by a magnificent selection of French wines) was likely to be the finest the legislators had ever tasted, and the conversation was regularly the most fascinating they ever heard. Jefferson always led the conversation, dazzling his guests by talking with equal ease of architecture, history, science, theology, music, mathematics, or art—everything but current politics, which subject was forbidden. Reading between the lines of the accounts of these occasions, one sometimes suspects that the talk was more brilliant than deep and that it frequently had the flavor of a lecture by Polonius. Moreover, the congressmen were for the most part a mediocre lot, having less talent, wealth, education, and social experience than their predecessors in the early Federalist Congresses. In any event, Jefferson's guests were usually overwhelmed: few congressmen were immune to the president's personality, and most returned to the congressional pit with renewed faith in his wisdom and virtue.

There was more, of course, to Jefferson's power over the national legislature than his magnetism at dinner, but that was a cardinal element. Another element was his deployment of Gallatin as the administration's unofficial liaison man with Congress. Gallatin knew and was on friendly terms with most Republican congressmen, having served for some time as their floor leader, and he could work informally with them on proposed legislation without violating their sensibilities in regard to executive encroachment. That made it possible for the president to have an effective voice in making legislative policy, and yet avoid Hamiltonian trappings of a monarchical-ministerial system.

Still another element was the Republicans' system of organization in Congress. Republican members of both houses met in caucuses to determine policy, and that was normally enough to establish all the discipline necessary for carrying out the party's program. There was, however, always a danger of factionalism within the party, and in order to check factional disputes, something extra was needed. In part, this was provided by investing the Speaker of the House with great power, and by choosing as Speaker Nathaniel Macon of North Carolina—a plodding, sincere, impeccably honest man whose lack of imagination and guile would have made him trustworthy even if his purity of Republican principles had not.

The next necessity was for a floor leader, which by recent custom devolved upon the chairman of the Ways and Means Committee. There some friction developed. The chief pretender to both roles was William Branch Giles of Virginia, who had earlier served as Madison's ablest lieutenant when Madison headed the "republican interest" in Congress; but instead, Macon appointed another Virginian as head of Ways and Means—his brilliant, caustic, erratic twenty-eight-year-old friend, John Randolph of Roanoke. Giles, as it happened, soon became ill and returned home, and when he came back to Washington, it was as a member of the Senate, in which he promptly became the president's leading spokesman. Meanwhile, Randolph took over as the Republicans' floor leader in the House, which caused the president some discomfort. Randolph was a man of pure political principles, but he was also a bit crazy, and was devoid, as well, of ability to compromise. His close friends in the House—Macon, Joseph Nicholson of Maryland, and Joseph Bryan of Georgia—exercised some moderating influence upon him; but Jefferson, sensing that he might one day prove a menace, sought vainly to find a leader to replace him.

Down in the ranks, Republican congressmen were of two broad descriptions. Perhaps something under half were men of relatively modest origins who, on the one hand, were social democrats if not egalitarians, or at least personally comported themselves as if they had not a superior on earth; and were, on the other, tough, opportunistic, alert to every chance for increasing their influence or wealth and not especially scrupulous about how they did it. Though such men were to be found in all parts of the country, more of them came from the West and from the Middle States and urban wing of the party than from the South. Most of the others, to a lesser or greater degree, fit the description that John Quincy Adams wrote of one of them: "He was a man of moderate talents and respectable private character, full of Virginian principles and prejudices, a mixture of wisdom and Quixotism. . . . He scarcely ever spoke; never originated a measure of any public utility, but fancied himself a guardian of the liberties of the people against Executive encroachments. . . . Jealousy of State rights and jealousy of the Executive were the two pillars" of his political fabric. He "always had the satisfaction of being in his own eyes a pure and incorruptible patriot. Virginia teems with this brood more than any other State in the Union, and they are far from being the worst men among us. Such men occasionally render service to the nation by preventing harm; but they are quite as apt to prevent good, and they never do any."[7]

Both types wanted artful management, but despite the absence of a reliable floor leader in the House, Jefferson—with Gallatin's able assistance—was quite up to the task. In the early days of the administration, in fact, managing the House was a relatively minor problem, for it was in the Senate that the Republicans had greatest cause for concern. Jefferson counted sixty-six Republicans and thirty-seven Federalists in the House, a majority that seemed so secure that no amount of factionalism could shake it. In the Senate the Republicans had an edge of only four votes, eighteen to fourteen, and enough Republicans were absent from time to time to make the balance very nearly even. Fortunately for the Republicans, Vice-President Burr was there, to control events with his adroit political hand and to break ties with his vote. Or rather, so it appeared.

A great deal of the Republicans' program for reform was negative, which is to say that it was aimed at undoing as much of Federalism as possible. In short order, for example, Congress repealed those of the Alien and Sedition Acts that had not already expired, Jefferson pardoned all ten persons (mostly Republican newspaper publishers) who had been convicted under the Sedition Act, and Congress voted to restore with interest all fines that had been levied under the act. Almost as quickly, Congress abolished most of the internal taxes—the hated excise, carriage, and direct property taxes—that Federalists had enacted in 1798 to help pay for the quasi war with France. As part of the same package, Congress set about the business of reducing the military establishment and slashing army and naval appropriations.

41

The task of undoing the Hamiltonian system fell mainly upon Gallatin. Gallatin's primary goal, which Jefferson not only shared but repeatedly said was the most important tangible objective of his presidency, was to reduce the public debt and ultimately abolish it. The ideological underpinning of this aspiration, as indicated, was the belief that debt, public or private, was inherently bad, and that the national debt as created and managed by the Hamiltonians was doubly so because it infected American government and society with the noxious germs of the corrupt British system. Gallatin also accepted Republican ideology in regard to taxes, which meant, after the internal taxes were repealed, that approximately 90 percent of all federal revenues came from a single source, namely, duties on imports. Gallatin believed that if people were relieved of onerous taxes in normal circumstances, they would gladly pay them during a war or in other emergency situations. He also believed that the best way for a government to build its credit was to pay its debts. Hamilton's view, on the other hand, was that Gallatin was making a dangerous mistake on both counts, that the public debt and the machinery and legislation for collecting all forms of taxes must be kept at least nominally operative at all times, so that they might be readily expanded or activated during emergencies.

The revenue structure thus being a "given," Gallatin sought to achieve his goal by cutting expenditures. Like most Republicans (and like most reformers at most times), he was entirely convinced that civilian expenditures of the government were extremely wasteful, and he instituted a vigorous program designed to eliminate the waste. With the wholehearted cooperation of both Congress and the president, he infused the government with a regularity and efficiency that the more freewheeling Federalists had never practiced. Appropriations, for instance, had previously been voted in lump sums by departments, and department heads and other high officials were left free to use the money at their discretion—with the result that funds intended for one purpose were often used for another. Indeed, money had sometimes been spent with no authorization at all, Congress being presented with a bill after the fact. The Republicans in Congress never went so far as to adopt Gallatin's recommendation for line-budget appropriations—ironically, because they trusted him implicitly and did not want to tie his hands—but they did make their appropriations much more specific than the Federalists had, and Gallatin policed every expenditure with meticulous care.

It turned out, however, that precious little waste was there to remove. The Federalists, for all their cavalier manners, proved not to have been throwing money around needlessly, and though irregularities had been common, actual peculation or other wrongdoing had been almost nonexistent. Thus, despite his zeal and his precisely methodical administration, Gallatin was unable to make any appreciable dent in civilian expenditures.

That left the military. Under legislation passed March 16, 1802, the army was cut to one regiment of artillery and two of infantry and to a total strength of 3,350 officers and men. All soldiers that were supernumerary to this establishment were discharged with a modest bonus. No provision was made for a quartermaster general or commissary; instead, economy was effected by placing the army's paymaster general in charge of clothing the troops and by vesting military agents, one at each post, with authority to feed and supply the soldiers. Economy was not the sole purpose of this reform: the Jeffersonians aimed at creating a small but well-trained army and at placing the main burden of national defense upon the militias. Toward the first end, positive steps were taken, for the same basic law of 1802 established the Army Corps of Engineers and the military academy at West Point; but Congress balked at the president's proposal to reorganize the militia system and infuse it with discipline.[8] The result was expensive economy, for the army was rendered so small as to be ineffectual and nothing was provided in its place.

Efforts to trim the naval budget were likewise less than satisfactory. The Federalists had, on the eve of Jefferson's inaugural, voted to dispose of all the smaller vessels acquired since the Navy Department had been created in 1798, to pare down to thirteen frigates—which were, by the way, the best fighting ships of their class in the world—and to keep only six of them in active service, the others to be laid up in ports. To maintain the reduced establishment, they appropriated only $3 million a year. The Jeffersonians promptly laid up the remaining frigates, suspended construction and all but minimal maintenance, and cut the annual appropriation to $1 million.

In regard to the navy as to the army, however, Jefferson and Gallatin had a positive program, or rather what more properly might be called a pet idea. They believed that navies were more of a menace than a boon, not only because they entailed an arrogantly aristocratic officer caste but also because they extended a nation's hostile boundaries and thus its likelihood of stumbling into war. What was needed was an inexpensive potential for defense without

43

the potential for mischief that accompanied an attacking force, and the Jeffersonian answer was the maritime equivalent of militias, namely gunboats. According to Jeffersonian theory, gunboats measuring about fifty feet in length, of shallow draft, equipped with oars as well as sails, and armed with one or two cannon were ideally suited to protect American harbors from foreign marauders, and had the added advantage of costing very little for construction or maintenance. Following that theory, the Jefferson administration was prepared to let the nation's magnificent Humphreys frigates rot at the wharves, and in 1805 it began to build a "mosquito fleet" of gunboats in their place.

The long-range implications of these false economies were to reduce the military capacities of the United States to virtually nothing, and thus to tie the nation's hands in its foreign relations far more than Hamiltonian policy ever had. On a different scale they seemed justified, for the fiscal soundness they seemed to make possible promised to strengthen the country more than a temporary loss of military potential weakened it. But there was the rub: for reasons quite beyond the administration's control (and to be described later), average peacetime expenditures for military purposes actually increased rather than decreased while Jefferson was in office.[9]

And yet, under Gallatin's management the United States government was able, during the presidency of Thomas Jefferson, to reduce its debt from $80 million to $57 million and to accumulate an additional treasury surplus of $14 million, despite the unanticipated expenditure of $15 million for the purchase of the Louisiana Territory. The key factor in this impressive achievement was an abnormal circumstance that blinded Jefferson and Gallatin to some harsh realities and would, in time, lead them quite astray: because of the profits of the neutral carrying trade, and ultimately because of the policies of the British government which permitted that trade, American commerce was inordinately prosperous during Jefferson's first few years in office, and with that prosperity the revenues of the American government were inordinately swollen. In sum, the success of the Jefferson administration in purging American government of corrupt British influence was directly dependent upon the will of the British government.

So much for reform based upon ideals. In two other areas of proposed changes, involving public lands and the judicial branch of government, the Jeffersonians were concerned more with money and power than with ideology—though it should be added that in these as in most matters their interests and their ideology were complementary. In any event, they moved vigorously in both areas, but their efforts met with mixed success.

The question of the public lands was complex, the more so because in regard to it the only significant differences between Federalists and Republicans were matters of interest, not of principle. The public domain consisted of millions upon millions of acres of unoccupied land between the Appalachians and the Mississippi, and nearly every important politician—indeed virtually every solvent American with capital or credit and even the least spark of avarice—had attempted to gain a piece of that vast turf, not with the intention of farming it but with a view toward selling it at a handsome profit to actual settlers. Federalist Congresses had facilitated such speculative activity by making the terms and conditions of direct land sales from the government to settlers more or less prohibitive, and Republicans did nothing substantial to change that scheme of things when they gained the ascendancy.[10] Nor did Republicans differ with Federalists in believing that a primary objective of American foreign policy should be to enhance the value of western lands (as well as secure the nation's frontiers) by obtaining control of the waterways and ports on the Gulf of Mexico, though for various reasons they disagreed over the most efficacious means toward that end. But in certain key respects, having to do with whose titles were valid and whose were not, disagreements were both numerous and intense.

The first area of dispute arose from confusion over which governmental authority had owned the land in the first place. Except in western Pennsylvania, where a monumental snarl of speculative claims had developed, everything north of the Ohio River was relatively simple, for that territory had become the property of the national government at the end of the Revolution. The territory that became Kentucky was more involved. It was originally a part of Virginia; and before consenting to Kentucky's becoming a state, Virginia had granted a great deal of the land as bounties to Revolutionary War veterans and others, so that neither Kentucky nor the United States had an unclouded title to the unoccupied lands in the state. North Carolina had gone even further before allowing Tennessee to be spun off as a separate state: it had granted or sold titles to almost every square foot of Tennessee to North Carolinians. Tennessee, on becoming a state, promptly reclaimed the land or regranted it to its own citizens.

45

Georgia alone continued, after the adoption of the Constitution, to hold all the land it claimed by virtue of its earlier charter as a colony of the British Crown, namely that between the Atlantic and the Mississippi. Land titles in Georgia were even more clouded than they were to the north, for two reasons. One was that Indians occupied most of the area, and were not only able and willing to defend it, often with the connivance of Spanish authorities, but were also guaranteed their rights by treaties with the United States, most especially treaties signed by the Washington administration in 1791 and 1792. Since the Constitution provided that treaties—along with constitutional acts of Congress and the Constitution itself— were the supreme law of the land, paramount to state constitutions or laws, all that land was legally nonexistent as far as white speculators and settlers were concerned.

The other reason for confusion was that the legislature of the state of Georgia had entirely disregarded such niceties and had sold the land anyway. Rather, the legislators had sold their votes to speculators and had all but given the land away. In 1789 three "Yazoo Land Companies"—one each in South Carolina, Tennessee, and Virginia, and named after the river that flows through what became the state of Mississippi—were organized, and the Georgia legislature sold them title to 16 million acres for a payment to the state of $200,000, plus large private payments to the legislators. During the next seven years the legislature canceled various earlier sales as fraudulent, but it also resold the land several times over: the land in twenty-four counties, amounting to 8.7 million acres, was so frequently granted that patents for it totaled 29 million acres by 1796. As titles were canceled, speculators dumped their claims on northerners.

The most important group of seemingly guileless buyers, concentrated in Connecticut and Massachusetts, was called the New England Mississippi Land Company, on which a band of speculators unloaded titles to 11 million acres of Yazoo lands for $1,138,000. The New Englanders made their purchase on the very day in 1796 that the Georgia legislature repealed and repudiated all its preceding Yazoo land grants, including the ones that the New Englanders bought. But the Yankees were not as witless as they seemed: the stockholders and officers of their company included prominent and wealthy men from both parties, who forthwith set out to use their political clout to obtain either confirmation of their title or suitable compensation from the federal government. During the presidency of John Adams they worked through their Federalist lobbyists and congressmen, but all their efforts failed. When Jefferson became president, their prospects brightened, for the Jeffersonians were politically weakest in New England, and were quite willing to make friends there by doing something they were eager to do already, which is to say exert the power of the federal government in behalf of land speculators of their own political persuasion.

The Jeffersonians moved swiftly to resolve the situation in the interest of all Republicans concerned. A token of good faith, as it were, was offered with the appointment to the postmaster general-ship of Gideon Granger of Connecticut, one of the leading Yazoo investors from New England. More tellingly, Jefferson appointed Madison, Gallatin, and Attorney General Levi Lincoln as commis-sioners to negotiate with Georgia regarding the state's western lands. Under the ensuing agreement, signed by both governments on April 24, 1802, Georgia ceded its claims to what became the states of Alabama and Mississippi, and the federal government paid Georgia $1,250,000. In addition, the United States agreed (a) to liquidate, by purchase or otherwise, Indian land claims in what remained of Georgia, and (b) to set aside one-tenth of the acquired lands for the compensation of Yazoo claimants. By the time the terms of this "treaty of 1802" were fulfilled, Congress would appropriate as much money for the acquisition of Georgia lands, already a part of the United States, as it would for the entire Louisiana Purchase, which approximately doubled the territorial extent of the nation. More-over, the pact would ultimately become the basis for Andrew Jack-son's "death-march" policy of Indian removal.

But that was in the future. More immediately, the problem entailed in these arrangements was that both parts of the deal—Georgia's nullification of its granting acts in 1796, and the terms under which it sold its western lands to the national government six years later—were of dubious constitutionality; and that brought the federal judiciary into the equation. The judiciary was, in fact, already much involved in cases concerning speculative land titles, and questions of jurisdiction over such suits were intimately related to the Federalists' Judiciary Act of 1801. In the Judiciary Act of 1789 state courts had been given trial jurisdiction over most, but not all, private civil litigation. By 1800, in literally thousands of instances, settlers and rival groups of speculators had brought actions against one another in suits involving millions of dollars and millions of acres. A hopeless tangle resulted. The cases sometimes involved conflicting jurisdiction (whether Kentucky land suits should be set-tled in Kentucky or Virginia courts, for instance), and sometimes

47

seemed to involve an absence of courts with any jurisdiction (the Georgia situation, for instance). Sometimes, too, the cases had become caught up in political fights that jeopardized the very existence of state courts; such was the situation in regard to the claims of the Holland Land Company in Pennsylvania and those of the purchasers of the confiscated Fairfax Estate in Virginia's Northern Neck. Most importantly, the cases involved conflicts between individuals and states: in 1800, as one historian has put it, "private interests, frequently on a grand scale, stood opposed to the interest of the state government in Pennsylvania, Georgia, Virginia, and Kentucky."[11] State governments had the upper hand until 1801, but then the new law removed jurisdiction over most of the cases from state courts to federal courts. In no small measure, the hostility of the Jeffersonians toward the Judiciary Act of 1801 derived from that transfer of jurisdiction.

The stakes in land speculation were grand, and other Republican economic interests were involved in the courts as well. For example, the Federalist-dominated court system had consistently ruled in favor of British creditors against their American debtors, which meant mainly Virginia and Maryland tobacco planters; and the courts upheld the constitutionality of the carriage tax of 1794, which was entirely discriminatory, falling as it did principally on southern plantation owners. Too, there was the matter of power. The federal courts were all that stood between the Republicans and total domination of the national government. That fact rankled doubly when Republicans reminded themselves that they controlled two branches by virtue of the will of the people, whereas Federalists controlled the other by virtue of chicanery and executive appointment. Beyond that, there was sheer pique. The Federalists, not satisfied with taking money from their pockets and power from their hands, threw a deliberate insult into the package as well. Jefferson so regarded, anyway, that portion of the 1801 act which reduced the number of justices on the Supreme Court from six to five, by providing that when the next vacancy occurred it should not be filled. Since the retirement of one justice was imminent, that was an intentional diminution of Jefferson's powers and would keep the Court entirely Federalist.

But there was even more to the Jeffersonians' war against the federal courts than money, power, and personalities. Underlying it all was a deep-seated attitude about the law and about courts in general. At bottom, the Jeffersonians really did not believe in law

—or not, at any rate, in the historical English concept of law as something fixed, immutable, handed down through the ages. Rather, they believed in government by the good and the wise, acting in the interest of the whole and restrained only by the virtue of an enlightened and informed people. The colonial Virginian system of justices of the peace—who exercised legislative, judicial, and executive functions—was one of their models. Another was the ancient Saxon system, wherein justice was dispensed according to the common law by judges who were elected and readily removable by vote of the heads of families. Still another was the plantation system, wherein the master ruled absolutely, but only if he ruled wisely and well: the check upon him was the opinion of his peers. In other words, law was a convenience and a norm that could and should be set aside when the needs of society—as judged by its wisest and most virtuous members—so dictated. Jefferson summarized this view repeatedly in his voluminous correspondence. "On great occasions," he wrote, "every good officer must be ready to risk himself in going beyond the strict line of the law, when the public preservation requires it; his motives will be a justification." Again, "a strict observance of the written laws is doubtless *one* of the high duties of a good citizen, but it is not *the highest*. The laws of necessity, of self-preservation, of saving our country when in danger, are of a higher obligation."[12]

So believing, the Jeffersonians were prepared to repeal the Judiciary Act of 1801, and hang the constitutionality of the question. To be sure, the constitutional question was a tricky one: judges held their seats for life unless removed by impeachment, and thus it could be argued that to abolish the judgeships created by the 1801 act was to remove judges unconstitutionally. But that, in turn, involved a trickier question, namely, who was to decide what was constitutional? On three or four occasions since the Revolution, state courts had exerted the power of judicial review and had declared legislative acts unconstitutional, and in the conventions that ratified the federal constitution, several people—including John Marshall—had asserted that federal courts had the power to pass on the constitutionality of acts of Congress and on acts of state legislatures. But in every instance in which state courts had exercised the power, they had been severely rebuked (and at least once overruled) by the state legislatures, and the doctrine had not been tested in the Supreme Court.

The Supreme Court forced the issue in December of 1801. William Marbury, one of Adams's midnight appointees to a justiceship of the peace in the District of Columbia, had not received his commission and had asked the Court for a writ of mandamus ordering Secretary of State Madison to deliver the same. The Court responded by issuing a show-cause order to Madison—an action widely regarded as a warning by the Court that it would challenge any efforts to repeal the Judiciary Act of 1801.

Rigorously undaunted, the Republicans introduced a repeal bill into the Senate on January 6, 1802. Debate proceeded, as expected, on strict party lines, but then the friends of an independent judiciary found an unexpected champion: the vote was tied, and Vice-President Aaron Burr cast the deciding vote to reconsider. (That finished Burr with the Republican party. Jefferson had repeatedly heard accusations that Burr had conspired a year earlier to steal the election from him, and had as often discounted them. Henceforth he was disposed to believe the stories, and other charges against Burr as well.) After further debate and various amendments, however, a majority was mustered and the bill was passed. Early in March the House added its approval. A few days later Congress passed a law that effectively postponed the next meeting of the Supreme Court for a year. A few weeks after that, Congress passed the Judiciary Act of 1802, which incorporated all the reforms of the 1801 act that were consistent with the Republicans' partisan and personal interests. President Jefferson signed all three bills into law.

That ended the first round. The second came when the Court next sat, in its February term of 1803. Right away, in the case of *Stuart* v. *Laird*, the Court decided an extraordinary case in an extraordinary way: it asserted its right to pass upon the constitutionality of acts of Congress, but it exercised that right by declaring the Judiciary Act of 1802 constitutional. Then it considered the case of *Marbury* v. *Madison*. The Jeffersonians expected the Court to lay itself open to political attack by issuing the mandamus that Marbury had requested, but instead John Marshall, who wrote the decision, outflanked the party of his cousin. Marshall ruled that section 13 of the Judiciary Act of 1789, under which Marbury had brought his suit, was unconstitutional on the ground that it gave the Supreme Court original jurisdiction in such cases, whereas the Constitution directed that the Court's jurisdiction be original only in certain specified kinds of cases and that it be appellate in all others. The writ of mandamus was therefore denied. The political implication of the decision was that the Republicans might dump all the Federalist appointees they pleased, without fear of interference from the Supreme Court—though in verbose obiter dicta,

Marshall scolded the president in advance for being such a scoundrel as to take advantage of the opportunity. The larger implication was the string attached: Marshall gave Jefferson a free hand, but only on condition that the president accept the Court's power to pass upon the constitutionality of acts of Congress.

That was going a bit too far. Jefferson and his followers did not challenge the right of the courts to decide matters of constitutionality; the principle that they did insist upon was that each branch of the federal government, and the state governments as well, shared that right equally. Marshall's calculated arrogance was another matter entirely. For some time, the less restrained Republicans had been insisting on sweeping the courts clean of Federalism; James Monroe, for instance, had suggested that the Judiciary Act of 1789 should have been repealed along with that of 1801, so that the entire bench might have been vacated. In the wake of *Marbury* v. *Madison*, such voices became a majority.

Coincidentally, means to the desired end were suggesting themselves at just that moment. Republicans in Pennsylvania, dominating the state legislature, had brought impeachment proceedings against the virulent Federalist state judge William Addison, whose partisanship, indiscretions, and explosions of temper had alienated even members of his own party on the state bench. Many federal judges had behaved in quite that manner, and when the state senate convicted Addison and removed him from office, just as the Marbury decision was being handed down, Republicans in Washington determined to follow Pennsylvania's example. On March 3, 1803, they took the first step on a trial run: in the House, they voted to impeach federal district judge John Pickering of New Hampshire, a man whose shortcomings were not high crimes and misdemeanors but drunkenness and insanity. If those reprehensible but quite nonconstitutional defects should result in conviction and removal from office, the entire federal court system could be picked clean.

The resolution of the Republicans' conflict with the courts would be some time in coming, and while the issue was pending, Federalists and judicial purists trembled with concern, for they believed that an independent judiciary was crucial to the perdurance of constitutional government. To the Jeffersonians, however, the question was of considerably less moment. They were keen with enthusiasm to overhaul the judiciary, to be sure, and from time to time the courts did things that sent them into great spasms of rage. But the fact of the matter was that judicial reform was not vital to their program. Even before impeachment proceedings against Judge Pickering were begun, the domestic part of their "Revolution of 1800" had been substantially and successfully completed.

And what they had accomplished was truly revolutionary. They had placed the public debts in train toward early extinction; and with the debts, the whole corrupt "monarchical" system that Hamilton had erected would expire as well. They had abolished most domestic taxes, had emasculated the standing military establishments, and had repealed a great deal of restrictive and oppressive legislation. To do all that was to defy every precedent. It was simply not in the nature of government to pay its debts, abolish taxes, deliberately restrict its ability to coerce, or voluntarily reduce its authority; rather, the tendency had always been the other way around.

For the moment, the Jeffersonians had reversed the flow of history.

3

★★★★★

THE REPUBLICAN TACK:
ABROAD, 1801–1803

Domestic reform was only half of the Jeffersonian revolution, for the basis of America's relations with other nations also wanted a fundamental reordering. In immediate and practical terms, it is true, the Jeffersonians sought pretty much the same things in foreign relations that the Federalists did. In orientation, style, and philosophical outlook, however, their approach was quite different. The Jeffersonians changed the reference point of American foreign policy from northern commercial centers to the southern plantation. They changed the style from that of Hamilton and Adams (who were both, though in separate ways, quite in the European tradition) to that of Virginia and Thomas Jefferson. And they changed the ideological base, from Walpolean to Bolingbrokean.

In Viscount Bolingbroke's plan of opposition to the Financial Revolution, obsession with independence was the international counterpart of obsession with retiring the public debt at home, and so it was with the Jeffersonians. In his inaugural address, Jefferson spoke of a need to avoid "entangling alliances" with all nations, but his attitude was rooted far deeper than in a mere concern with formal treaties between governments. As secretary of state, he had seen the United States turn its back on Revolutionary France, despite a treaty of friendship and alliance, because America's financial and commercial commitments made it dependent upon the favor of Great Britain, and he was determined to rid his country

53

of all such shackles. Yet even that was not all. Independence, or self-reliance, was at the very core of the eighteenth-century gentry's notion of manhood, and virtue and manhood were interchangeable concepts: a nation could not simultaneously be virtuous and dependent, any more than a man could simultaneously be a gentleman and a sycophant. The trouble was that the game of international relations, as it was played in the courts of Europe, turned not upon manly virtue but upon wile, intrigue, and hypocrisy. Moreover, as Jefferson knew from personal experience, it was a seductive game; and Jefferson was determined to keep his nation out of it, even as a once-burned, twice-wise father steers his sons away from gambling houses and harlots. On this subject he was almost fanatical. He would avoid intimacy with the powers of the Old World as he would avoid a vile and fatal contamination; he used such words as "cankers" and "sores" in talking of Europe's society, and "madmen" and "tyrants" to describe its rulers; he thanked an "overruling Providence" for being "separated by nature and a wide ocean" from a Europe that he described as the "exterminating havoc of one quarter of the globe."

Jefferson's way of implementing his foreign policy was uniquely his own, and it corresponded closely to his style in handling domestic affairs. Madison played, in the international arena, a role that was a counterpart to the one that Gallatin played in the domestic: he was all propriety, reserve, caution, and protocol, and he worked himself to the emaciation point into the bargain. The president assumed a mánner that seemingly clashed with but in fact complemented the secretary of state's stiff formality, treating diplomats with calculated casualness, with a threadbare and homey simplicity that was somehow elegant, with a New-World innocence that was somehow sophisticated and cosmopolitan, with an insistence upon equality that somehow demonstrated his superiority.

For a time that style was as persuasive in foreign affairs as it was in domestic: as president, Jefferson was a superb diplomat. Edward Thornton, the young British minister to Washington, was smitten with Jefferson; he regularly painted the president's intentions in the most favorable colors when reporting to his superiors in London. Louis Pichon, the French chargé d'affaires, thought Jefferson to be among the staunchest allies of his master, Napoleon. Even Don Carlos Casa Yrujo, the Spanish minister, came to regard the president as a personal friend who was well disposed toward His Catholic Majesty Charles IV. That was Jefferson's design:

allow the sovereigns of Europe to think of him as their pawn, so that in fact they would become his.

Diplomacy, of course, was only one of the determinants of relations between nations, refined though it was as a supplement to naked force. In the new world ushered in by the American and French revolutions, by Napoleon and Pitt, and by Jefferson himself, there were broadly speaking four other sets of determinants: ideology, national interest, domestic politics, and the aspirations and capabilities of other contending nations.

Ideology had been introduced into international affairs by the American and French revolutions. If one ignores the lessons of the past, as ideologues are wont to do, the innovation appears to have raised the plane of international relations, to have elevated them from a base in mere national self-interest and aggrandizement to a base in morality and justice. In fact, however, the change reintroduced barbarism into the relations between nations of the Western world. Upon the abandonment of religious warfare in the late seventeenth century, the openly avowed aims of the foreign policy of Western nations had moved toward the bald pursuit of power and plunder, but the effect was a civilizing one. Codes of behavior became progressively more strict; both diplomacy and war came to be governed by international law, which is to say by rules of the game as strict as those that governed jousting, dueling, or chess. Conversely, when international relations once again became moral or ideological crusades, they ceased to be a sordid game, and when they stopped being a game they stopped having rules; for those who are possessed of holy truth, secular or sectarian, have neither the need nor the ability to compromise or give quarter.

The experiment was short-lived, and by 1801 Jefferson was the only head of state around who was still even partly motivated by ideals in the conduct of foreign relations. (Napoleon did occasionally keep up the pretense: instead of conquering countries, for instance, he "liberated" them.) To the extent that ideology did govern Jefferson's doings, the effect was curiously mixed. On the one hand, the commitment could reduce his flexibility by locking him into positions from which escape was virtually impossible. On the other, ideology provided steel for his sword; for when set on a course, he could pursue it far more relentlessly and ruthlessly than could even the arch bandit Napoleon.

National interest, the second determinant, was subject to various definitions, depending upon who did the defining. Broadly speaking, however, whether one sought to aggrandize or merely to protect what the United States already had, the national interest dictated policies in two general areas—one concerning maritime trade, the other concerning land and frontiers. Ocean-borne commerce had been thriving since the early 1790s. The most spectacular aspect of the commercial boom was the war-born neutral carrying trade; the larger, underlying part, which affected far more people, was the traditional business of exporting American goods to foreign markets and importing goods from them. The continued prosperity of both kinds of trade was dependent upon the vicissitudes of international politics.

The carrying-trade bonanza arose from the fact that, in wartime, France and its ally Spain did not have merchant marines large enough—given the depredations of the superlative British Royal Navy—to carry more than a fraction of the regular trade with their colonies in the West Indies and on the American mainland. Accordingly, both nations had opened the trade to neutral carriers. At first the British had refused to allow that. They invoked the so-called Rule of 1756, which held that trade that was illegal in peacetime could not be legalized in time of war, and under that rule they seized a large haul of American vessels which were attempting to capitalize on the opportunity. For reasons of its own, however, Britain had abruptly reversed its policy with a legal fiction, called the doctrine of the "broken voyage," that particularly benefited the United States. Americans who carried goods from French or Spanish West Indies islands to the United States, unloaded most of their cargoes, took on American goods, and then sailed for Europe with a mixed cargo—all of which was marginally legal in peacetime— were allowed to do so from 1794 onward. American sea captains, for their part, only went through the motions of breaking their voyages and mixing their cargoes, but that was enough to satisfy the British, and the trade boomed.

Federalists tended to regard this profitable scheme of things with enthusiasm, and also to consider it as one of the fruits of their own diplomacy, since the spirit of it was incorporated into the Anglo-American Jay Treaty of 1794. Republicans, less sanguine, pointed out that the arrangement was not in fact a part of the treaty at all, but rested instead upon unilateral Orders in Council which could be reversed at the whim of the British government. Jefferson and his followers wanted it in writing: they wanted freedom of the seas guaranteed by treaty.

The state of things in regard to regular trade was more fluid and more complex. What the Americans had for sale abroad were the products of their farms, forests, and fisheries. These were mainly foodstuffs—wheat, rice, fish, and, on a much smaller scale, beef and pork—but also included lumber, wood products, and two important nonfood agricultural staples, tobacco and cotton. What they bought abroad was manufactured cloth, tools and machinery, sugar, salt, and wines and liquors. In gross terms, just over a third of their exports normally went to the West Indies, just under a third went to Great Britain, most of the remainder went to the European continent, and small amounts went to South America and the Far East. More to the point is an itemized breakdown. The markets for cotton and tobacco were European: cotton was sold almost exclusively to Britain, tobacco about half to Britain and half to the Continent. American lumber and food were sold mainly in the West Indies: practically all the meat, three-quarters of the fish, two-thirds of the lumber and the wood products, and more than half the flour. Rice went more or less equally to the West Indies, England, and the Continent. As to imports, sugar (along with molasses, rum, and a crucial item, hard money in the form of gold and silver) came from the West Indies; wines and liquors came from southwestern Europe and the wine islands; and the overwhelming majority of manufactured goods came from Great Britain.

International politics influenced the flow of goods and the profitability of trade in a variety of ways. Least interfered with was the import trade, for producers were normally avid to sell their goods to Americans or anyone else, but even that trade was not entirely unfettered. Britain, for instance, would not allow American vessels of more than seventy tons burden to trade in the British West Indies, and it often imposed blockades on the ports of its enemies. Markets for American goods, especially in the West Indies, were subjected to a labyrinth of restrictions, deriving from traditional mercantilist policies of parent governments in Europe, which were likely to be waived or altered on short notice for reasons of military or economic expediency. To make matters more difficult yet, the economics of American trade were such that direct trade was rarely feasible. That is, American merchants did not normally ship, say, wheat to England and return with a cargo of cloth which they exchanged for more wheat at home, and so on. Rather, to make ends meet, they had to trade three or four or even five ways, quite commonly with countries that were at war against one another, and/or with their colonies.

There was not much that the United States government could

do about these variations, except to hope that someday trade might become more regularized. Theoretically, the Jeffersonians sought freedom of trade, but in practice—given both their interests and their prejudices—they were not especially vigorous in pursuing the subject. In that respect they differed markedly from the Federalists, who in theory approved every nation's right to restrict the trade of its domains, but in practice worked diligently to open new markets for American goods and American merchants.

National interest regarding the land was fairly clear-cut. Indians in the northwest and southwest must be kept pacificated, the Canadian and southwestern frontiers must be kept secure, and the navigation of the Mississippi (including the right of deposit and transshipment at Spanish New Orleans) must be kept free. On these matters, however, the relative militancy of the American political parties was the reverse of what it was in regard to commerce. The Federalists were the more passive party: they had negotiated treaties that at least nominally guaranteed everything the United States genuinely needed, and they were content to leave it at that. The Republicans sought a great deal more, and were aggressive in seeking it. They wanted the Indians substantially removed, if indeed not annihilated. They were also highly sensitive in regard to the navigation of the Mississippi—or at least those on the Atlantic seaboard were. Actual settlers in Tennessee and Kentucky were, for the most part, raisers of cattle and swine whose markets were to the east, over the mountains, and were accessible by way of long, arduous, but entirely traditional drives. Great landholders and owners of speculative titles in the area, on the other hand, foresaw the development of the cotton kingdom, and saw that control of the southwestern rivers was a *sine qua non* of their future success. To them, the right of deposit at New Orleans—which was guaranteed for three years by Pinckney's Treaty of 1795 and was continued informally afterward by the grace of Spain—was far from enough. They would not be content until the United States actually owned New Orleans and all the Gulf Coast eastward to Apalachicola Bay.

At that point the national interest intersected and blended into the third determinant of international relations, namely popular opinion—or, more properly, domestic politics, and, more properly yet, the expression of local and private interests through the machinery of politics. The general program of the Jeffersonians in regard to the southwest has been mentioned: by obtaining control of the Gulf Coast they could simultaneously work in the national interest, extend the cotton belt, reward land speculators among loyal Republicans, and create new political friends in New England. But there were complications, stemming from the facts that the territory belonged to Spain and that Spain was under the thumb of France. Since the outbreak of the wars of the French Revolution, the Republicans had struck a pro-French, anti-British stance, the Federalists just the opposite. At first, ideology and interest had coincided, for Spain was among France's most devout enemies, and thus to support revolutionary France was entirely compatible with entertaining designs upon Spanish territory. When Spain changed sides in the mid nineties, it became awkward for Republicans to remain pro-French, and their embarrassment became acute during the United States' quasi war with France, 1798–1800. Meanwhile, Napoleon came to power, establishing what amounted to a military dictatorship, and thus the Republicans could scarcely continue to hold that they supported France as a champion of republicanism and liberty.

Logic dictated a total reversal of positions; but in the game of popular politics it is often impossible to follow a logical course, and so it was in 1801. For one thing, Republicans were not immune to the rule that politicians must appear consistent and never admit they have been wrong. For another, to oppose France was ipso facto to become a partner if not an ally of France's archenemy Britain, and that ran counter to everything the Republicans held dear. Alternatively, one could pray for peace: if the war ended, the United States could take an aggressive stance toward Spain without becoming involved in the dispute between Napoleon and England. As it happened, peace came to Europe only a few months after Jefferson took office, with the signing of the preliminary treaty of Amiens between France and England on October 1, 1801. No one doubted that war would resume, soon or late, and what Napoleon contemplated in the interim was entirely inimical to American expansionism. But Jefferson did not know that, and so Amiens seemed to be a heaven-sent opportunity.

In the meantime, Jefferson had occasion to ingratiate himself with Napoleon by doing something he and his party wanted to do anyway. The richest European possession in America, save only the Mexican and South American gold and silver mines, was the Caribbean island of Hispaniola, containing French Saint-Domingue in its western half and Spanish Santo Domingo in its eastern. Until the early 1790s St. Domingo (as Americans referred to the entire island) had been by far the most important West Indies market for goods of the United States. Since then, however, it had been torn by slave uprisings, insurrections, and civil war. When Jefferson took office, it had emerged as a de facto black republic under the wily and brilliant leadership of the mulatto general Toussaint L'Ouverture. Napoleon, as a part of a grand scheme that Jefferson was not yet aware of, planned to reestablish French control of the island. In the undertaking, the cooperation of the United States would be important, perhaps vital.

Jefferson and his party were favorably disposed toward the venture, for stories of slaves slaughtering their erstwhile masters had sent waves of horror through the heart of Jefferson country; but the matter was not simple. As indicated, the Adams administration, hostile toward slavery as well as toward France and avid for commercial opportunity, had opened diplomatic relations with Toussaint and had reopened American trade with the island. The carrying of American foodstuffs and European arms to St. Domingo constituted a large element in the commercial prosperity of the United States. It also constituted a veritable lifeline to the black revolutionaries.

Napoleon had some idea of how important the trade was on both sides, and he instructed Louis Pichon to sound out the Jefferson administration on the subject. The chargé talked with Madison about it four months after Madison took office, but in good diplomatic fashion, Madison hedged. He assured Pichon that the United States would do nothing to undermine French rights to the colony, but added that he did not want to get into difficulties with Toussaint. Unsatisfied, Pichon called on President Jefferson. After some discussion, during which Jefferson reminded Pichon that the United States could not easily abandon such a lucrative trade, but also admitted that he did not approve the existing policy of supporting Toussaint, Pichon put the question directly to him: Would the United States act jointly with France if the French undertook to restore their supremacy over the island? Without evasion, Jefferson replied that it would, and he went on to say that France must first make peace with England, after which "nothing would be easier than to furnish your army and fleet with everything, and to reduce Toussaint to starvation." He added, somewhat naïvely, that he believed England would lend its assistance to the suppression of the black rebels.[1]

Such was the Jeffersonian Republicans' maiden voyage into the seas of diplomacy.

The fourth and most important determinant of America's relations with the rest of the world was the aims of other nations.

Napoleon had designs of his own, as did England and even Spain; and so powerful were the Europeans, relative to the United States, that their designs weighed more in determining what the United States could do than did ideology, politics, and considerations of national interest combined.

As if to demonstrate the futility of the Americans' supposition that they could be masters of their own destiny, the petty tyrant of a petty African satrapy—the pasha of Tripoli—declared war on the United States almost immediately after Jefferson was inaugurated. For some time the United States, like most other commercial nations with weak navies, had paid annual bribes, or "tributes," to the various Barbary Coast princes, in exchange for which the several beys and deys and pashas refrained from engaging in piracy upon private shipping of the paying nation. The pasha of Tripoli, a newcomer who had usurped the throne from his brother, had extraordinary expenses, having to support the large number of wives he had acquired along with his brother's crown and being indebted to those who had supported his usurpation. Moreover, he was jealous when he learned that Tripoli was receiving a smaller tribute from the United States than Algiers and Morocco were. Following local tradition, he declared war by cutting down the American flag.

Responding to threats that preceded the ceremonial declaration, Jefferson dispatched four vessels to the Mediterranean under Commodore Richard Dale: the 44-gun frigate *President*, the 38-gun *Philadelphia*, the 32-gun *Essex*, and tiny *Enterprise*, 12 guns. The fleet was hampered by Jefferson's orders to engage only in "spirited defense" of American shipping—the president took the position that offensive action, without congressional authorization, would be an unconstitutional waging of war—but Dale did impose an effective blockade, and *Enterprise* annihilated a 14-gun corsair without losing a man.

The war, such as it was, dragged on for four years, and in due course American action became decisive. In the meantime the war had two significant consequences. The first was that it disrupted harmony in the administration: Secretary of the Navy Robert Smith wanted to pursue a more vigorous course, Gallatin wanted to cut back so as to save money, Madison and Jefferson vacillated, and Commodore Thomas Truxtun, the senior and ablest proven officer in the navy, got into a hassle with the administration and resigned. The second was that Gallatin's economizing efforts were undermined: despite all the slashing of expenditures for the navy as a whole—and the serious crippling of it in the doing—the cost of maintaining the small fleet in operation in the Mediterranean kept naval expenses nearly as high throughout Jefferson's first term as they had been when he took over.

But the Tripolitan War was a relatively trivial affair, at least for the first two years; what genuinely mattered were the aims and activities of France, Spain, and England. The plans of Spain and England can be summarized briefly, for they were essentially reactions to Napoleon's initiative. The Spanish, unable to wrest themselves free from the Corsican's dominance, had adopted an ingenious strategy. Manuel de Godoy, the most powerful man in the Spanish government (the king being an effiminate fop and the queen being Godoy's mistress), had generously arranged to cede to France first Santo Domingo and then, in a secret treaty signed October 1, 1800, Louisiana. Neither possession was defensible; neither had any value to Spain; and they could be nothing but an expensive burden to France. Moreover, as the clever Godoy may have anticipated, the cessions whetted Napoleon's colossal ego and insatiable greed, and set him to thinking anew of restoring France's long-lost American empire. Preoccupied with that foolhardy course, he just might get off Spain's back, at least for a time.

Great Britain, for its part, was determined to frustrate Napoleon in all his designs, sooner or later destroy him, and ultimately eliminate France as a rival in the race for European domination of the world. The United States figured into Britain's plans in two ways. First, the British proposed to win American friendship and support by facilitating American commercial prosperity in every way that was compatible with English interests. Second, as soon as the British learned of Spain's retrocession of Louisiana to France, they laid plans for seizing it once war was resumed—not to keep, but to present to the United States, on the theory that the Americans could hold it and thus thwart Napoleon. To Americans the rewards, real and potential, of both aspects of British policy were large; but so were the implications for American foreign policy. To anyone of the Jeffersonian persuasion, the costs of Britain's friendship seemed likely to be prohibitively high, entailing the sacrifice of any hopes for reaching the cherished goal of independence. (Indeed, a reminder of America's subordination to Britain lay upon Jefferson's desk even as the peace treaty was being signed at Amiens. During the war just ending, the British had periodically replenished the manpower of their navy by impressing seamen from American vessels, on the claim that the men were deserters from the Royal Navy. There were pending American applications for the release of about two thousand men. More than half were soon discharged, but eight hundred were held for further evidence, and a hundred were detained as proven British subjects.)

Napoleon, not really needing the Spanish bait—since reestablishment of France's empire in America had never ceased to be a primary aim of French policy—was busily engaged in a grandoise new effort toward that end. His attitude regarding the United States, whose interests were most vitally affected by the undertaking, was one of contempt masked by duplicity. The first part of the adventure, the retaking of St. Domingo, was placed in the charge of Napoleon's brother-in-law, Gen. Victor E. Leclerc, who sailed from France late in 1801 and occupied Cap Français on February 6, 1802. Leclerc's instructions in regard to the United States were treacherous in themselves, for American shipping was to be allowed only during the campaign against Toussaint, and prohibited thereafter; but in practice Leclerc behaved even more contemptuously toward Americans. There were twenty American vessels in port when Leclerc arrived, and Leclerc not only seized them but also imprisoned some of their masters, including the naval hero Capt. John Rodgers. Despite the indignation this aroused, and despite a formal protest filed by the American minister in Paris, Robert Livingston, Jefferson assured Pichon that the United States would respect all the French actions "in their full vigor."

The second part of Napoleon's plan was quite another matter, for that entailed the occupation of Louisiana. In the summer and fall of 1802 the French general Claude Victor, under Napoleon's direction, assembled a fleet, men, and supplies in Holland, preparatory to sailing for New Orleans the following winter. Jefferson knew none of this, but rumors of the retrocession of Louisiana had long since begun to reach him, and that was enough to throw him into a state of alarm that bordered on panic. As early as May of 1801, he had written to his son-in-law Thomas Mann Randolph that he feared the "inauspicious circumstance" of retrocession—a fear apparently based on a letter which Rufus King, the Federalist holdover as American minister in London, had sent to Madison late in March. In that letter and in subsequent messages sent during the summer, King informed Madison that British officials assumed the retrocession had taken place and believed that Napoleon had designs on the entire Mississippi Valley, the Great Lakes country, and Canada. The following winter, just as Leclerc was landing in St. Domingo, Jefferson got confirmation of the retrocession. In March of 1802 the news became public.

Desperately, Jefferson undertook a maneuver—which may or may not have been bluff—which he hoped would deter the French from actually taking possession of New Orleans. In a word, he threatened Napoleon, but he did so in a circuitous, unofficial way, through a private letter addressed to Livingston and delivered by the president's old personal friend Pierre S. Du Pont de Nemours. Du Pont, who was returning to his native France on a visit, was asked to read the letter and then seal it before delivering it personally to Livingston; Jefferson expected and hoped that Du Pont would then impress upon the French government the "inevitable consequences of their taking possession of Louisiana." By this means, Jefferson could privately threaten war without issuing an official ultimatum, and thus keep his options open.

Specifically, Jefferson said that "there is on the globe one single spot, the possessor of which is our natural and habitual enemy. It is New Orleans." Possession by Spain was tolerable, at least temporarily, because of "her pacific dispositions [and] her feeble state"; but not so with France. "The day that France takes possession of N. Orleans fixes the sentence which is to restrain her forever within her low water mark. It seals the union of two nations who in conjunction can maintain exclusive possession of the ocean. From that moment we must marry ourselves to the British fleet and nation." The United States would "turn all our attentions to a maritime force," and upon the resumption of hostilities in Europe, an Anglo-American force would not only eject France from the New World, but would also take over Spanish America—without which Spain could not provide France with the subsidies it needed to finance its wars. Thereafter, the combined force would hold "the two continents of America in sequestration for the common purposes of the united British and American nations."[2] That was going a great deal further than the "Anglophile" Federalists had ever gone.

It was also a potent threat, and Jefferson had already assured himself, through his talks with the English minister Edward Thorton in Washington and through Rufus King's talks with British officials in London, that Britain would welcome the arrangement. Whether he could have brought himself to go through with it, or indeed whether he even seriously considered doing so, is open to question. Clearly he did not want things to come to that. Blithely ignorant of the extent of Napoleon's schemes (and having long refused to believe reports, even from unimpeachable sources, that France planned ultimately to restore its American empire), he suggested that Livingston inform the French that if they thought Louisiana really necessary as a granary for St. Domingo, they might win American acquiescence by ceding New Orleans and West Florida to the United States.

The matter came to sudden climax in the fall of 1802, in a way that was as confusing as it was unexpected. In mid October Juan Morales, the Spanish intendant at New Orleans, issued a proclamation closing the port to all foreign shipping and withdrawing from Americans the right of deposit there. Just who ordered him to do so remains a bit of a mystery, as does the question of motives. Minor Spanish officials did not act without instructions from someone, and there is evidence that the orders came from high in the government and included instructions that Morales should conceal from everybody the source of his authority. The action was entirely compatible with Godoy's scheme of causing trouble for France without overtly challenging her. If that was the plan, it worked, for the general American public instantly assumed that France was responsible, and a great clamor for counteraction swept the country.

It was a delicate moment for the Jefferson administration. The quasi war with France had ended but twenty-four months earlier, and the embers of hostility still smoldered, ready to burst into flame. Should they be sufficiently fanned—and Federalists were eagerly fanning them—Jefferson could be forced into adopting the policy of alliance with Britain that he had outlined to Livingston; and though the president may have loved popularity, as the Federalists charged, that love was not a fraction as strong as his aversion to having his hands tied. Accordingly, he took the official position that Morales had acted solely on his own initiative, with neither prodding from France nor instructions from Madrid. Then the president and his party leaders engaged in some adroit maneuvering.

In his annual message to Congress (December 15, 1802) Jefferson pointedly refrained from making any reference to Louisiana. Two days later—in what was made to appear as a spontaneous action hostile to the president, but in actuality was carefully orchestrated in advance—the House of Representatives adopted a resolution calling for the president to submit all papers in his possession that were relevant to the withdrawal of the right of deposit at New Orleans. That stratagem accomplished a dual purpose, as it was designed to do. It convinced Pichon that Jefferson, despite his cooperative demeanor in his official relations with France, would be forced by his own partisans to adopt an aggressive policy, and therefore that his unofficial threats must be heeded. Moreover, it disarmed Federalists who really did want to force Jefferson into adopting an aggressive policy, for it confined the congressional inquiry to the narrow matter of the right of deposit, thus leaving the president free to deal with the larger issue—France's possession of Louisiana—without political interference.

At that point the most potent of all determinants of history, chance and misinformation, entered the drama. Jefferson's offhand suggestion to Livingston that France might want to cede New Orleans and West Florida—an idea half-wished and half-baked—struck the fancy of Du Pont. On the basis of quite unreliable information, Du Pont became convinced that France would sell both territories for $6 million, and after some exchange of correspondence he convinced Jefferson. As it happened, under the Convention of 1800, whereby French and American grievances had been settled, France owed Americans roughly $4 million for spoliations of American shipping, and through simple arithmetic Jefferson leaped to the conclusion that the desired areas could be had for a net outlay of $2 million. Forthwith, conferences were held; the House met in secret session; Jefferson appointed outgoing Governor James Monroe of Virginia as minister extraordinary to France and, if necessary, Spain. Then Congress voted a secret appropriation of $2 million "to defray any expenses which may be incurred in relation to the intercourse between the United States and foreign nations."

It was pie-in-the-sky diplomacy if ever such existed. Given Napoleon's ambitions, Monroe had about as much chance of buying New Orleans as he had of buying Paris. Even Jefferson felt, except in his most euphoric moments, that it was a futile gesture and that war with France would still be necessary. And yet the mission resulted in the most spectacular diplomatic coup in American history.

When notified of his appointment, Monroe was in process of setting out for Kentucky to tend to some land speculations he had there; and though he canceled the trip, he had to make various alternate arrangements before he could sail for Paris. As a result, he was unable to depart from New York for more than two months. In the interim, news arrived that Morales had received orders to turn New Orleans over to the French—Victor's expedition—as soon as appropriate officials arrived.

It was now or never, and Federalists were quick to cry for a more active policy than the administration was following. Alexander Hamilton himself, writing under the pseudonym Pericles, pointed the way. Since war was clearly justified, Hamilton said, the governing considerations were matters of expediency rather than principle. In those terms, there were only two possible courses: "First, to negotiate, and endeavor to purchase; and if this fails, to go to war. Secondly, to seize at once on the Floridas and New Orleans, and then negotiate."[3] Jefferson was taking the more cautious first route; Hamilton was advocating the bolder second. Federalists in the Senate, led by James Ross of Pennsylvania, introduced a set of much-publicized resolutions authorizing the president to call out 50,000 militia and spend up to $5 million for taking the area by force, but after some debate Republicans defeated the proposal. The Federalists, eliciting a good deal of popular support, charged the Republicans with being pusillanimous; Republicans, somewhat feebly, charged the Federalists with being rash. Jefferson stuck to his course, and at last, in March of 1803, Monroe sailed.

The delay turned out to be important, for it gave Napoleon time to learn that his American adventure was doomed. As fate would have it, an extremely cold winter froze Victor's fleet in port in Holland, and there it remained. What was more telling, news arrived from St. Domingo that Leclerc's expedition, begun most auspiciously, had turned into a catastrophe. For a time Leclerc had registered one triumph after another: he had tricked Toussaint into going voluntarily to France, ostensibly to be decorated but actually to be imprisoned, and his military campaigns, conducted with ruthless efficiency against an enemy demoralized by the loss of leadership, had promised to restore control of St. Domingo in short order. But then yellow fever attacked the French, and between the disease and the rallying of the blacks for guerrilla warfare under new leaders, no fewer than twenty thousand French soldiers were wiped out in a matter of weeks, one of them being Leclerc himself.

Abruptly and decisively, Napoleon moved to cut his losses. "Damn sugar, damn coffee, damn colonies," he said. "Irresolution and deliberation," he declared, "are no longer in season; I renounce Louisiana. It is not only New Orleans that I cede; it is the whole colony, without reserve."[4] In that spirit he scrapped his entire American adventure, turned his attention to plans for new conquests in Europe, and instructed subordinates to raise funds for his proposed military campaigns by arranging to sell Louisiana to the United States. Talleyrand, the French minister of foreign affairs, stunned Livingston by making the offer on the eve of Monroe's arrival. Livingston stalled; after so many months of futile negotiations, he assumed that Talleyrand's offer meant France was not in a tenable negotiating position. Word of Senator Ross's resolutions had reached Paris, though it was not known that they had been rejected—which might have been an element in Napoleon's calculations—and Livingston hoped to learn from Monroe that the United States had already seized New Orleans. When Monroe arrived the next day with no such news, the two Americans conferred, decided that Napoleon's offer was too good to turn down if a reasonable price could be obtained, and agreed that Bonaparte's capriciousness made it imprudent to wait for further instructions from Washington. That very evening, Livingston met with Napoleon's minister of finance, François de Barbé-Marbois, and they agreed privately on the terms: the United States would pay 60 million francs and assume all American claims against France up to another 20 million, the total being around $15 million. On May 2, 1803, in an agreement back-dated to April 29, a treaty of cession was signed.

When news of the purchase reached the United States, joy was not entirely universal. New England Federalists tended to disapprove the acquisition out of a general fear that eastern commercial interests would be sacrificed for the sake of territorial expansion and out of a more specific fear that New England's influence in the national councils would be weakened by the growth of the West. The Massachusetts Federalist George Cabot expressed the sour view of both his section and his party: "The cession of Louisiana," he wrote to Rufus King, "is an excellent thing for France. It is like selling us a ship after she is surrounded by a British fleet. It puts into safe keeping what she could not keep herself; for England would take Louisiana in the first moment of war, without the loss of a man." Since France was unable either to settle or protect the area, Cabot concluded, "she is therefore rid of an incumbrance that wounded her pride, receives money, and regains the friendship of our populace."[5] Other Federalists claimed that had Hamilton's advice been followed and had the Ross resolutions been adopted, the United States could have had the territory—and West Florida, too—for a fraction of the purchase price. Their position was given substance by the ensuing course of events, for England and France were back at war two weeks after the Louisiana purchase agreement was signed.

But such carping, for the most part, merely reflected the Federalists' narrowly partisan recognition that the general popularity of the purchase would be devastating to them politically. The administration had avoided war and pulled off a real estate transaction that boggled the imagination. The boundaries of the acquired territory, though not clearly defined, extended from the Gulf of Mexico to the headwaters of the Mississippi and Missouri rivers, stretching nearly 1,500 miles north from the Gulf and extending the American border 250 miles west from New Orleans and a thousand west from the Great Lakes. All told, it added 828,000 square miles to the United States, nearly doubling the nation's size. Jefferson, in his jubilation, declared that the purchase would enable the United States to remain a nation of farmers and land developers—and thus to avoid the evil of urbanization that had corrupted Europe—"for a thousand years." He also declared that he saw "nothing which need ever interrupt the friendship between France and this country."

There were, however, some complications—legal, fiscal, constitutional, and administrative. The legal complication was that the Louisiana territory was not France's to sell. It had been solemnly agreed, when Spain retroceded Louisiana to France, that France could not sell it to a third party, and Napoleon had confirmed that agreement with a vow to Spanish authorities which he made less than nine months before he offered the territory to the United States. Moreover, Napoleon had never fulfilled the conditions whereby he had obtained the retrocession in the first place.

Casa Yrujo, the Spanish minister, entered these objections in strongly worded notes to Madison, implying that if the United States took possession it would, in effect, be receiving stolen property. Rigorously unmoved, Madison dismissed the objections as "too futile to weigh," and the cabinet resolved (on October 4) to take New Orleans forcibly if Spain refused to turn it over peaceably.

The fiscal complication was that the purchase increased the public debt of the United States by nearly 20 percent, and that was a serious matter to an administration whose concern with retiring the debt virtually amounted to a fixation. The terms of sale specified that $11,250,000 of the purchase be paid in 6 percent "stock" (bonds) irredeemable for fifteen years; the remaining $3,750,000 was to be paid in gold or American treasury notes, with which France was supposed to satisfy American claimants. Gallatin wanted it all to be payable in notes, so that he could retire them as rapidly as possible (the interest would run to $675,000 a year, or $10,125,000 total on a simple basis; at compound interest, the method of payment more than doubled the purchase price), but his protests were in vain. Moreover, France arranged in advance to sell the stock to Baring Brothers of London and to Hope and Company of Amsterdam for $9,750,000 cash less accrued interest (or $8,830,000), giving the bankers a profit close to $2.5 million. Not only did that run counter to Gallatin's frugal grain, it contradicted a cardinal principle of Republican financial theory—namely that when foreigners held large amounts of the public debt, America's ability to act independently was severely impaired. Clearly, the treasury could have saved many millions of dollars had not Monroe and Livingston (and, for that matter, Jefferson and Madison) been in such a hurry to consummate the deal.

The financial considerations, however, like the legal, were simply waved aside. Gallatin concurred in the decision, believing that he could retrieve the funds somehow. When the time came for him to do so, he was ready with a proposed means: slash naval expenditures even further.

The constitutional complications were more subtle. Earlier, when the purchase of New Orleans alone had been under contemplation, Jefferson had expressed doubts as to the constitutionality of acquiring territory on the ground that the power was not specifically enumerated in the Constitution; but Gallatin, Madison, and Attorney General Levi Lincoln more or less convinced him that the power was inherent in the very fact of nationhood.[6] When he learned that Monroe and Livingston had agreed to buy not a mere town but a vast empire, his doubts returned, and he decided that the only proper course was to go through with the deal and ask the people to indemnify the action with a constitutional amendment. In keeping with that idea, he drafted an amendment to submit to Congress along with the treaty. Accepting, with reservations, the argument that the government had the authority to *acquire* territory, he addressed the amendment to legitimatizing the incorporation of such territory into the Union. In his draft, he provided for incorporation only of the area below the 31st parallel, where most of the white inhabitants resided. In the huge remaining area, Congress would have no power to grant lands except to eastern Indians in exchange for lands they held east of the Mississippi. Full incorporation of the entire area, Jefferson believed, would drastically alter the constitutional nature of the Union, and his amendment would have postponed such an alteration by leaving it to possible future amendments.

The impracticality of that approach soon became manifest. The president wrote his proposed amendment early in July, before learning that the treaty specifically guaranteed all whites in the territory full benefit of the "rights, advantages and immunities" of American citizens, and also gave French and Spanish ships trading with New Orleans a twelve-year exemption from the duties they paid as aliens in other American ports—a direct contravention of the constitutional requirement that duties must be uniform through-out the territory of the United States. Upon learning this, Jefferson redrafted his amendment and began a campaign to gain support for it by writing letters to all the important members of his party.

With some effort, he managed to overcome his scruples. One element in his conversion was a dispatch that arrived from Living-ston, saying that Napoleon had had second thoughts about the wisdom of the transaction and would withdraw it if the Americans made any changes in the treaty or took a single hour longer than the stipulated six months to ratify it. Though it is entirely unlikely that Napoleon wanted to back out—indeed, he doubtless issued the threat to prod the Americans into action, lest *they* have second thoughts and simply take the territory for nothing—Livingston's let-ter alarmed Jefferson, who called upon Congress to convene in mid October, three weeks earlier than was scheduled, in order to ensure that ratification could take place before the deadline at the end of the month. The president's closest advisors pressed upon him the argument that to couple ratification with a constitutional amend-ment could occasion delay that might be fatal to the purchase. Probably the consideration that weighed most heavily with Jefferson was that almost none of the people to whom he wrote about the constitutional barrier seemed to regard it as any barrier at all—al-though, as some New England Federalists pointed out, full incor-poration of the territory meant that more states would ultimately be admitted to the Union by treaty than were original parties to the federal compact, and that would be an utter negation of the states'-rights doctrine with which the Republican party was identi-fied. Of the few Republicans who did confront Jefferson's consti-tutional questions, the old revolutionary propagandist Thomas Paine, he of *Common Sense* and "the times that try men's souls," was possibly the most persuasive. "The cession makes no alteration in the Constitution," Paine wrote to Jefferson, "it only extends the principles of it over a larger territory, and this certainly is within the morality of the Constitution."[7] That cut to the heart of the matter, and in that spirit Jefferson abandoned his reservations.

The administrative complexities had to do with ascertaining just what the territory was and with establishing some kind of authority over it. By far the largest part of the area, that north of the Arkansas River, was a matter of widespread indifference. Jeffer-son, out of unquenchable curiosity (he had heard wondrous tales of great animals and salt mountains and self-replenishing salt plains in the Trans-Mississippi West, and he was burning to know whether such stories were well founded), had previously persuaded Congress to underwrite what became the celebrated Lewis and Clark expedition, and now he sent the explorers out with a reasonable excuse. Otherwise, however, the area was generally regarded as of little consequence to the United States, at least for the time being.

Of greatest concern was the question whether West Florida was included in the purchase, for that, after all, was what Monroe had been sent to buy along with New Orleans. If historical legitimacy was to be the criterion, West Florida was decidedly not a part of the package. Prior to the 1800 retrocession, Spain had held not one but three distinct territories on the western and southern frontiers of the United States. One was Louisiana, which France had owned by right of discovery until it ceded the colony to Spain in 1762, toward the end of the Seven Years' War. Louisiana extended from the Mississippi River (including the island of Orleans) westward to some vaguely defined part of what became Texas, and from the Gulf northward to Canada. Spain's claim to the other two territories, West Florida and East Florida, rested on a separate and more complex title but was based ultimately on the right of discovery. West Florida extended from the island of Orleans east to the Perdido River (just west of Pensacola) and from the Gulf to the thirty-first parallel, and thus comprehended the rivers and harbors in what became the states of Mississippi and Alabama. East Florida, beginning at the Perdido, included all the territory encompassed by the present state of Florida. Only Louisiana had been retroceded to Napoleon in 1800, and though he could sell what Senator William Plumer called a quitclaim deed to Louisiana, he had no valid historical claim at all to the Floridas.

But the matter was not so simple as that. Clearly, Napoleon had intended to make West Florida a part of his American empire, and various documents attested both that intention and Spain's unwillingness to contest it. The Americans preferred to believe they acquired from Napoleon everything Napoleon believed he had acquired from Spain. Monroe and Livingston tried to get some official confirmation of that position, but when they asked Talleyrand to say that West Florida was a part of the Louisiana Purchase, the Frenchman grew coy. "You have made a noble bargain for yourselves," he said, "and I suppose you will make the most of it."

The Jeffersonians acted upon these various problems with just such a view. The Senate, which needed no prodding from the president, promptly ratified the treaty. Then Congress, delayed only slightly by Federalist efforts to embarrass the administration by demanding to see all the papers pertaining to Monroe's mission—a position which, in the dispute over Jay's Treaty a few years earlier, Republicans had insisted was a congressional right—effectively provided for government of the area by presidential fiat until permanent arrangements could be made. Not long afterward, on February 24, 1804, Congress passed the Mobile Act, setting up a customs district east of New Orleans and thereby laying statutory claim to West Florida. Meanwhile, Jefferson claimed all the Gulf Coast from the Perdido River to Matagorda Bay and, alternatively, to the Rio Grande, and he instructed Monroe to proceed to Madrid to obtain confirmation of the claim.

All that would soon prove to be wishful thinking: in the summer of 1804 Napoleon would declare flatly that West Florida was not a part of what he had sold to the United States. Moreover, the complications attending the "noble bargain" would, in time, turn out to be trivial snags in comparison to the larger implications of the purchase, for those were thorny in the extreme.

But early in 1804 such problems were invisible. Had history ended with the adjournment of the first session of the Eighth Congress on March 31, 1804, it could have been written that the Revolution of 1800 had been completed as thoroughly and successfully in foreign affairs as in domestic. The achievements of the Jefferson administration during its first three years rivaled those of Washington's first three; they would never be matched again, not by Jackson, by Lincoln, or by either Roosevelt. Popular approval of the president was very nearly unanimous west of the Hudson River, and even in New England those who faulted him were a narrow and privileged minority.

4

★★★★★

TURBULENCE IN DOMESTIC WATERS: 1804–1805

No American doubted, in the winter of 1803–1804, that the acquisition of Louisiana would permanently influence the course of the nation's history. Most believed, as well, that the shorter-range implications would also be large, though perceptions of those implications were diverse. Rank and file Republicans saw nothing but enhanced opportunities: land speculators fairly drooled at the prospect for profits, planters on exhausted tobacco farms quickened in the expectation of an expanded market for their surplus slaves, and the party faithful everywhere smelled the political gains that would result from the popularity of the purchase. Many Federalists, by contrast, and practically all New England Federalists, were inspired with a fear that doom was coming even faster than they had prophesied in 1800: they were torn between a dread that the nation would be split into two or three separate republics and, what was equally painful to contemplate, that it would remain one nation under the domination of southern slaveholders and western heathen.

President Jefferson and his intimates, taking the grander view, rose above the mundane considerations as they rose above the paranoid fears. From their vantage point, it was clear that acquiring New Orleans and the Louisiana territory had secured the frontiers of the United States to the west, the northwest, and the southwest, and had reduced the likelihood of war with France to almost nothing. As to the possibility that the nation might one day be divided

into several sovereign entities, Jefferson faced that with total equa-
nimity; it simply did not matter much to him whether one or three
or five republics inhabited the continent, so long as they were all
republics. It did matter to him whether the Floridas, East and
West, remained under European control, and he was prepared to
expend his best diplomatic efforts to see to it that Florida became
a part of the American republic or sisterhood of republics. That
now became his primary goal.[1]

For a while, for eighteen or twenty months after the purchase
treaty was ratified, everyone had the luxury of following up the
great event in his own way—opportunists avariciously, the New
Englanders with crazy schemes, Jefferson and his intimates with
shrewd wisdom—until events in Europe came to overshadow everything Americans did. Even during that period of respite (or of
illusion), however, serious problems arose. For the first six months
of 1804 it appeared that the Jefferson administration might have
made considerably larger commitments than it could live up to.
Scarcely had the administration weathered that storm than domestic
political squabbling threatened to tear apart the Republican coalition and, indeed, the Union itself. Then the party pulled itself
together and scored a resounding victory at the polls, only to be
rent by dissension when Congress reconvened in December. Before
that session of Congress adjourned, the Jeffersonians suffered their
first genuine reversal.

And at that point the trials of the Republican revolution were
just beginning.

The first intelligence to arrive in Washington from the outside
world in 1804 seemingly had nothing to do with the government's
major preoccupation of the moment. Congress and the executive
were busy working out the details of providing Louisiana with a
government that would be consistent with the purchase treaty, the
Constitution, and republican principles, which was a thorny enough
problem in itself. The news had to do with that irrelevant absurd-
ity, the Tripolitan War. As it turned out, however, the two problems
were intimately related.

In the early part of the preceding summer, just as news of the
Louisiana Purchase was reaching America, the Jefferson administration had almost offhandedly vested command of the Mediterranean
squadron in Edward Preble. Preble was a sour down-east Maine
man, a forty-two-year-old disciplinarian with broken health and a
stomach ulcer that kept him in continuous pain. His first act upon

taking command of the 44-gun Humphreys frigate U.S.S. *Constitution* was to complain to Secretary of the Navy Robert Smith that his crew was "nothing but a pack of boys"; his next several acts were efforts to make the boys into men, toward which end he had a goodly number flogged and two hanged for insubordination. When he arrived at Gibraltar in August of 1803, he did something that transformed the men's bitterness into awe, and gave them a foretaste of the glory and pride—both of which qualities were anathema to good Jeffersonian Republicans—that would attend being one of "Preble's Boys." In darkness and fog, he was challenged by a British naval commodore, arrogant as only such could be, who identified himself as Sir Richard Strachan, claimed to be commanding "His Britannic Majesty's ship *Donnegal*, 84 guns," and demanded that Preble send his boat on board. "This," Preble replied, "is the United States ship *Constitution*, Edward Preble, an American commodore, who will be damned before he sends his boat on board of any vessel. Strike your matches, boys." Strachan backed down, and when day broke, it turned out that his ship was only a 38-gun frigate; but Preble had convinced the young men of the infant American navy that he would not be daunted, and he soon set sail for Africa, determined to scour the seas forever of Arabic scum.

At first, as well as in the long run, Preble succeeded totally, but in between he suffered a reversal, and news of that reversal was what dismayed official Washington early in 1804. Preble imposed a blockade, not only of Tripoli, but of Algeria and Morocco as well, and for the first time in living memory, piracy vanished from the Mediterranean: no pirate at sea could return home, and none in port could slip past the Americans and go to sea. Then, however, came a disastrous episode. As a routine part of his operations, Preble entrusted the blockade of Tripoli to the 38-gun frigate *Philadelphia*, Capt. William Bainbridge. To accompany *Philadelphia* Preble sent the smaller, more maneuverable 20-gun sloop-of-war *Vixen*, for the North African coast had shallow and dangerous waters and its winter winds blew toward the shore and were treacherous. Bainbridge, less seasoned than Preble, sent *Vixen* in pursuit of escaping corsairs, which left *Philadelphia* unprotected a few days later when a westerly gale appeared and corsairs set out to beat the one-ship blockade. *Philadelphia* gave chase, ran aground, and was captured.

The meaning of this episode to the navy was rather different from what it was to the executive branch of the United States government. To Preble it was a bitter blow, but in larger terms only a tactical reversal; in response he made such adjustments as were necessary to keep the blockade intact, and meanwhile he considered the most viable ways of minimizing the damage from the loss of *Philadelphia*. The senior American officer who remained captive after Bainbridge was released, twenty-two-year-old David Porter, coolly turned his prison into a naval war college—wherein the Americans retained their sanity and their aplomb, despite frequent torture, by playing theoretical war games. But to President Jefferson, and especially to Secretary of the Treasury Gallatin, the demise of *Philadelphia* was a calamity of an entirely different sort: it meant that Gallatin's hope of financing the interest on the Louisiana Purchase by cutting naval expenditures had been shattered.

What ensued was likewise of different import in the Mediterranean and in Washington. The Tripolitans entertained no thoughts of attempting to use *Philadelphia* as a ship of their own on the high seas—that was alien to their style and their experience—but figured instead to offer her for sale to the British or the French navy. Preble, mistakenly believing that the enemy would be as eager to fight as he was, thought in terms of preventing the Arabs from getting *Philadelphia* to sea. Recapture was impossible, given the heavy fortifications in Tripoli, so Preble decided on an effort to destroy the frigate. He assigned the task to Lt. Stephen Decatur and sixty men, aboard a small captured Arabic vessel, renamed *Intrepid*. The *Philadelphia* was guarded by two hundred men on board and thousands of Tripolitans ready on shore, not to mention heavy shore artillery; and yet Decatur and his men slipped into the harbor, destroyed *Philadelphia*, killed scores of Tripolitans, and escaped without the loss of a man. Lord Admiral Horatio Nelson, the greatest sailor of the entire era of fighting sail, called Decatur's raid "the most bold and daring act of the age." Preble, for his part, was ready to follow the raid with a campaign that would utterly emasculate the pirates.

In Washington, news of the destruction of *Philadelphia* was seen only as another financial reversal, as another strain on a treasury that was already overburdened. That is not quite accurate: in the broader range, it helped convince the Jeffersonians of something they were already wishfully thinking, that small (and cheap) gunboats were more valuable for shore defense than were great (and expensive) frigates and ships of the line. In time, when the Tripolitan campaign was over and done, Decatur's heroic act—or rather, the Jeffersonians' misreading of it—would cost the navy millions in appropriations.

The administration's concern over the expenses of Preble's campaign was not quite so narrow as it appeared from the quarter-deck of U.S.S. *Constitution*. There was a grave weakness in the Republican system of finance, and though Jefferson and Gallatin were unable or unwilling to perceive it, it surfaced in early 1804. By repealing virtually all internal taxes, the Republicans had made federal revenues dependent upon the vicissitudes of the import trade, and the trade in turn varied with the comings and goings of war in Europe. Placed on a chart, the contours of American revenues precisely followed the course of the Anglo-French struggle, though with a six-month to one-year time lag because of the system of collection; and the contours of Republican foreign policy mirrored the revenue curve with equal precision, for the supply of money delimited what could be done. In short, Gallatin's financial system, far from making the nation independent in international relations, made it more dependent than ever before.

In 1804 the Republicans were able to deceive themselves; indeed, they were able to regard the predicament in which they found themselves as confirmation of the soundness of their fiscal philosophy. What happened was this. The interest expense on the bonds and notes issued to finance the Louisiana Purchase ran to $675,000 a year on a semipermanent basis and to another $225,000 on a short-term basis, for a total of $900,000. Revenues in 1803, reflecting the interval of peace in Europe, fell drastically, from $12.6 million to $10.6 million; and with revenues down by $2 million and expenses up by nearly $1 million, the inability to cut the naval budget was a severe blow indeed. With singular lack of grace, Jefferson and Madison began to grumble about the precipitousness with which Livingston had snapped at the offer of Louisiana, and to point out that he could have obtained much better terms. Gallatin met the interest payment by dipping into treasury reserves, depleting them by a whopping 25 percent. All three men were convinced anew of the wickedness of a public debt, and they cast about for new means of continuing their program of trying to retire it.

For that purpose, Gallatin hastily improvised a financial proposal which he estimated would increase revenues by $826,000, and Congress enacted the proposal on March 26, 1804. The bookkeeping involved was less than forthrightly honest. The law was officially styled "An Act Further to Protect the Commerce and Seamen of the United States against the Barbary Powers." It provided for an additional 2½ percent in ad valorem duties on imports carried in American vessels, and an additional 12½ percent on goods imported in foreign vessels; it authorized the president to build or lease additional naval craft; and it required that the "Mediterranean Fund" be kept as a distinct account, so that it might be spent on nothing but war against the Barbary pirates. Gallatin promptly set out to juggle his books in such a way as to stay within the law and yet make the proceeds of the fund available for general expenditures. That is to say, he saw to it that regular naval appropriations were reduced far below actual operating costs, applied the money thus "saved" to general purposes, and made up the shortage from the Mediterranean Fund. In the words of the foremost historian of Jeffersonian finance, "had Hamilton used the same technique of separating permanent from extraordinary expenditures, Gallatin would have been the first to call it a snare and a delusion, and in that he would have been justified."[2]

The Mediterranean Fund saw the administration through the financial squeeze of 1804: revenues for the year were up, to $11.6 million. By the end of the year the fiscal effects of the resumption of hostilities in Europe were being felt, and before the end of the following year Gallatin would be wallowing in a treasury surplus. That development would seriously influence the course of Jeffersonian foreign policy.

Meanwhile, Congress was following through in regard to an unfinished aspect of the Republican program, namely the cleansing of the federal judiciary. Federal district judge John Pickering of New Hampshire, who had been impeached by the House early in 1803, came up for trial in the Senate in March of 1804. Being totally insane, Pickering could not appear in his own defense, and on that ground his son asked that the judge simply be removed and thus not be made to suffer the disgrace of impeachment. But the circumstances brought to light a defect in the Constitution. There was no way to get rid of a federal judge for incompetence; there was only the process of impeachment and conviction for high crimes and misdemeanors. Moreover, Pickering's impeachment was a trial run, anyway, its real design being to test the process as a means of overcoming the Federalists' domination of the judiciary, which would otherwise last for many years. Accordingly, the Senate proceeded with the trial and, by a vote of nineteen to seven—one more than the constitutionally required two-thirds majority—found Pickering guilty and ordered his removal from office (March 12, 1804).

That set the stage for a maneuver of much grander moment. The most vulnerable justice on the Supreme Court was Samuel

Chase, a bluff and outspoken Marylander who had aroused the hatred of Republicans by the unrestrained vigor with which he tried cases under the 1798 Sedition Act, by his fierce and unseemly outbursts of temper from the bench, by his insulting castigations of young Republican lawyers, and by his harangues of grand juries with highly partisan political rhetoric. Though it was quite customary for judges to deliver partisan orations to grand juries, in May of 1803 Chase, in addressing a grand jury in Baltimore, became so extreme as to lay himself open as a target for possible impeachment. He denounced a variety of recent reforms, notably the adoption by Maryland of universal manhood suffrage, on the ground that when the propertyless were allowed a voice in government, "mobocracy" was sure to follow. He declared that certain and impartial justice, under the rule of law, was indispensable to the freedom of all men in their persons and property, and he charged that the Judiciary Act of 1802, by shaking the "independence of the national judiciary . . . to its foundation," had imperiled "all security for property and personal liberty." Then he struck at the heart of the danger, as he saw it, namely the ideas that Jefferson had written into the Declaration of Independence, which Chase himself had signed in his younger and more radical days: "The modern doctrines by our late reformers, that all men in a state of society are entitled to enjoy equal liberty and equal rights, have brought this mighty mischief upon us; and I fear that it will rapidly progress until peace and order, freedom and property, shall be destroyed."

These were scarcely popular sentiments; they may also have been unsound, foolish, or even wicked. But they were Chase's honest opinions, and according to republican precepts he had every right to hold and utter them. The proper defense against error was truth, reason, and enlightened public discussion; for as the simple, honest Republican Speaker of the House, Nathaniel Macon, asked in response to the outcry, "is error of opinion to be dreaded where enquiry is free?" But Macon's view was not the view of his co-partisans. To most Jeffersonians, the federal judiciary stood as a barrier to the realization of the kind of society they envisioned for America, and Chase's utterances were both a confirmation of the evil and an occasion for ridding the nation of it.

It was the president himself who suggested that Chase's announced opinions be made the subject of impeachment proceedings. To Congressman Joseph Nicholson he wrote: "Ought this seditious and official attack on the principles of our Constitution, and on the proceedings of a State, to go unpunished? And to whom so pointedly as yourself will the public look for the necessary measures?"[3] Nicholson conferred with Macon (who, having been shown the light, saw it), and it was agreed not only that Jefferson should be kept out of the affair, as he requested, but that John Randolph, rather than Nicholson, could take the lead most effectively. Accordingly, on the very day that the Senate voted to convict Pickering, it was Randolph who moved that impeachment proceedings be instituted against Justice Chase. The House so voted, and a tentative list of articles of impeachment was drawn up and published before Congress adjourned, ending its first session. Completion of the matter was scheduled for the second session, commencing in December.

Even as the attack on the judiciary was being mounted, indicating political self-confidence that bordered on arrogance, the administration was confronted with a political development that appeared, for a time, likely to portend dire consequences. The threat arose from the squeeze in which northern Federalists found themselves. On the one hand, they were exercised over most of what the Jeffersonians were doing, not merely the impeachments but also the sectional nature of Jefferson's achievements, the advantages as well as the preoccupations of his policies being preponderately in favor of the South and the West. On the other, they were beginning to recognize that they were remarkably inept at the kind of popular politics in which the Jeffersonians were so superbly gifted, and thus might never be able to fight back effectively. One of the requisites of a successfully functioning two-party system is that neither side comes too close to total victory, for in that event the losers are likely to resort to drastic measures, to challenge the very foundations of the system itself. That is where the Federalists found themselves early in 1804.

In their frustration, even the more responsible Federalists became willing to raise a delicate issue. The most tenuous fibers in the fabric of union concerned slavery. In one of the great compromises made by the convention which had drafted the Constitution, it was provided that slaves would count as three-fifths of a person for purposes of reckoning both the distribution of direct taxes and the apportionment of representation. But direct taxation was out as long as the Jeffersonians were in, which meant that the benefits of the compromise were one-sided: slave states received the advantage of outsized representation without having to carry a proportionate part of the tax burden. Thus, for instance, New York and New England together had about sixty thousand more free inhabitants than did the entire slaveholding South, and as entrepôts they doubtless paid considerably more in import duties; yet the South had thirteen more seats in the House of Representatives (65 to 52) and twenty-one more electoral votes (81 to 64). If the Louisiana Territory were opened to slaves, the malapportionment would increase. It was that pivotal part of the system to which the moderate northern Federalists addressed a challenge in January and February of 1804.

They tried in two ways, and though both failed, the very effort portended serious political division in the future. The first attempt came in Massachusetts, where Federalists in the state legislature proposed a constitutional amendment abolishing the "three-fifths clause." Only modest support for the proposal was forthcoming even in New England, and none came from elsewhere, so it died. A more nearly successful effort, aimed differently, was made in Congress, where Federalists attempted to prohibit slavery in the entire area of the Louisiana Purchase. Though the Federalists in Congress were far outnumbered, they gained support from some northern Republicans, and southern Republicans proved to be divided. All the southerners wanted the area open to slavery, but some wanted to prohibit the importation of slaves there from abroad, so as to increase the market in the lower South for the surplus slaves of the upper South. As a consequence of this divisiveness, the legislation providing for the government of Louisiana somewhat limited slavery in the territory. No slave could be either imported there from abroad or taken there if he had been imported from abroad since 1798, and no slave could be taken into Louisiana at all except by an American citizen "removing into said territory for actual settlement, and being, at the time of such removal, *bona fide* owner of such slave."[4]

But frontal attacks upon what would later be called the slavocracy were inherently futile, for the power of the party of liberty, southern style, was simply too formidable. Recognizing that, and believing that Republicans were bent upon saddling the United States with the triplet evils of democracy, slavery, and atheism, a radical fringe of northern Federalists, under the leadership of Timothy Pickering of Massachusetts, emerged with a plan of purification. Pickering, who was no relation of the ousted judge, was a man of even more peccadillos—for example, he had refused for a time to resign as John Adams's secretary of state, though requested to do so by the president, on the ground that he needed the salary to support his large family. He was also more extreme in his views than were such hard-shelled and high-principled Federalists as Alexander Hamilton, Rufus King, Fisher Ames, and George Cabot. Being more extreme, he believed that he saw more clearly; and what he saw was that the only way to save the Union was to get all right-thinking people out of the Union before it was too late. He hatched a plot, the essential feature of which was that New England should secede from the United States and form a separate country. He gathered support, among ordinary Yankees if not among the "Essex junto" of Federalist leaders, but he became convinced that his plan could work only if New York were included as a member of his northeastern confederation.

To venture into New York politics was to open a can of worms, or rather of vipers. The Federalist party in that state, though containing a glittering galaxy of leaders (including Hamilton, John Jay, Rufus King, and Gouverneur Morris), was hopelessly outnumbered by Republicans. It could count on support only in the lower wards of Manhattan, on a few of the old Hudson River manors where patroons still controlled the vote, and among frontier farmers—perhaps a third of the electorate. The Republicans, however, were not one party but three: one headed by Aaron Burr, another by the Livingston family, and a third by George Clinton and his nephew De Witt Clinton. Burr had pulled the three factions together for the presidential election of 1800, but they promptly came unglued in time for the triennial gubernatorial election of 1801. Then, and for the next two years, the citizens of New York were treated to a display of slander and vilification, aimed mainly but by no means exclusively at Burr, which was stupifyingly scurrilous even by the unrestrained standards of the time.

In the circumstances, the Federalists might easily have recaptured the governorship in 1804, but for one shortcoming: they could find nobody respectable who was willing to run. Popular politics was a game for young men, and all the great Federalist leaders were years past having the stomach for it; and besides, King was the only one among them who had survived the vituperative political wars of the 1790s with his reputation wholly intact. They asked him to be the candidate, and he flatly refused.

Enter Vice-President Burr, who had been read out of the national party by Jefferson, for whatever reason, but was at the prime of his personal gifts. Restlessly ambitious, possessed of virtually irresistible charm, unburdened by scruples except for a need to comport himself with good humor and good taste, Burr was loved by every man and woman and child who met him, save possibly by those who took themselves or their careers seriously. Hamilton and Jefferson agreed on very little, but they were of one mind in regarding Burr as a menace. New York Federalists, taking the shorter view, saw in the vice-president a man who could carry his Republican following with him into any party alliance and who, with solid Federalist support, could gain control of the state. They made overtures. Burr responded, and accepted their informal nomination. Timothy Pickering quickened at the news, seeing in Burr the kind of man who could steer New York out of the United States of America into the United States of New England, and apparently Pickering made overtures also. It is one of the legends of American history that Pickering and Burr struck some kind of arrangement, and rumors that they did so were abundant; but as with most of Burr's doings, there is no firm evidence either way.

In any event, Burr made the race. To run against him, the Republicans agreed for a time upon John Lansing, an old-time anti-Federalist of such deep dye that he had walked out of the Constitutional Convention of 1787 in an effort to sabotage the very creation of the Federal Union. Hamilton, hating and fearing Burr with an intensity that transcended politics, argued that Federalists should support Lansing on the ground that he was at least an honest and decent man. Then Lansing, stunned to learn what everyone else in New York knew, that as governor he would be expected to be a mere tool of De Witt Clinton, withdrew. Next the Republicans put up Morgan Lewis, an utter mediocrity who differed from Lansing only in being a lackey of the Livingstons, not the Clintons, and in knowing and accepting his role. Hamilton embraced Lewis as ardently as he had earlier embraced Lansing.

The campaign was one of the most vicious in American history, and few have had such profound consequences. The immediate outcome was that Burr lost: Hamilton led more Federalists away from the party than Burr could bring Republicans into it, and so Lewis received nearly sixty percent of the votes. On a larger plane, Timothy Pickering's scheme was flushed down the drain, at least for a time, and thus the threat to the Union withered away. On a plane at once grander and narrower, Burr found something in Hamilton's demeanor during the election to be offensive—just what is a mystery, for Burr had been subjected to far viler charges than Hamilton hurled at him in 1804 and had shrugged them off—and in response, Burr challenged Hamilton to a duel. The election was held late in April, the duel in July. Alexander Hamilton died as a result of wounds suffered in the duel. Politically, Aaron Burr very nearly died also. Very nearly, but not quite. Two more acts in his drama remained to be performed, both of major import.

Important as the politics of 1804 were to the success of the Republican revolution, they were overshadowed, in the president's inmost being, by a personal event. Shortly before Congress had adjourned in March, Jefferson's twenty-five-year-old daughter, Maria Jefferson Eppes, had given birth to a daughter, then had fallen severely ill; and in April, just as the New York gubernatorial campaign was reaching its climax, Maria died. To an old friend, Jefferson wrote that he had lost half of all he had and that the prospects for his evening years now hung on the thread of a single life, that of his daughter Martha Jefferson Randolph.

Fortunately for the president, it was not necessary for him to take an active part in the political campaigning of the summer and fall. The only internal problem concerning the Republicans' national ticket, the choice of a successor for Burr as vice-president, was settled early and with a minimum of friction: a congressional caucus overwhelmingly chose George Clinton as the nominee. The same caucus selected a committee from its own ranks to supervise the national campaign, and most state Republican organizations (faction-ridden New York and Pennsylvania being the two conspicuous exceptions) functioned with machinelike precision. The president himself was immensely popular, and Republican publicists could claim monumental achievements for his administration. Except for a few comments about the federal judiciary and the purchase of Louisiana, the claims could have been torn directly from the pages of Bolingbroke's *Craftsman* as a litany of what an idealized Tory revolution of the 1730s would have been all about. The Jeffersonians, the Republicans declared, had abolished internal taxation, purged government of "superfluous and useless judges," dispensed with "several thousand unnecessary officers," reduced the land forces and as much of the navy as possible, lessened the expenses of civil government, reduced the public debt by "several millions of dollars," made "provision by law for the entire discharge of the public debt in about fifteen years," and preserved peace while effecting "by negociation in a few months what it would have taken years of hostilities to acquire," namely the Louisiana Territory.[5]

Against all that, the Federalists were helpless. Disorganized and dispirited already, they were totally demoralized by their failure in New York, by Hamilton's death, and by the shame attendant upon having backed the man who had killed him. Without putting their hearts in it, they went through the motions of agreeing upon candidates for president and vice-president, Charles Cotesworth Pinckney of South Carolina and Rufus King of New York. There was simply no contest. Jefferson swept even New England, except for Connecticut, and won 162 of the 176 electoral votes. Republican success in the congressional elections was equally sweeping: they increased their hold on the Senate to a 27 to 7 margin, and on the House to a whopping 116 to 25. The two-party system was all but dead.

The appearance of virtual unanimity, however, was deceptive. When one party succeeds overmuch, the victors are as likely to succumb to factionalism as the vanquished are to extremism; and Republican factionalism reared its head viciously when the Eighth Congress (elected in 1802) assembled for its final, lame-duck session in December of 1804. The occasion was the debate over congressional approval of the administration-sponsored measure to compensate claimants for Yazoo land purchases. The Madison-Gallatin-Lincoln commission had recommended that 5 million acres of land acquired from Georgia by the Convention of 1802 be used to satisfy the claimants, and congressional acceptance of the proposal had been expected as a matter of routine. But John Randolph of Roanoke decided that the entire transaction was fraudulent, and in the wake of his spectacular attack on the measure the House was torn with dissent.

Randolph was already famous for his vitriolic rhetoric, but until now it had been turned only against Federalists, and only Federalists seemed to have noticed what a bizarre creature he was. Tall, emaciated, spectral in appearance, he had a face as devoid of hair as a ten-year-old's, and a voice to match—which led one enemy to suggest that he had been castrated "either by nature, or manual operation" so as to be "fixed for an Italian singer." In truth, nature had done the job, and his phallic shortcomings no doubt help to explain the exaggerated belligerence that he displayed toward all men save his most intimate friends. In any event, fellow Republicans now began to feel the acid outpouring of his invective, as they would increasingly in the future, and turmoil was the result.

The eruption began on January 29, 1805, when Samuel Dana of Connecticut, chairman of the House Committee on Claims, presented a resolution endorsing the administration committee's Yazoo recommendations. Then and for several days to come, Randolph arose to denounce the proposal as reeking of "the spirit of Federalism," as "plunder of the public property" in behalf of a "set of speculators." Echoing the Bolingbrokean language that Madison, Jefferson, and other Republicans had used to castigate the Hamiltonian fiscal system a few years earlier, he charged that the scheme was "a monster generated by fraud, nursed in corruption." His supporters marveled at the fluency of his classical allusions, though some listeners thought that if Randolph sought to emulate a Cicero attacking a Catiline, his references to "brothel-houses & pig stys" were more than a little "course & vulgar."[6]

After raging in that manner for some time, Randolph grew specific: he charged that Postmaster General Gideon Granger, as chief lobbyist for the New England Yazoo claimants and as the dispenser of considerable patronage in the form of mail contracts, had bribed several members of Congress to support the proposed compensation. In the ensuing uproar, Granger denied all charges—though it seems entirely probable that they were well founded—and demanded a full-scale investigation of his conduct. The demand was effectively ignored, and Granger, after the fashion of the day, published a long tract purporting to absolve himself of all wrongdoing.

Meanwhile, most Republicans in the House, whether from guilt or fear, refrained from fighting back as Randolph's tirade continued. Only a few offered demurrers, and only one retaliated in kind. Matthew Lyon, erstwhile martyr to the Sedition Act, a crude, vulgar frontiersman who had earlier represented Vermont and now represented Kentucky, reckoned himself as being among the congressmen that Randolph was attacking, and he was not the sort of fellow who took insults meekly. Once, on the floor of the House, he had responded to an insult by spitting upon and physically attacking a Federalist congressman from Connecticut; on another occasion he had chastised a political enemy with a set of fire tongs. On the present occasion he confined himself to words, but his words were choice. Describing himself as a plebian, he taunted Randolph as an idle aristocrat who wallowed in wealth derived from unearned lands and slaves, as a pompous, pretended man of learning who was in reality ignorant of the most elementary facts of life. Then he got personal: he characterized Randolph's speeches as the "braying of a jackal" and the "fulminations of a madman," and he thanked God for having the face of a man, "not that of an ape or a monkey." It was generally believed that Lyon was trying to provoke Randolph into a duel, and Randolph was at that point trying to provoke Dana into one. Neither duel materialized: Dana, a good Yankee, was not even tempted to rise to the bait, and Randolph refused to condescend to challenge a social inferior, as Lyon clearly was. Besides, he probably realized that Lyon would have chosen some barbaric form of weaponry and butchered him.[7]

The upshot of all this was that the Yankee bill was temporarily shelved. It would come up again; and when it did, it would afford the administration a great deal of discomfort.

Haggling over the Yazoo issue stopped abruptly on February 4, 1805, not because anybody involved changed positions, but because Randolph had to turn his attention to a far graver matter—management of the prosecution in the impeachment trial of Justice Samuel Chase. No other trial in American history, save possibly the impeachment trial of President Andrew Johnson sixty-three years later, would be half so important, and none involved more fundamental philosophical and constitutional principles. What was at stake was not merely the career of an intemperate and highly partisan judge, but the transcendent questions, whether the popular will and individual liberty were compatible, and if not, which had priority. Moreover, though the contending parties defined their positions in terms of the much narrower issue of the proper construction of the constitutional impeachment process, both did so in such a way as to make their answers to the larger questions unmistakably clear.

The Republicans took their stance unreservedly in favor of the will of the people. For three elections in a row the people had declared themselves in favor of Republican principles and Republican candidates, by a greater majority each time and most recently with a very nearly unanimous voice. And yet, as a result of an unwise provision in the Constitution (which its authors had inserted with the deliberate design of restraining the will of the people), the Supreme Court remained a bastion of thrice-rejected Federalism, only one of the six justiceships being held by a Republican.[8] The sole way to bring the judiciary into harmony with the will of the nation, and with the other two branches of government, was to interpret the impeachment process loosely and then prove in impeachment trials that the judges' behavior on the bench had not been acceptable.

William B. Giles of Virginia, erstwhile Republican leader in the House and now the president's right arm in the Senate, expressed the attitude as well as the intentions of his party. He scorned the Federalists' cry for an "independent judiciary," charging that it was a euphemism for an attempt to establish an aristocratic despotism. If, he said, the judges of the Supreme Court should deviate so far

from true republicanism as "to declare an Act of Congress unconstitutional, or to send a mandamus to the Secretary of State, as they
had done, it was the undoubted right of the House of Representatives to impeach them, and of the Senate to remove them." It was
improper, he believed, to liken impeachment to a criminal prosecution. Rather, "removal by impeachment was nothing more than a
declaration by Congress to this effect: you hold dangerous opinions,
and if you are suffered to carry them into effect, you will work the
destruction of the Union. We want your offices for the purpose of
giving them to men who will fill them better." Disdaining equivo-
cation, he indicated that "not only Mr. Chase, but all the other
Judges of the Supreme Court, excepting the last one appointed,
must be impeached and removed."[9]

The opposition position—that shared by Chase and his friends
and by most old-guard Federalists—began with a strict construction
of the constitutional definition of the impeachment process. The
Constitution specified that all federal officers "shall be removed
from office on impeachment for, and conviction of, treason, bribery,
or other high crimes and misdemeanors" (Article II, Section 4). In
the absence of any language that would justify extending the
grounds of impeachment beyond those explicitly cited, argued Chase
and his supporters, it would be patently unconstitutional to impeach
and remove on the principles that Giles enunciated.

But that was merely the Federalists' legal position; their underlying philosophical attitude ran far deeper. The basic premises were
well summarized by Chase's counsel during the trial. "All governments," said Joseph Hopkinson, "require, in order to give them
firmness, stability, and character, some permanent principle, some
settled establishment. The want of this is the great deficiency in
republican institutions." But that deficiency had been overcome in
the United States Constitution by provision for a permanent judiciary which was independent of the ebb and flow of popular whim.
Without such a feature, "nothing can be relied on." Luther Martin
was even more succinct. "We boast," he said, that ours is a "government of laws. But how can it be such, unless the laws, while
they exist, are sacredly and impartially, without regard to popularity,
carried into execution?" Only an independent judiciary could per-
form this function, and thus protect "our property, our liberty, our
lives."[10]

Philosophically, then, the Republican position was democratic;
the Federalist position was constitutional and libertarian. To the
Federalists, the Republican position was narrowly and despicably

political; to the Republicans, the Federalist position was narrowly and despicably aristocratic.

The outcome of the trial depended upon which theory of impeachment prevailed, which is another way of saying that it depended on whether the trial was conducted on a political basis or on a legal and constitutional basis. In a purely political trial, Chase had not a chance, for the Republican majority in the Senate was more than the required two-thirds. In a trial conducted on a strictly legal and constitutional basis, there was no possibility of conviction; for, whatever the seriousness of Chase's indiscretions and improprieties, they by no means amounted to high crimes or misdemeanors.

And the kind of trial it would be depended, by virtue of a supreme irony of history, largely upon a fugitive from justice. Aaron Burr, though defeated and discredited, though under indictment in New York for dueling and in New Jersey for murder, still had a month to serve as vice-president, and in that capacity he would preside over the Senate during the trial. As one Federalist newspaper commented, it had traditionally been "the practice in Courts of Justice to arraign the *murderer* before the *Judge*, but *now* we behold the *Judge* arraigned before the *murderer*."[11]

Republicans were scarcely leaving the matter to chance. Randolph had his spleen worked up, that being a most potent way of preparing for a political trial; and Giles, as majority whip, was diligently lining up doubtful Republican senators so they would view the trial politically. Jefferson himself courted the wayward vice-president. Burr, the ultimate cynic, had expected to be treated rather well—Randolph had remarked of the duel that if Burr had no greater stain on his character than the blood of Alexander Hamilton, he should have Randolph's vote for any office short of the presidency, and that was approximately the attitude Burr had anticipated from the Virginians, now that they needed him again—but even he was a bit overwhelmed by the favor he received. Again and again he was dined at the White House and subjected to the president's warmth, wit, and charm. And there was more: Jefferson, in what was couched as a magnamimous fit of gratitude for Burr's past services and as concern for his future, offered the outgoing vice-president the patronage in the newly established Louisiana Territory.[12] Burr cheerfully accepted, and his stepson, his brother-in-law, and one of his cohorts acquired the three most important offices in the territory, including the governorship.

Inasmuch as these plums were offered as something earned, however, and not as a bribe, Burr received them in that spirit and proceeded according to the dictates of his conscience. What his conscience dictated was decorum and propriety. He had the Senate chamber adorned with red, green, and blue velvet, in ostentatious imitation of the garb of the British House of Lords when that august body sat in impeachment hearings. He conducted the trial according to rules so strict that—at first—Federalists complained that he was being unduly harsh upon Chase and his counsel, and Randolph was duped into contrasting Chase's lack of decorum on the bench with Burr's abundance of it.

That doomed the prosecution. Witnesses were paraded, and they demonstrated beyond question that Justice Chase had behaved himself improperly as charged; but it became increasingly clear that he had done nothing that could be considered as legal grounds for conviction and removal. Moreover, in the austere atmosphere that Burr had created, it was daily evident that the managers of the prosecution—John Randolph, Joseph Nicholson, and Caesar Rodney of Delaware—were no match for the brilliant counsel that Chase had assembled—Luther Martin, Joseph Hopkinson, and Robert Goodloe Harper.

Though the president remained officially aloof from it all, he followed the proceedings carefully, and at least twice the statements of the rattled prosecution must have caused him a great deal of discomfort. Nicholson, attempting to prove that noncriminal activities could be grounds for impeachment, argued hypothetically that if a president attempted to influence congressional proceedings by offering government appointments, he could not be indicted but could and certainly should be impeached and removed from office. Given Jefferson's wooing of Burr—not to mention the fact that the president had rewarded all three key witnesses against John Pickering with government jobs—that theoretical example struck painfully close to home. And Randolph, perhaps deciding to have a little malicious fun in what was clearly a losing cause, castigated Chase by dwelling at length on a comparison of Chase's intemperance with the propriety that always marked John Marshall's deportment on the bench. Hating Marshall as he did, and seeing him as the archenemy on the Court, Jefferson could scarcely have found Randolph's antics amusing.

The climax came on March 1, when the senators voted. "The Sergeants-at-Arms," Burr announced to the packed assembly, "will face the spectators and seize and commit to prison the first person who makes the smallest noise or disturbance." Then he had the secretary read the first of the eight articles of impeachment, after which he twisted the knife by the language he used in polling each senator: "Senator Adams of Massachusetts! How say you? Is Samuel Chase, the respondent, guilty of high crimes and misdemeanors as charged in the article just read?" He used precisely that language two hundred and seventy-two times, as each senator was polled on every charge—including such high crimes and misdemeanors as scolding a young attorney, haranguing grand juries, and expressing unpopular opinions. Then Burr ordered the names of the senators and their recorded votes to be read for verification. At last he announced the results: Chase had not been found guilty by a constitutional majority on any article. On five articles there was not even a simple majority for conviction.[13]

Responses to the verdict were varied, as were the appraisals of what had gone wrong. Randolph and Nicholson stormed back over to the House and proposed a pair of constitutional amendments which that body promptly passed, though the amendments never went any further. Randolph's would have provided for removal of federal judges by the president upon recommendation by a simple majority of both houses of Congress; Nicholson's would have empowered state legislatures to recall senators at any time. Jefferson fumed, called impeachment a "bungling way of removing judges," and said it was "a farce which will not be tried again." As to diagnoses of what had happened, it was clear that the nine Federalist senators had hung together for acquittal and six of the twenty-five Republicans—two apiece from Vermont and New York, and one each from Ohio and South Carolina—had joined them on every vote. Some people suggested that the deviant northern Republicans were piqued at Randolph because of his sabotaging of the Yazoo settlement and had taken it out on him with their votes for acquittal. Others blamed the House managers for not having prepared their case with sufficient attention to legal niceties.

None of that especially mattered. It was a victory for law and a defeat for democracy. The integrity of the federal judiciary was saved, and thereby the Constitution of the United States was saved also. And the man most responsible was named Aaron Burr.

The defeat, however, cost the administration little. To be sure, the Court remained Federalist; and it would continue, despite intermittent political sniping, to be dominated by John Marshall for another thirty-one years, by which time both Jefferson and his party were dead. But the president had wisely divorced himself, publicly, from the impeachment affair, and its failure impaired neither his prestige nor his popularity, both of which remained nearly as great as Washington's had been. Furthermore, Jefferson's view of constitutional interpretation was sounder than Marshall's—legal theory to the contrary notwithstanding—and in the long run it prevailed. That is to say, there would be no single, final arbiter of the supreme law of the land. The federal courts would continue to pass upon the constitutionality of acts of government, in accordance with the theory of judicial review, but so, in fact, would other branches of the federal government and the several state and local governments as well. That was as Jefferson always maintained things should be.

Nonetheless, the defeat in the Chase impeachment trial rankled. Moreover, it was but the first in a succession of defeats. Indeed, all the happy hours had passed: Thomas Jefferson's luck had run out.

5

★★★★★

TURBULENCE IN EUROPEAN
WATERS: 1805–1806

It is in the nature of the presidency that matters of domestic reform, however engrossing they may be for the incumbent at first, lose their appeal after a time. The chore of manipulating or currying favor with congressmen, necessary though it is, grows tedious and even demeaning, and the attraction of dealing with foreign affairs, wherein one has a much freer hand, becomes well-nigh irresistible. So it was with Jefferson by the winter of 1804–1805. Randolph's disruptive activities and the impeachment "fiasco" made the prospect for close future dealings with Congress distasteful, to say the least. Jefferson would scarcely have been human if, in the afterglow of his overwhelming reelection, a voice deep inside him had not whispered that he now had earned the right to stand above that sort of thing.

The broader, beckoning international arena, by contrast, was becoming more challenging by the day. The game was deadly dangerous: France and England were locked in a struggle for dominance of the Western world, and any nation that managed to be neither devoured nor reduced to puppet status could count itself blessed. And yet the opportunities were as great as the risks, as American commercial prosperity and the acquisition of Louisiana abundantly attested.

Thomas Jefferson was a wily and resourceful player in this perilous game, one of the most gifted of them all, even in an age that numbered Napoleon and Talleyrand, Pitt and Castlereagh, and Godoy and Metternich among the contestants. But there were two crucial weaknesses in his approach to it. One was implicit in the ideology of Republicanism. The Republicans' world-view included a naïve, secularized form of demonology in which certain groups were rigidly typed as evil; and high on their list of devils was the government of Great Britain. Accordingly, they failed to understand that the British people were entirely loyal to Crown and country and that indeed they tended to despise Americans for having rebelled against mother England. Moreover, Republicans were incapable of recognizing or admitting that the United States was inherently dependent upon Britain in some respects and was her natural ally in others; and thus when they had to deal with her at all, they felt partly sullied and partly as if they were doing her a favor.

The second shortcoming was related to the first: consciously or unconsciously down-grading as well as distrusting Great Britain, Jefferson, like most Republicans, never fully grasped the significance —to Britain and to the United States—of British sea power, and he never fully understood that what happened on the seas was as important as, and inextricably connected with, what happened on the battlefields and at the negotiating tables. Thus he virtually took the seas for granted as he concentrated his efforts, single-mindedly, on the next major goal of American foreign policy, the acquisition of West Florida. He assumed that commercial prosperity and the attendant burgeoning of federal revenues—without which most of his achievements would have been impossible—would continue to come as a matter of course, as if they were due to America as a right. They came, in fact, only at the suffrance of the hated British government; but so far was Jefferson from facing this harsh reality that he even expected to be able to use the Royal Navy when it suited his convenience.

Those weaknesses, deriving from Republican ideology and from something personal in Jefferson's makeup, were compounded by a pair of difficulties inherent in the office of president. The first was that of the "lame duck": in his second term the president loses a great deal of his ability to manage things because his party adherents almost invariably temper their loyalty to him with concern over who is to be his successor four years hence. Though the idea that a president should serve only two terms was scarcely a hoary tradition as yet, Jefferson made himself a lame duck by announcing shortly after his reelection that he would follow Washington's precedent and step down at the end of his second term. He also let it be known that his preference for a successor was Madison, which caused a great deal of consternation among the followers of John Randolph in Virginia, the Smiths in Maryland, William Leib and William Duane in Pennsylvania, and the Clintonians in New York. These dissidents, loosely and with varying measures of sincerity, backed James Monroe as a prospective alternate candidate, and set out to undermine Madison. Toward that end, they were apt to oppose any foreign-policy initiatives that seemed likely to reflect credit upon Madison.

The other problem is that, though the chief executive is relatively free in handling foreign affairs, he is not totally so: the approval of the Senate is necessary for making treaties, and that of the House as well is necessary for obtaining appropriations. The need to deal with Congress not only impairs the president's flexibility, it also consumes a great deal of time—with the result that, when the pressures and opportunities of international politics are rapidly changing, as they were from 1805 onward, it becomes difficult if not impossible for the president to move as swiftly as the occasion demands.

In these circumstances President Jefferson vacillated, made some bad guesses, got some bad advice, and settled on a policy decision to which he committed himself almost irrevocably—only to learn, with a sickening realization, that his policy had become obsolete by the time it was adopted. By the spring of 1806 he had lost control of events; by early summer he had begun to consider a resort to desperate means.

The Jeffersonians' efforts to obtain the Floridas went through several phases, the first of which was characterized by open and rather artless negotiation. In the summer of 1804, when Napoleon first announced that West Florida had definitely not been included in the Louisiana Purchase, the administration chose to respond as if there had been an honest misunderstanding, and instructed James Monroe (who had replaced Rufus King as minister to England) to go to Madrid to assist Charles Pinckney in clearing up the matter. Monroe, in keeping with his unhurried approach to diplomacy, did not leave London until October and then elected to go to Madrid by way of Paris, there to sound out the French before proceeding to Spain.

In Paris, Monroe proved remarkably resistant to accepting what he learned. Livingston greeted him with the news that Barbé-

Marbois had recently suggested that the United States might acquire both Floridas by paying France 60 million francs, and in no other way; clearly, Livingston reported, "France wishes to make our controversy [with Spain] favorable to her finances." Refusing to believe this, Monroe wrote a long letter to Talleyrand, stressing the justice of America's claim to West Florida and asking for France's "good offices" in so persuading Madrid. Weeks passed before Talleyrand answered, during which time Monroe heard various reports that led him to believe that France would do as he had requested. When Talleyrand finally granted him an interview—not yet having answered his letter—the Frenchman's only comment about Monroe's mission to Madrid was that "you will have much difficulty to succeed there." A few days later Talleyrand's chief assistant, Alexandre Maurice Blanc de Lanautte, Comte d'Hauterive, was more to the point. Both parties must make sacrifices, d'Hauterive told Monroe: "Spain must cede territory, and . . . the U. States must pay money." Convinced that Napoleon knew none of this, believing that Talleyrand and others were merely seeking bribes for themselves, and remembering the infamous "XYZ Affair" of 1797, Monroe finally decided that he was wasting his time in Paris. On December 8 he set out at last for Madrid.[1]

While Monroe was en route, three developments bearing on his mission took place, all of them unfavorable. One was that Talleyrand finally answered his original letter, the gist of the reply being a flat refusal to help and a reiteration of France's position that the Floridas belonged to Spain. The second was that Talleyrand wrote to Napoleon, urging a hard line on the matter—advice the emperor scarcely needed. The third was that Spain became France's military ally once again, declaring war against England on December 14. Just after Monroe reached Madrid, an even more unfavorable event occurred: on January 4, 1805, France and Spain signed a secret treaty whereby France agreed to guarantee Spain's territorial integrity in Europe and to ensure "the return of colonies seized from Spain in the course of the current war."[2]

The Spanish, thus knowing and understanding more than Monroe did, were prepared to turn a deaf ear to his pleas, threats, and arguments. Pinckney had already negotiated his way to a total standstill by insisting that Spain not only give formal recognition to the Louisiana Purchase, including Florida, but also dip into its almost exhausted treasury and compensate the United States for alleged damages suffered in Spanish waters during the Franco-American quasi war of 1798–1800. Monroe's presence changed the situation not at all: he stayed in Madrid seven months, engaged in a lot of conferences, wrote a lot of letters, and accomplished nothing.

Monroe was quite confused by the stalemate, for it seemed to this honest and simple republican that French support of the American position was both reasonable and just; and for a time Livingston's successor in Paris, Gen. John Armstrong of New York, was likewise guileless and mystified. Monroe reasoned that it was to France's interest to aid the United States, since France (as well as Spain) relied on Americans to carry cargoes between her blockaded colonies and home ports. It never occurred to Monroe that America's need of the trade was at least as great as France's. Moreover, to his way of thinking, the United States held clubs over France, in a way: there was always the possibility of an Anglo-American alliance, should a favorable settlement with Spain not be forthcoming, and American willingness to cut off trade with the rebellious blacks of St. Domingo might also hinge on such a settlement. Unwilling to believe that Napoleon, his erstwhile benefactor, could fail to comprehend such clear reasoning, Monroe concluded that Talleyrand and other devious ministers were keeping facts from their master. Armstrong thought along similarly naïve lines at first, but it did not take him long to tumble to the reality that he was dealing with nothing more nor less than Corsican Mafiosi. "De l'argent—beaucoup d'argent is what they want, & what they insist on, and it is (they say) the only means of terminating our differences." Indeed, he perceived, Napoleonic France regarded Spain and the United States as "a couple of oranges in her hands which she will squeeze at pleasure, and against each other, and that which yields the most will be the best served or rather the least injured."[3]

Back at home, angrily reading the dispatches that reported this succession of non-developments, the president of the United States reacted far more realistically than either his ministers in the field or his advisors in Washington. He hinted at a new attitude toward the problem in the instructions he wrote for James Bowdoin, Jr., whom he sent to replace Pinckney in the late spring of 1805. Spain, he declared, had "met our advances with jealousy, secret malice, and ill faith." Therefore, despite the desire of the administration to maintain friendly intercourse with all nations, the time had arrived to get tough. The negotiations regarding West Florida had dragged on entirely too long; their outcome, wrote Jefferson, would determine "whether our relations with [Spain] are to be sincerely friendly, or permanently hostile."[4]

To his cabinet members, Jefferson was more blunt: in circular letters written from Monticello in August, he proposed that West Florida be seized forthwith, and he requested the cabinet's views toward seeking an English alliance to head off any possible French retaliation. Otherwise, he argued, Spain would continue to hold out, relying on the "omnipotence of Bonaparte" to protect its possessions. As to an English alliance, he maintained that it would be easy to arrange, for "the first wish of every Englishman's heart is to see us once more fighting by their sides against France."[5]

The cabinet, or rather the influential members of it, dumped ice water on the idea. Navy Secretary Robert Smith agreed with the plan with only mild reservations, but Gallatin and Madison were strongly opposed to it. Gallatin wrote the president a long and tedious tract entitled "Spanish Affairs," which was filled with legal and moralistic philosophizing but came down to an argument that attacking Spanish possessions would cost too much money. Madison, in a series of letters, merely expressed reservations about war with Spain but was vehement in opposition to an alliance with Great Britain. The British were never to be trusted, he said; and besides, France was likely to be too tied up in Continental affairs to be of much help to Spain in any event.

Unconvinced by this resistance, Jefferson continued to think that war with Spain was the most advantageous course to pursue; and in those mysterious ways that attend the wishes of popular presidents, the press began to inform Americans about what a vicious neighbor they had on their southern and western borders. But then, quite suddenly, the decision was taken out of the president's hands, and an alternative opened.

Timing is crucial in international relations, and Jefferson's timing, fortuitously superb in 1803, was unlucky from 1805 onward. As a result, relations with Britain disintegrated, opportunities were lost, and the administration began to be buffeted by the winds it had earlier turned to American advantage.

Since the Louisiana Purchase the Jeffersonians, though steering a neutral course between the belligerents, had attempted to curry favor with France and Spain and had remained somewhat cool toward Britain. In theory, at least, the slight but continuous pressure thus exerted would ultimately persuade Britain to settle its differences with the United States in a way that would be favorable to the Americans. In 1803 King had negotiated a partial repudiation of the right of impressment, but it was rejected because the Americans were confident that they could do better. In 1804 Monroe had Britain ready to concede a good deal more; but neither he nor the president was in a hurry, and so nothing was concluded before Monroe left for Madrid.

When he returned to London in the summer of 1805 Monroe found a drastically altered situation. The friendly, or timorous, ministry of Henry Addington, Viscount Sidmouth, had fallen and had been replaced by the much tougher ministry of William Pitt. The Pitt government was skeptical of the ability of the Jefferson administration to make "any great, vigorous, or persevering exertion," and was determined to give it a test. For that purpose, a dozen American vessels en route to France from the West Indies were seized for violation of the Rule of 1756, which had been effectively suspended for more than a decade.[6]

A violent wave of protest swept the United States, and the occasion called for a hard line from the administration—for, as Monroe wrote, the seizures were clearly an "experiment" to determine "what the United States will bear." But it was at just that point that Jefferson had lost his patience with France and Spain and had decided to take West Florida by force, for which he would need the support of the Royal Navy. Accordingly, when news of the seizures arrived, Jefferson sloughed it off, since he was in process of adopting his most cordial manner toward Britain. The Pitt government, neither knowing nor caring what manner of scheming was going on in the mind of the president, read this response as confirmation of the administration's weakness, and instituted an extremely harsh policy toward American commerce on the high seas.

The first step was a tacit repudiation of the Anglo-American rapprochement that had prevailed since 1794. On July 23, 1805, Sir William Scott handed down his prize-court decision in the case of the American merchantman *Essex*. The ship had carried a cargo from the French West Indies island of Martinique to Charleston, and thence to London, where it was seized as unlawful. Since the ship had American customs-house papers showing entrance at Charleston, it was protected under the doctrine of the broken voyage; but Scott now overturned this doctrine by ruling that the owner had to be able to prove that the original intention had been to terminate the voyage in the American port. In one blow, the legal fiction underlying American prosperity as a neutral carrier was destroyed. In the ensuing weeks and months, the British navy seized scores of American vessels for violation of the newly restored Rule of 1756.

Jefferson vacillated. For a time he remained intent upon taking West Florida by force, and for that long—through September and into October—he continued to hope that the new British policy was a temporary aberration. Meanwhile Republican newspapers, following earlier cues, went on drumming up popular hostility toward Spain in anticipation of a war message. But then Madison's and Gallatin's arguments began to have their effects upon the president, and so did news of further British seizures, and so did reports that Britain had resumed the practice of impressing seamen from American vessels. Then came news that Napoleon was scoring a series of awesome military victories on the Continent, which promised to make him virtually the unchallenged master of Europe—and incidentally reminded Jefferson that it could be costly to be in Napoleon's bad graces, even as it could be advantageous to be in his favor.

Hard on the heels of that intelligence came powerful temptation in the form of a dispatch from Armstrong. In Paris, Armstrong had struck up a friendly association (and, Bowdoin charged, a secret and corrupt business connection) with an American expatriate named Daniel Parker, a wily and unscrupulous manipulator who apparently had ties with the principal banking houses and with every important venal politician in Britain, France, and Holland. Through Parker, Armstrong held various conferences with highly placed Frenchmen—mainly agents of Talleyrand—and obtained assurances that if the United States would entrust its desires "to the decision of the Emperor," Napoleon would arrange the sale of the Floridas for a price of seven to ten million dollars. Into the bargain, if the United States showed firm attachment to France during the presently intensive phase of the war, the emperor would see to it that the Gulf boundary of Louisiana be extended 400 miles westward to the Colorado River. That would give the United States title to the Gulf Coast from the Florida Keys almost to Corpus Christi. Armstrong so informed Madison in a letter written on September 14 and received in Washington five or six weeks later. Informally, he also passed along the suggestion that the United States should maintain its warlike posture toward Spain, which would make it easier for Napoleon to convince the Spanish that it was better to sell the Floridas "and get the proceeds of an honourable sale, than to loose (sic) them by American cupidity & conquest."[7]

The temptation became irresistible when Gallatin's account of the state of the treasury, belatedly reflecting the increased revenues attending the renewal of the commercial boom a year before, showed a large surplus. Gone was the indignant rejection of bribery that was manifested earlier in 1805: bribes as a means of obtaining what one covets are somehow less odious when one's pockets are full. The prospects for a bargain as great as the Louisiana Purchase had seemingly opened up, if the United States would but supply the cash; and as Jefferson now told Madison, "we need not care" who actually got the money.[8]

Thus did Jefferson make the most important—and the most fateful—decision of his entire presidency. By mid November, shortly before Congress was scheduled to reconvene, the administration decided to reverse its positions again: to take a stern line against the latest British outrages, to offer some kind of sop in order to show its good faith to Napoleon, and to ask Congress for the money, so as to be ready for this second great windfall when it came.

The first task would be easy enough to accomplish; the second and the third, in light of the popular hostility that had been aroused against France as well as Spain in recent months, would be rather more difficult. To obviate the difficulty, Jefferson determined to be more or less candid with Congress and to be considerably other than candid with the citizenry at large. He prepared two messages for the upcoming congressional session: one official and for public consumption, the other to be read behind closed doors. The public version, delivered in the formal annual message presented on December 3, 1805, was belligerent toward Spain and suggested the need to prepare for war. The private version apprised Congress frankly of the new turn of events and asked for a secret appropriation of $5 million to supplement the $2 million which had been secretly appropriated in 1802 and was still unspent.

Once again the administration's timing was spectacularly bad. In the first place, the switch back to hostility toward Britain was grossly premature. Soon after Congress convened, news arrived of the most decisive naval battle since the defeat of the Spanish Armada more than two centuries earlier: on October 21, 1805, Lord Admiral Horatio Nelson and the Royal Navy had engaged the combined French and Spanish fleets in the battle of Trafalgar, and destroyed them so thoroughly that neither France nor any other nation would be able to challenge the naval supremacy of the British for a hundred years to come. Thenceforth, even if the United States should obtain the entire Gulf Coast from the Florida Keys to the Rio Grande, such possession would be meaningless without Britain's permission to go to sea.

In the second place, the administration neglected to take John

Randolph into account, though that strange man had given ample warning that he was prepared to cause serious trouble in this very session of Congress. In addition to sheer perversity, Randolph was moved both by a devout hatred of Madison and by a determination to prevent the secretary of state from succeeding Jefferson in the White House. He suspected that Madison was responsible for the administration's shift in foreign policy, and he was petty enough to attempt to frustrate the new policy on that ground alone. Beyond that, he had become the self-appointed guardian of morality in government, and to him the new effort to buy Florida reeked of corruption.

In the latter sentiment he was not alone: Jefferson's secret message inspired considerable shock in Congress. In the House, the body empowered by the Constitution to initiate appropriations, the request was turned over to a special seven-man committee, the first and second members of which were Randolph and Nicholson. Though the pledge of secrecy remained inviolate, Randolph denounced the proposal to his fellow committee members, as well as to Gallatin, Madison, and Jefferson himself, as a "base prostration of the national character," and he vowed that the president would not get away with his effort to throw upon Congress the odium "of delivering the public purse to the first cut-throat that demanded it." Six of the seven committee members shared his opinion, the lone exception being the freshman congressman Barnabas Bidwell of Massachusetts. The committee did nothing for three weeks— Randolph scornfully took a week's holiday in Baltimore while the president anxiously waited—and then it not only voted to refuse the request, but also attempted to force the administration to adhere to its public position, offering a substitute resolution to raise troops for defense of the southern frontier "from Spanish inroad and insult, and to chastise the same."[9]

When the committee made its report on January 3, 1806, however, other Republicans moved two substitute resolutions which were designed to give the president what he had asked for—one appropriating funds for "extraordinary expenses" in foreign relations, the other continuing the Mediterranean Fund for a new term of years.[10] A fierce debate ensued. In the next ten days, to Jefferson's chagrin, Randolph gained the support of a majority of the more respectable Republicans, including twelve of the twenty-two from Virginia. The president cracked the party whip, throwing all his prestige behind the measure and gaining votes mainly among northern Republicans; but even the most faithful party members complained. When the vote came on January 16, the appropriation passed, seventy-six to fifty-four, but it was a costly victory for the administration, and not only because of the schism it opened in the party. What was more important, Jefferson invested his political capital so deeply in the fight that he became almost irreversibly committed to the foreign-policy line he had so precipitately adopted. Henceforth there could be no turning back.

The bill passed the Senate and was signed into law on February 13. What with various administrative delays, however, another month passed before Madison wrote to Armstrong, authorizing him to proceed with the effort to consummate the purchase. By the time Armstrong received the letter, six months had passed since the original hint at an offer. A great deal had happened in Europe in the interim.

Meanwhile, Congress and the administration were at work on the second part of the package, devising a suitable sop for Napoleon. There was no problem in determining what that should be: Napoleon, Talleyrand, and the French chargé Louis Turreau had demanded that the United States prohibit trade with all parts of St. Domingo that were under control of black rebels, which is to say most of it. Republican Senator George Logan of Pennsylvania introduced the appropriate measure. In vain, Federalists and a few northern Republicans argued that it would reduce the government's revenues by several hundred thousand dollars, that it would wreak havoc on American merchants and seamen by abolishing the most important trade left to them after the recent British orders, that it was designed to destroy a people fighting for republicanism and independence, and that it was a disgraceful capitulation to orders from Napoleon. The last charge upset even Randolph; and though as a slaveholder he could not bring himself to vote against the measure, he did abstain. The other southerners voted for the bill without qualms, and it passed overwhelmingly and was signed into law on February 28. Out of lust for land, the Jeffersonians sentenced the black revolution in St. Domingo to death by starvation.[11]

The third step was to adopt a line of resistance against British maritime policy, but on that matter there was some confusion. Congress needed no prodding, for the British seizures had elicited cries of outrage even in New England; but no one could think of any countermeasures that were likely to be effective. The hard fact was that as long as Pitt remained in power, no form of protest short of war could be expected to have any effect whatever; and the administration was by no means prepared for war, having emasculated its navy and being unable to build a new one because of the way it had just opted to tie up its revenues. Some support was roused for an embargo, but since that was generally regarded as a step preparatory to war, the idea was stillborn. Federalist Senator John Quincy Adams offered resolutions denouncing the British actions as an encroachment upon the independence of the United States. Though Congress was just then in process of comprising American independence and sacrificing the independence of St. Domingo in the same act, no one pointed out the irony, and the resolutions were adopted; but the resolutions were scarcely a form of action that would instill sober second thoughts at Whitehall.

The problem was compounded by the fact that the administration was ambivalent on the subject. The president and the secretary of state were agreed that a tough line should be taken, yet neither was especially eager that the tactic should prove successful, for if a new accord with Britain were worked out, the negotiations with Napoleon to obtain Florida would be seriously jeopardized. Besides, from Madison's point of view there was an additional reason for preferring that no quick settlement with Britain should be forthcoming: that might make a hero of Monroe and thereby boost his claims for the presidency in 1808. In view of these considerations, Jefferson and Madison agreed merely to give Congress a nudge in an appropriate direction, and count on Congress to come up with a scheme that would strike a suitable stance without being likely to accomplish anything.

The nudge was provided in a lengthy pamphlet that Madison wrote and Jefferson enclosed in a brief message to Congress. In the main, the pamphlet was a complex and prolix legal argument, the essence of which was that Britain's position was indefensible in international law. The policy to pursue in forcing Britain to reverse itself was left largely implicit, but everyone knew what Madison advocated in general on that score, for he had been advocating it as a means of curtailing Britain's high-handed measures on the seas since the wars of the French Revolution broke out in 1793. The basic idea was to curtail the importation of British manufactured goods into the United States. Madison had long insisted that in the ensuing economic dislocations, three hundred thousand unemployed British laborers would march on London and ultimately force Government to mend its ways. John Randolph sneered that the secretary of state had hurled a sheaf of paper against eight hundred ships of war, but most congressmen reckoned that some variation of Madison's approach should be followed.

The Congress, however, promptly got out of hand; for the legislators, lacking the guile of the president and the secretary of state, earnestly sought a tactic that would work. The first proposal toward that end emanated from Congressman Andrew Gregg of Pennsylvania, who offered a bill forbidding the importation of all goods produced by Great Britain or its colonies. Supporters of the bill, mainly northern Republicans, proposed to go much further in the same direction. For instance, Jacob Crowninshield of Massachusetts (who had made a fortune in trading with France, not Britain) declared that if total nonimportation did not work he would be ready to threaten war, but he believed that Britain would back down when faced with the monetary loss that war would entail. He pointed out that British subjects owned $16 million of the original public debt of the United States, $8 million of the stock issued to buy Louisiana, and $4 million in stock of the Bank of the United States, and were owed $10 or $12 million in private debts—all of which could be confiscated in case of war. Others of Gregg's supporters enthusiastically seized upon Crowninshield's idea and suggested that confiscation be adopted as a means of coercing Britain without a war.[12]

Gallatin was thrown into a veritable panic by such talk. He pointed out to his good friend and brother-in-law Nicholson that the Gregg bill would cost the government $5 million in revenues per annum, and therefore would bring on national bankruptcy. At Gallatin's request, Nicholson introduced a substitute bill that would cut off the importation of only those British goods that the United States could do without or produce for itself. Such "necessary" (and revenue-producing) items as Jamaica rum, coarse woolens, salt, and Birmingham hardware would be expressly exempted.

Another Republican faction, associated with Senator Samuel Smith and his brother the secretary of the navy, was willing to go along with either Gregg's or Nicholson's version of nonimportation, but wanted to take a tougher line in other respects. This group proposed that funds also be appropriated for a massive naval build-up and then, after Britain had thus been informed that the United States meant business, that a tough-minded man of mercantile affairs, namely Senator Smith himself, be sent to London to negotiate a settlement. This "war party" was defeated on the matter of building up the navy, but an agreement was reached—against the president's wishes—that the proposal to send a special minister would be made an integral part of any bill that might be passed.

Debate on the two bills occupied the entire month of March

and went on into April, and as it did, still another Republican faction had to be reckoned with. Randolph and his following of southern "old Republicans" denounced Gregg and Crowninshield and their adherents as candidates for bedlam, and charged that the Smith faction was even less rational. It was insanity, Randolph said, for the "great mammoth of the American forest to leave his native element and plunge into the water in a mad contest with the shark." Instead, Randolph would opt for total nonintercourse—that is, he would call all American ships home and keep them home until the hungry beasts of Europe had exhausted or devoured one another. At first Randolph had most of the southern members with him, for all that was at stake was American commercial prosperity, which they were not at all loathe to sacrifice. But then he went too far: he declared himself in open opposition to the president and Madison, and charged that secrecy, duplicity, and corruption had marked all their conduct since they took up with the sinister "Yazoo interests."

The administration had no choice but to intervene, and it did so, skillfully and decisively. Smith was virtually read out of the party: in a calculated affront, Jefferson let it be known that William Pinkney, another Marylander and a Federalist at that, would be sent on the mission that Smith coveted. He also let it be known that henceforth the Smiths need not expect any patronage. Randolph was effectively undermined by the loss of his two most respectable supporters: Jefferson veritably seduced Macon away, and Nicholson, who had long been in financial trouble, suddenly resigned his House seat to take a better-paying position as a Maryland judge. As to the northern Republicans, flattery, charm, patronage, and reason were applied to induce them to abandon the Gregg resolutions in favor of those offered but not supported by Nicholson.[13]

And fate intervened. As the debate was reaching its climax, news arrived that William Pitt had died in January and that his ministry had been succeeded by a coalition headed by Lord Grenville and including as foreign secretary Charles James Fox, notoriously a friend of America. That development made the debate academic, for it was nearly certain that Fox would reverse Pitt's maritime policy. Moreover, news that arrived almost simultaneously from the Continent doomed the whole complex scheme of trying to buy the Floridas. Napoleon had won the most brilliant military victory of his career at Austerlitz, which put Europe at his mercy and removed the urgent need for funds that had led him, six months earlier, to think of forcing Spain to sell.

In sum, had Jefferson simply adhered to his original policy—the one with which he was still publicly identified—he could have had Florida for the taking, could have treated the British problem as a transient unpleasantness that only momentarily disrupted commerce, and could have held his party, as well as the nation's honor, more or less intact. Instead he was, by virtue of the tactics he had employed to bend Congress to his will, irrevocably committed to a policy which was part impossible and part unnecessary.

The charade was acted out: before Congress adjourned, it passed Nicholson's limited nonimportation bill, but promptly suspended the bill's operations until November 15. Thus armed, Pinkney was sent as a special emissary to join Monroe in London, and ultimately to replace him.

One senator remarked, upon leaving Washington, that the president had "aged ten years" during the congressional session.

There was yet another problem or, rather, a loose end that proved uncommonly difficult to tie up. On the public record, the United States was committed to a warlike posture toward Spain, and for all the world knew, that was a bona fide commitment. The Spanish minister, Yrujo, lodged a formal protest with the secretary of state upon reading Jefferson's hostile annual message; Madison, lacking any precedent or protocol—he could scarcely tell Yrujo that Jefferson was pulling Spain's leg—curtly replied that it was improper to protest communications between departments of the government. Yrujo persisted, making himself a considerable nuisance, and in exasperation Madison had Jefferson order Yrujo to leave the country. Yrujo flatly refused to do so, and there was no law by which he could be made to leave; but the situation meant there was no official way for the United States and Spain to communicate except through the American minister to Madrid, James Bowdoin, who happened to be spending all his time in London and Paris.

The absence of ability to communicate raised some interesting possibilities, and interesting things began to happen. One was the adventure of Francisco Miranda, a Spanish colonial who had been trying for the better part of two decades to stir up support for an independence movement in Spanish America. Among others, Alexander Hamilton, Revolutionary France, and the British ministry had flirted with the idea of backing him as a means of striking at Spain, but Spain had never stayed still long enough as anybody's enemy to make it seem worth while to follow through. Now, early in 1806, Miranda showed up in New York, attracted by the American government's display of bellicosity toward his parent country, and suddenly it appeared that his life's dream was on the brink of fulfillment. From friends and cohorts of erstwhile Vice-President Aaron Burr he got enough financial assistance to acquire and fortify the ship *Leander*, to lay in a supply of small arms, and to recruit a large number of volunteers for a grandiose filibustering expedition. That in the works, he headed for Washington to obtain the blessings and, hopefully, the support of the government of the United States.

What happened in Washington became the subject of some controversy and no small number of conflicting stories. Clearly, Miranda had several meetings with Madison and was entertained most cordially at the households of both the president and the secretary of state. Then he departed for New York and his waiting shipload of arms and adventurers, announcing en route to all and sundry that the government of the United States was supporting or at least winking at his mission to liberate Spanish America. Whatever Madison had promised Miranda, he was appalled at the openness, or the brazenness, of the revolutionary's claims, and he denied them all.

Yrujo, for his part, was fully aware of all this, since it was in every newspaper, and he duly alerted appropriate Spanish authorities in time to ensure that Miranda's venture would prove abortive. Lacking a means of communicating directly with the United States government, he had no legal way of protesting the administration's complicity in the affair, but he did have an indirect means and he employed it. He beseeched Turreau, the French chargé, to protest for him; and Turreau, who was not at all fond of Madison, took special delight in bringing pressure to bear on the secretary of state. In response, the administration felt obliged to make at least a token act of dissociation from Miranda. Accordingly, William S. Smith—a Burrite and the surveyor of the port of New York, who had assisted Miranda—was removed from office and indicted along with Samuel Ogden, owner of *Leander* and a heavy investor in the venture.

Which brings Aaron Burr back onstage for his final public performance. Burr had been in the wings, in fact, since he left government a year earlier, and he had not been waiting idly. He had traveled to South Carolina to visit his daughter, Theodosia, and his son-in-law, Joseph Allston, during the course of which trip he had ventured into East Florida; and he had spent most of the summer and fall of 1805 in the West, where he found the citizenry eager for war with Spain, even as their president was at the time. He also found that most Republican political leaders throughout the West were warmly disposed toward him; and in New Orleans he found a number of wealthy malcontents who were scheming to pry the city loose from the United States. Somewhere along the line he conceived a plan, albeit a dim one, of recouping his political fortunes by rallying around himself a few thousand westerners—rallying people to his banner was the easiest thing Burr ever undertook— and, with New Orleans as a base, attacking whatever Spanish possessions seemed ripest. In a fit of euphoria he promised Theodosia that he would make her empress of Mexico. His promises to his daughter were the only ones he ever felt compelled to keep, if it were possible to do so.

Among others in the West, he sounded out two soldiers, of sorts. One was a rough-and-ready land speculator, violent Hispanophobe, erstwhile congressman, and currently brigadier general of Tennessee militia named Andrew Jackson. Jackson fell instantly under Burr's spell and vowed to back him with men and arms for any expedition against Spain that Burr should name. The other soldier was an old comrade in arms, a veteran of service as a young officer with Burr during Arnold's heroic campaign against Quebec thirty years earlier. He was James Wilkinson, governor of upper Louisiana and perhaps the most treacherous and scurrilous of all the scoundrels and adventurers who infested the southwestern frontier. For years, Wilkinson had been commander of the American forces defending the United States against Spain in the Southwest, and for most of that time he had been the recipient of regular annual bribes from the crown of Spain. It is difficult to imagine that Burr, the utter master of intrigue, did not soon tumble to Wilkinson's duplicity; but Wilkinson was a factor to be reckoned with in any expedition into the area, so Burr pretended to take Wilkinson into his confidence as a co-conspirator in a grand scheme whose details were not yet firm. Wilkinson snapped at the bait, and dutifully notified his Spanish patrons.

In all likelihood Burr was not merely playacting when he shrouded his plans in mystery, for the probability is that he had no clear plan. He was later charged with conspiring to lead the western states in armed revolt against the United States. Doubtless he would not have scrupled against doing so, but (except in New Orleans) he found almost no support for, and a great deal of opposition toward, such an enterprise; and so, with a characteristic shrug of the shoulders, he abandoned the idea—save as it might be useful for scaring up support from persons or governments who would regard it as an interesting prospect.

Having laid his complex trail, Burr returned to Washington

about the time Miranda showed up there, seeking support as Miranda was; but Burr no doubt learned, as Miranda did not, that President Jefferson had adopted a dual policy toward Spain. Burr then engaged, personally and through intermediaries, in discussions with officials of three governments. From the British minister Anthony Merry, he attempted to obtain both financial backing and the support of the Royal Navy by suggesting (what Merry was pleased to hear) that the western Americans were eager to break away from Jeffersonian tyranny and were equally eager to attack Spanish America, and that Burr planned a venture which, with the blessings of Great Britain, would accomplish both ends. To Yrujo, Burr and his agents likewise intimated that the westerners wanted both to secede and to attack Spanish territory, but they told the Spaniard that with aid from Spain, Burr would see to it that they seceded and threw themselves under the protection of the Spanish crown instead. Merry, though suspicious of Burr, gave Burr's proposal a qualified endorsement in his recommendations to his superiors. Yrujo, though alerting Spanish officials in America and at home to expect an attack from American forces under Burr's generalship, also contributed several thousand dollars toward Burr's campaign on the off chance that it might be designed against the United States.

The third government Burr approached was that of the United States: he dined privately with the president on a number of occasions between December of 1805 and April of 1806. Neither man left any record of what was said, and thus whatever passed between them must be a matter of conjecture. It need not, however, be uninformed conjecture. For one thing, any idea that the calls were purely social can be readily dismissed, for the two men were scarcely enamored of one another's company. For another, it is clear that Jefferson was aware, from a variety of sources, that Burr was contemplating some kind of military or quasi-military operation in the Southwest. Rumors to that effect were rife, and several people, including Gen. William Eaton and Federal District Attorney Joseph Daveiss of Kentucky, told the president in February and March that Burr and Wilkinson intended to lead the western states out of the Union and/or to attack Spanish West Florida and Mexico. Jefferson professed not to believe his informants; most were pointedly told not to concern themselves with the matter because it was none of their affair. In light of what Jefferson knew and of what he did—or rather did not do—about it, one could infer that he had suddenly become indifferent or careless in regard to the southern and western frontiers, which is inconceivable; or that he had suddenly learned to trust Burr, which is nearly so; or else that he had reason not to fear Burr and indeed to believe that Burr's venture could prove advantageous to the administration and to the nation. Only the last squares with what is known about the two men, what their circumstances were at the time, and what they did in the ensuing months.

It has been customary to approach the "Burr Conspiracy" from Burr's point of view; it is more fruitful to approach it from Jefferson's. The president's private correspondence during this period reveals several changes in mood. In January and February of 1806 he was anxiously concerned over the battle in Congress. In March and April he went through about a month of elation, amounting almost to euphoria, over his success in beating back his enemies, especially Randolph. By the time Congress adjourned, that happy glow had vanished, and Jefferson repeatedly sounded a partly wistful, partly wishful suggestion that belligerence toward Spain was the best course, after all.

The flow of international events augmented this last mood. Spain was assuming an increasingly bellicose stance, and the president had received reliable reports that the Spanish were enlarging their garrisons at both Pensacola and Mobile and were moving troops from Mexico toward the Sabine River. The number of Spaniards involved was small, but they were probably more than a match for the corrupt and incompetent Wilkinson, if indeed Wilkinson did not, in a showdown, completely betray the United States. Should war come—as Jefferson was beginning to hope it would—the Spanish would have found the western Americans itching for a fight but totally unorganized. Moreover, given what had just taken place in Congress, the administration could not, prior to an actual Spanish attack, either increase the size of the regular army or mobilize the militias. In other words, it could not prepare for defense officially. What it could do unofficially was another matter.

That situation made Burr potentially useful. It would have been greatly in the interest of the United States, and would in no way have compromised Jefferson's integrity, to use Burr's ambitions as a means of resolving the military dilemma. One needed only to suggest to Burr that it would be entirely acceptable for him to raise volunteer troops for an attack on Spanish territory, and even to hint to prospective recruits that the government of the United States had authorized him to do so and had supplied him with blank commissions—provided, of course, that Burr must absolutely not deploy the troops unless war with Spain broke out.

Burr would have readily agreed to such an arrangement, for he was hedging his bets in several ways. First, though he had been advocating (and dreaming of leading) an expedition against Spanish North America for fully a decade, he had prepared a stopgap or backup plan against the possibility that he might have to wait even longer. Shortly after leaving Washington he obtained title to the so-called Bastrop grant of a huge tract in the Spanish borderlands, and he told all his recruits—albeit with a wink and the recognition that they understood far more interesting things to be in the offing—that he was recruiting them as settlers on that tract. If war did not come soon, the settlement could actually be made, and it could be used as a base for an assault on a near or distinct morrow, whenever the war that Burr regarded as ultimately inevitable should come.

Second, Burr was not leaving the matter of war entirely to chance and diplomacy. One reason for ringing Wilkinson in on the scheme was that Wilkinson was uniquely in a position to provoke war with Spain: given the state of diplomatic relations between the two countries, any skirmish between Spanish forces and the troops under Wilkinson's command, if conducted on soil even remotely claimed by the United States, could be regarded as the opening of hostilities. In that event Burr could proceed to rally forces and attack West Florida and Mexico on the pretext (or legitimate ground, if it so developed) that Spain and the United States were at war. His expedition would thus be legal, be in the interests of both the administration and the country, and be a springboard for a spectacular resumption of his political career.

Finally, should the British government come through with sufficient backing—financial and naval—Burr could afford to move irrespective of the outcome of the dispute between Spain and the United States. In that event he would be able to take New Orleans and use it as a base for establishing a new American empire.

Only the last of Burr's prospective courses could have occasioned concern to Jefferson. The president, for his part, believed that nothing of the sort was likely to happen, and believed Burr could be readily thwarted if he attempted such a thing. In sum, from Jefferson's point of view, Burr might prove useful; if not, he was expendable.

That Jefferson was willing to treat with Burr at all, however, is a measure of the toll the presidential office was exacting.

6

★★★★★

THE RAGING STORM: 1806–1807

Jefferson's second term was becoming a painful ordeal. Disappointment and frustration followed one another in endless succession, and before the term was half over, events at home as well as on and beyond the seas had ceased to respond to his bidding. It is customary, in accounting for the calamity of his second term, to attribute it to circumstances. He was a man of high ideals and lofty moral principles, as the accounting usually reads, who was caught between the hungry British shark and the even more ravenous Napoleonic tiger, and he strove nobly but in vain to extricate his administration and his country from an impossible situation.

The truth is at once simpler and more complex: the failings were of Jefferson's own making, and they flowed logically if not inevitably from the interaction between Republican ideology and the policies adopted during Jefferson's first term. The primary goals of the Republican revolution, sought with obsessive zeal, were retirement of the public debt and territorial expansion, specifically the acquisition of Spanish territory on the southern and southwestern frontiers of the United States. Given world circumstances, both ends might have been most efficaciously pursued by a policy of accommodation with Great Britain and a policy of aggressive opportunism toward Spain and its ally France. The Jefferson administration followed quite the opposite course, and yet because of special conditions that prevailed during the first term it registered spectacular successes both in managing the debt and in expanding the nation's boundaries. But those special conditions had vanished by the winter of 1805–1806, never to return; and a policy of accommodation with Britain and aggressiveness toward France and Spain now became the *only* policy that was consistent with the primary aims of Jeffersonian Republicanism.

And therein lay the dilemma the Jeffersonians had made for themselves: they simply could not follow the necessary path. As to bellicosity, they were willing to fight Spain (a pushover) and did not fear war with Britain (they could always "defend" the United States by staying off the seas); but they were possessed of an uneasy feeling, rational or otherwise, that a war with France could mean loss of territory to Napoleon's seemingly invincible armies. To the Jeffersonians, no foreign policy that entailed such a risk was thinkable. As to accommodation with Britain, there were several barriers they could not overcome. One barrier was ideological and psychological. Since opposition to the English system lay at the very heart of the Republican revolution, to make common cause with England was to join hands with the devil. Another was more involved. The Jeffersonians, having emasculated the American armed forces in the interest of economy, were left with no way of making themselves heard abroad except through diplomacy and a professed moral commitment to abstract principles of international law. The British, given the conditions necessary to their continued existence as a sovereign nation, found it impossible to comport themselves strictly within the limits of those principles. They depended for their survival upon mastery of the seas, and though they were (after Pitt's death) willing to make concessions to the United States that they made to no other nation, they could not and would not waive their "right" to impress British seaman from foreign vessels and to issue orders determining who could trade with whom and in what commodities. Since both of these practices were in violation of the international law to which the Jeffersonians were committed, the Jeffersonians could not sanction them without compromising their moral integrity. Moreover, in that regard they were also bound by practical political considerations. For more than twelve years the Republicans had consistently and vigorously protested British naval policies, and they could not suddenly abandon that posture without a total loss of face. Finally, and perhaps most vitally, for the Jeffersonians to reach an accommodation with Britain on Britain's terms —however reasonable those terms might be—would have been to admit the obvious but unutterable fact that the success of the Revolution of 1800 was directly dependent upon the good will of Great

Britain. In other words, for the Revolution of 1800 to continue to succeed, it would have to deny and contradict itself.

British sea captains sometimes made it difficult for their civilian superiors to conduct their diplomacy in accordance with the niceties of that calling. The captains, though perfect gentlemen by their own lights, were wont to execute their duties with a heavy, even brutish hand. One instance of their bullish ways jeopardized the Pinkney mission before it began.

In April of 1806, after Congress had adjourned but before Jefferson headed homeward for Monticello, a three-ship British squadron was patrolling the American coast off New York, searching merchantmen for contraband. One of the British men-of-war, H.M.S. *Leander*, fired a warning shot across the bows of a merchant ship, that being the conventional way of announcing to the merchant vessel that she was to be searched, but the projectile far overshot its mark. Such inaccuracy was commonplace with the British navy, which, like the American, specialized in heavy and rapid fire rather than (as with the French navy) in precision; but this particular blast landed amidships an innocent American sloop, killing a crewman named John Pierce, brother of the small vessel's captain. Captain Henry Whitby of *Leander*, inured to death in time of war, regarded the incident as only an incident, albeit an unfortunate one. Captain Pierce regarded it as murder; and he returned to port, where he walked the length of Broadway, carrying in his arms the body of his dead brother. The citizenry of New York, normally rather crass in its attitude toward the perils of seeking profits from the fortunes of war, rose en masse to demand retribution, vengeance, and, in the harshest sense of the term, justice. A grand jury indicted Whitby for murder, and President Jefferson demanded his courtmartial and ordered the British ships to leave American waters.

All of which might have made James Madison's task of writing Pinkney's instructions rather more difficult—except that Madison was not anxious for the mission to succeed anyway. His instructions in fact made failure almost certain. The United States and Britain were at odds on a number of points, including the proper definition of contraband and of what constituted a legitimate blockade, but the immediate occasion for the Pinkney mission was the *Essex* decision, which cut off America's lucrative trade as a neutral carrier. Yet Madison instructed Pinkney to give first importance to still another matter, the impressment of American seamen. Indeed, he made the satisfactory settlement of that problem a *sine qua non* for any agreement between the two countries.

The question of impressment wants careful notice. Under British law, the Royal Navy was empowered in time of war to press into service, for the duration, any subjects it needed for manning its ships. Discipline and living conditions in the British navy were hard, and the conscripted seamen were apt to desert any time they thought they could get away with doing so. Ordinarily the most convenient means of escape was to jump ship in an American port or in a neutral port where there were American vessels. If the deserters signed on as American merchant seamen they could easily pass as Americans, for the differences in speech and mannerisms were not yet large. Moreover, the American merchant marine, which was continuously expanding because of the neutral carrying trade, could absorb several thousand new seamen a year and paid four or five times the wages of British seamen into the bargain.

To compensate for the drain of manpower, captains of the Royal Navy were authorized, whenever they were short-handed, to stop American vessels and recover any deserters they found. Since proof of citizenship was difficult and the captains were scarcely fastidious about seamen's rights, a goodly number of Americans were taken into British service along with actual deserters. Madison claimed that the number was in the thousands; Britain maintained that it was only a handful and that Americans were regularly released upon satisfactory proof of citizenship. Whatever the merits of the two claims, it was clear that the number of British deserters in the American merchant fleet was several times as large as the number of Americans who had been pressed into British naval service. It was also clear that no British captain would sail short-handed when replacements could be obtained from the first passing American vessel, and that no British government would jeopardize national security by depriving the captains of that source of manpower.

New England merchants were as indifferent regarding impressment as they were ardent regarding the reopening of the neutral carrying trade. This was not, however, the result of a callous disregard for human liberty in the pursuit of profit. Rather, the reason was that vessels from New England were manned almost entirely by locals; as one moved southward, dependence on outside seamen, including British deserters, progressively increased. Some Yankees charged that the preoccupation of Jefferson and Madison with impressment reflected nothing more than concern for the interests of the South. Defenders of the president and of the secretary of state have maintained that their concern stemmed from valuing human rights above property rights; and certainly the clamor raised by Republican press and politicians cast the matter in that light. The New Englanders' charge was no doubt groundless, but the defense is difficult to reconcile with the fact that the president and the secretary of state personally held property rights in human beings.

In any event, Madison insisted that impressment be the first order of business for Pinkney and Monroe, which doomed the mission and resulted in an estrangement that would ultimately lead to war. Moreover, the point on which Madison specifically insisted was so narrowly legalistic as to amount to nit-picking. The United States conceded that Britain had the right of impressment in British territorial waters, though it insisted that those waters extended no more than twelve miles offshore, contrary to the British position that they covered all the "narrow seas," meaning essentially the English Channel. On the opposite side, Britain did not claim the right of impressment in American waters or in neutral ports, nor did it claim the right to search American naval vessels. At issue was only impressment from merchant vessels on the "high seas," meaning the open ocean. Madison himself pointed out that most American vessels on the high seas sooner or later found themselves in British waters, where the right was not challenged, and that made the question at issue somewhat academic. But Madison contended that he was pressing for a principle that was, or ought to be, a matter of international law—namely the principle, accepted by no other nation, that merchant ships flying the American flag were extensions of American sovereignty, and to board them forcibly if they were not carrying illegal cargoes was to violate that sovereignty.

In the course of time, insistence upon that dubious principle would cost the United States thousands of lives, millions of dollars, and immeasurable humiliation.

Despite Madison's doctrinaire stance and despite Jeffersonian policy in general, it appeared in May of 1806 and for some time thereafter that America's international problems would be favorably resolved by the mere inertia of events. In London the newly formed Grenville-Fox government made a decision about its prosecution of the war which incidentally satisfied all the practical wants of the United States, if none of the theoretical. On May 16 Fox informed Monroe that Britain, in retaliation against Napoleon's efforts against British commerce, was declaring a blockade of all the European coast from Brest, in the northwest point of France, to the Elbe at Hamburg, Germany. The blockade would be strictly enforced, however, only in the narrow area between Le Havre, France, and Ostend, Belgium; except in that zone, American vessels that were not either carrying contraband or sailing directly between enemy ports would be unmolested. By this means the *Essex* decision was tacitly negated; Americans could resume the lucrative neutral carrying trade under the doctrine of the broken voyage.

In Paris, developments ran counter to the Jefferson administration's plans but not counter to the attainment of its objectives. Armstrong, upon receiving authorization to try to buy Florida through Napoleon, forwarded the authorization to Talleyrand, who took it to the emperor. The hoped-for miracle, a repetition of what had happened with Louisiana, did not come. Rather, Napoleon blandly said that he did not think King Charles IV of Spain could be persuaded to sell. Napoleon's announcement made it clear that if the United States wanted the Floridas or other Spanish territory, it would have to take them for itself.

That turn of events was actually advantageous, for it forced the president back toward his original position of bellicosity toward Spain. Moreover, the Spanish were just then providing him with a valid excuse for a renewal of belligerence: late in May, Jefferson received a report that a Spanish force had crossed the Sabine River into Orleans Territory and that additional invading forces were soon expected. That intelligence gave the president a golden opportunity to get himself off the hook on which (at Madison's urging) he had hung himself, and he seized the chance. Forthwith, he dispatched orders to Gen. James Wilkinson to leave St. Louis (his seat as territorial governor of upper Louisiana) and proceed at once to the Sabine area. If he met resistance, Wilkinson was to repel the Spanish by force.

That development, and one other, sealed Aaron Burr's plans. Burr had continued to flirt with a treasonable alternative to his more honorable plan of leading an American force against Spain in the event of war, but early in June that flirtation abruptly ended. Burr called upon Anthony Merry in a last attempt to get British naval and financial support for an expedition that involved taking New Orleans as well as the Floridas and Mexico. Pitt's death had made such support seem less likely, and now Burr learned that Merry himself had been recalled and would be replaced by a minister who was more favorably disposed toward the United States. That being that, only one western adventure was left open to Burr, and he made himself ready to undertake it. Preparatory to heading westward, he sent for his daughter, conferred with various associates, tried to raise some money, and—most importantly—waited for news that Wilkinson was marching to war.

The wait was vain, for Wilkinson was still in St. Louis, leisurely disobeying his orders from the president of the United States. Later he claimed that he had delayed his departure because his wife was ill. On May 13, before receiving the presidential orders, he had written to Burr about their designs. The letter has never been found, but from other evidence it is clear that Wilkinson was getting cold feet and was petulant over recent attempts by the Randolph faction to remove him as territorial governor. It is also clear that Wilkinson was implicated in the most treasonable of the various plans that Burr had considered.

By mid July, Burr had done all he could do in the East, except for one thing. In a last wild effort to prod Wilkinson into action, Burr and his cohort Jonathan Dayton wrote the general a pair of letters. All Wilkinson had to do, now, was obey the president's orders; but suspecting that something more than the call of duty would be necessary as an inducement, they chose to deceive him. Dayton's letter, dated July 24, 1806, played upon Wilkinson's fears: it suggested that Wilkinson's long-time perfidies had come to light and that in the next session of Congress, Wilkinson was to be stripped of his command as well as his civil office, leaving him disgraced and broken. "Jefferson," Dayton added, "will affect to yield reluctantly to the public sentiment, but yield he will." But, he coaxed, "you are not a man to despair, or even despond, especially when such prospects offer in another quarter. Are you ready? Are your numerous associates ready? Wealth and glory! Louisiana and Mexico!"[1]

Burr's letter, dated July 29 but sent with Dayton's, was an even more brazen set of lies. He claimed that enough money and men had been raised, that British naval support was assured, that Commodore Truxtun would lead an American fleet and would join with the British at Jamaica, and that the people of Mexico were "prepared to receive us." Burr himself would head west on August 1; he would then mobilize his forces, and would begin to descend the Ohio with the first five hundred or one thousand men on November 15. Between December 5 and 15 he would rendezvous with Wilkinson at Natchez. All this was couched in cipher; to ensure that Wilkinson received it, Burr sent one copy overland to St. Louis with Samuel Swartwout and another copy by sea to New Orleans with

Erick Bollman. Two or three days later, with his daughter and a few companions, Burr set out for the West—in his words, "never to return."[2]

As Burr headed westward, determined to have a war with Spain one way or another, the prospects for an amicable settlement with Britain continued to improve. Though the British press blamed the United States for the *Leander* incident and demanded war over it, the Grenville-Fox ministry apologized and recalled Captain Whitby for investigation. Talks with Monroe and Pinkney were delayed because Fox fell ill, and he died in September; but that did not alter anything, for the British appointed Lord Aukland (formerly William Eden) and Lord Holland, Fox's nephew, as ministers plenipotentiary to conduct the negotiations, and both were warm friends of the United States. Several sessions were devoted to seeking an arrangement regarding impressment that both parties could live with, but to no avail. Aukland and Holland pled with the Americans not to let the prospects for a long-term peace founder on a doctrinaire principle; they also pointed out that the British government was currently giving no cause for offense regarding impressments and intended to continue that policy. Surely, the British argued, it was better to defer the question of conflicting principles, if there were no practical clash, than to abandon entirely the hope of a friendly settlement.

Monroe and Pinkney asked whether it would be possible to obtain written assurances of the continuation of non-impressment in practice; the British promptly produced the necessary document. On November 9 they delivered to the Americans a formal diplomatic note which conveyed the British government's solemn assurances that orders had been given to the Royal Navy—and would be repeated and enforced—to observe the strictest caution in impressing British seamen and the strictest care in protecting Americans "from any molestation or injury." The note also pledged that any complaint would bring "immediate and prompt redress." Finally, the note urged an effort for "drawing closer the connexion between the two countries," and it invited the Americans to go ahead with the negotiations.[3]

Monroe and Pinkney followed the only reasonable course: they accepted the invitation. Though nothing would be said about impressment in the prospective treaty, the assurances of the diplomatic note expressly underlay any agreement that might be reached. To negotiate on that basis was to violate the letter of Madison's instructions, but not to do so would be to scratch the mission and risk a further estrangement that could lead to a naval war with Britain —in which, in contrast to a war with Spain, the United States would have nothing to gain and a great deal to lose.

Meanwhile, Burr's doings in the West could scarcely have attracted more attention had he hired a publicity agent. Rumors attended his every move, and reports regularly flew back to Washington. One such came from John Nicholson in Herkimer, New York, and another from Col. George Morgan near Pittsburgh; the former was vague, the latter a charge that Burr intended to secure the independence of the western states. Several others also cried alarm, but the most persistent was Joseph Daveiss, federal attorney for Kentucky, incidentally a brother-in-law of John Marshall's, and a Federalist so devout that he had assumed "Hamilton" as a middle name. In a series of eight letters, beginning in February and continuing into the fall, Daveiss warned Jefferson of a Burr-Wilkinson plot that involved virtually every important Republican west of the Appalachians—whom Daveiss named, for the most part accurately. At first Daveiss charged that Burr intended to separate the West from the Union as well as to attack Spanish territory, but subsequently he decided that the plot was aimed only against Spain. The president ignored Daveiss's letters, and later fired him for his trouble.

Burr had set up headquarters of sorts on an island in the Ohio River, technically in the state of (West) Virginia; the island belonged to a wealthy, gullible, eccentric Irish expatriate named Harmon Blennerhassett, who had eagerly joined Burr's cause and had come up with a goodly measure of financial support for it. From there, throughout September and October, Burr moved up and down the area between Cincinnati and Nashville, consulting and planning—as Daveiss charged—with most of the important Republican military and political figures along the way. The persistent rumors of a secessionist plot sometimes made it necessary to indulge in explanations, as for instance with the former senators John Smith of Ohio and John Adair of Kentucky. Burr consistently denied any secessionist intentions, insisting that his aim was to attack Spanish territory in the event of war and asserting that he had the blessings of the government for such an undertaking. In most places no explanations were necessary, and Burr received a hero's welcome. Late in September, for instance, he spent several days as the guest of Gen. Andrew Jackson; and on October 4 Jackson published in the

Nashville newspaper a notice alerting the Tennessee militia to ready themselves to march on the hated Spanish.

By that time the war loomed as a virtual certainty within a matter of weeks. The Spanish reinforcements had arrived east of the Sabine and, under Col. Simon de Herrera, had established an encampment at Bayou Pierre (near present Shreveport). What was more portentous, Wilkinson had finally bestirred himself, gathered his troops, and begun to march southward for the confrontation.

But it was not the Spanish that Wilkinson decided to confront. On October 8, 1806, encamped fifty miles from the Spanish force, he received Swartwout's copies of Dayton's and Burr's letters. Whether to protect himself or to sound out his subordinates, he showed the letters to a colonel and perhaps another officer or two. For nearly two weeks he did nothing more, save possibly to weigh his options; then on October 21 he sat down to write three fateful documents, which he sent by special courier to the president. The first was a supposedly anonymous paper, phrased as if Wilkinson had received rather than written it, stating that a powerful association had been formed to recruit a large force on the upper Ohio beginning November 20, that the men would gather auxilliaries as they proceeded down the river, and that they were scheduled to rendezvous in New Orleans about February 1, by which time they would number eight to ten thousand. There, with British naval support, they planned to debark for an attack on Vera Cruz, Mexico. No leaders or participants were named in this paper, and there was no mention of a plot to dismember the Union. The second document, a signed letter from Wilkinson to the president, was an elaborate denial that Wilkinson himself was in any way involved in the scheme. The third was a covering letter for the other two. In it Wilkinson said that, though the "anonymous" paper did not mention any danger to American territory, he was convinced that "the revolt of this Territory [Orleans] will be made an auxilliary step to the main design of attacking Mexico." Accordingly, Wilkinson added, he had decided to disregard his orders, to work out a quick compromise with the Spanish commander, and then to hasten to New Orleans "to be ready to defend that capital against usurpation and violence." On November 5 Wilkinson reached his "compromise" agreement with Herrera: they created a neutral zone *inside* what the United States claimed to be Orleans Territory, the Americans withdrawing east of the zone and the Spanish withdrawing west of it.[4]

Thence Wilkinson sped to New Orleans, where he began

making wholesale arrests—and where he wrote two more letters. In the first letter, addressed to the president, Wilkinson said that "this deep, dark, wicked, and wide-spread conspiracy" was even more dangerous than he had suspected, but that he would combat it with "indefatigable industry, incessant vigilance and hardy courage." The president must speedily reinforce him with men and ships; though if necessary, Wilkinson said, "I shall glory to give my life" to save the nation from the fiendish plot. Wilkinson's other letter went to the Spanish viceroy in Mexico City; it informed the viceroy of Wilkinson's great service to His Catholic Majesty in thwarting Burr, and demanded as compensation $110,000 in cash, plus a reimbursal for out-of-pocket money he had been "obliged to spend in order to sustain the cause of good government, order and humanity."[5]

Wilkinson's dispatches of October 21 did not reach the president until November 25. In the meantime, Burr was being thwarted in another quarter. Early in November and again two weeks later, Joseph Daveiss attempted to have Burr indicted, in Lexington, on charges of conspiring to levy war against the United States or Spain or both. Burr appeared in his own behalf, with young Henry Clay as his counsel, and disclaimed having any intentions other than to lead a force against Spain in the event of war or to settle his Ouachita lands if war did not come. On both occasions the grand jury refused to indict Burr; after the first dismissal tumultous cheering erupted, and after the second a public ball was given in Burr's honor. Nevertheless, Daveiss's continued pressure afforded embarrassment to President Jefferson—as it was designed to do.

But neither Wilkinson's spectacular charge nor Daveiss's legal activities, taken alone, would have been enough to stir Jefferson into action against Burr. To be sure, the president and his advisors were already jumpy: in mid October, in response to reports that Burr intended to start the war as a private undertaking, they had adopted measures to head him off, but on October 24 they had reversed themselves and had resolved merely to have him watched. Yet Burr could not be regarded as a danger as long as his avowed aims were consistent with Jefferson's own designs and expectations, which were based upon the belief that war with Spain was both imminent and desirable. That was the way things stood until the middle of November. What changed then were the administration's designs and expectations, and the main stimulus for change emanated not from New Orleans and Lexington but from Paris.

For Napoleon had determined upon an audacious scheme, and though its outlines were known only to the emperor himself, the

United States figured into it. Frustrated and enraged by the freshest display of British insolence—the blockade, which was touching his pocketbook as well as his pride—he had conceived the idea of imposing a counterblockade by land. The idea was a wild one, but it could be made to work if Napoleon controlled every foot of the European coastline between Iberia and Prussia, and if the United States cooperated. To secure control of northern Europe he set forth on September 25 for an invasion of Prussia, and in little more than a month, after a pair of brilliant victories, he marched into Berlin. To ensure that there would be no bickering between his "friends," Spain and the United States, he issued what amounted to an ultimatum: they must have no war. To make certain that the United States understood, he made it clear, through both Turreau and Armstrong, that the Americans would know his generosity if they cooperated and his wrath if they did not.

The advance warning of Napoleon's new policy, soon to be formally proclaimed in his Berlin Decree, was enough to inspire the administration to seek pacification rather than war on the Spanish frontier. That shift was made just before the reports from Wilkinson arrived and the news filtered in that efforts were being made to indict Burr in Lexington. Exit Aaron Burr.

When Jefferson received Wilkinson's October 21 communications on November 25, he immediately called a cabinet meeting. The problem was ticklish. Burr must be stopped, but the host of important Republicans who were involved with him must not be embarrassed; and besides, Jefferson had no special animus against Burr himself, even though he vacillated in his notions of Burr's intentions. What was decided upon was a proclamation that would halt the venture without naming anyone. The proclamation, issued on November 27, declared that "sundry persons," in defiance of the laws, were conspiring to attack Spain. It warned all such persons to withdraw from the enterprise, and directed civil and military officers of the United States to arrest any persons who attempted to carry out such an expedition.

That might have been that, for Burr had no real force to be stopped, and the administration made no effort to arrest him. He continued to move about unmolested, no more and no less innocently than before. But in the prevailing atmosphere, charged for months by rumors of secessionism and now supercharged by stories that Wilkinson was rounding up traitors in New Orleans by the score—he was in actuality arresting everyone who could have implicated him—the effect of the proclamation was electric. By the time Congress convened in December, panic was abroad in the land.

Throughout December and for the first two months of 1807 the arch conspirator and traitor James Wilkinson, acting in the name and with the authority of the United States, was trampling the Constitution and the Bill of Rights into dust. In New Orleans, Wilkinson arrested without warrants and held incommunicado three of Burr's couriers and lieutenants, Samuel Swartwout, Peter V. Ogden, and Erick Bollman. He denied them access to counsel, and when writs of habeas corpus were obtained in their behalf he had them clapped in irons and sent by sea to Washington. He also jailed their attorney, the judge, the judge's closest friend, the editor of the *Orleans Gazette*, former Senator Adair, and some sixty other citizens. None was specifically charged, all were denied their legal and constitutional rights, and several were transported in chains away from the vicinage, where they had a constitutional right to a speedy and public trial, and were shipped in secret to Washington. The president of the United States privately approved all Wilkinson's actions, his only reservation being that Wilkinson must remain within the limits, not of the Constitution, but of what public opinion would bear. Public opinion would just then bear a great deal, for the sensational nature of the proceedings in New Orleans convinced a large portion of the public—as Wilkinson intended it should—that the Burr conspiracy must have been powerful, nefarious, and dangerous indeed, for otherwise the government would scarcely have resorted to such drastic means to suppress it.

The ostensible center of the ostensible plot continued for a remarkably long time to be left alone. Rowdies and militiamen, upon reading the presidential proclamation, attacked, plundered, and virtually demolished Blennerhassett's island, and others seized a few dozen men who had signed on with Burr in Ohio and Kentucky; but nobody interfered with Burr and the hundred or so men who, ignorant of what was happening in New Orleans, accompanied him down the river toward his Ouachita lands. But Wilkinson had sent Jefferson a decoded copy of Burr's letter of the previous July 29— somewhat garbled so as to make the plot seem more dire, and emended so as to remove all traces of Wilkinson's complicity—and he had also released that version of the letter to the newspapers. In mid January, Burr saw a published copy of it and, deciding instantly that flight was the path of wisdom, fled. In Mississippi Territory he was apprehended and subjected to a burlesque of a grand jury hearing, one of the presiding judges of which was an old friend and comrade in arms of both Burr's and Wilkinson's, Peter B. Bruin, with whom Burr afterward stayed as a guest for a few days. Subsequently released on a bond of questionable legality, Burr learned that Wilkinson had sent agents to assassinate him, and this time he fled in earnest. Soon he was captured and sent overland to Richmond for yet another grand jury inquest.

Meanwhile the publication of the cipher letter, together with the news from New Orleans, inspired many in Washington to wonder why Jefferson was not doing anything about Burr. On January 18, 1807, John Randolph expressed his curiosity in the form of a demand: he introduced into the House a two-part resolution, the first part calling upon the president to deliver any information that he might have concerning an unlawful combination against the Union or a foreign nation, the second inquiring what the president had done and proposed to do about any such combination. In short order the resolution was passed, though the reference to what Jefferson *proposed to do* was omitted.

That forced Jefferson's hand, and four days later he presented Congress with a version of the "conspiracy" that was essentially identical to Wilkinson's version. He said that Burr had set out to attack New Orleans and/or launch an illegal assault on Mexico, and he asserted, inaccurately as well as improperly, that Burr's guilt had been "placed beyond question." Defending his own conduct, Jefferson averred (quite contrary to the facts) that he had first heard warnings about Burr in September and had issued his proclamation instantly upon receiving the first reliable confirmation of the plot, namely Wilkinson's dispatches of October 21, which the president included with his message. As to how serious the danger had been, Jefferson had it two ways: it was not serious enough to warrant any action from him beyond the proclamation, as witness the fact that the conspiracy had been destroyed and the danger was past; and yet it was serious enough to warrant Wilkinson's wholesale violation of the rights of accused accomplices, which was still going on. Finally, Jefferson publicly endorsed Wilkinson's actions, declaring that the general had acted with "the honor of a soldier and the fidelity of a good citizen."[6]

The message evoked different responses among Jefferson's followers and copartisans in Congress. In the Senate, the dominant element adhered to a form of Republican ideology that might be styled totalitarian libertarianism: believing that the government in their hands was dedicated to preserving human liberty, they were willing to resort to mass arrests and even to hangings in order to protect that government; and believing that the courts were dominated by enemies of liberty, they saw legal protection of the civil rights of accused persons only as subterfuges behind which traitors and other enemies of liberty could hide. In keeping with this perverse philosophy, the Senate suspended its rules and rushed to passage, in one day, a bill to suspend the privilege of the writ of habeas corpus for three months. The bill was aimed specifically at the prisoners Wilkinson was sending up from New Orleans, but it cast a far wider net. It was sponsored by Jefferson's friend and floor leader, William B. Giles of Virginia, and though it was probably not suggested by the president, he doubtless would have signed it into law had the House concurred in its passage.

The House was having no part of it, for the response to recent events there was a resurgence of a different form of Republican ideology—that of the doctrinaire libertarian who would abide the subversion of government and of society itself before willfully jeopardizing the rights and liberties of a single citizen. The House, led by Randolph and by Jefferson's son-in-law John W. Eppes, rejected Giles's bill by an overwhelming majority. A few days later the House went a great deal further, considering a bill making "further provision for securing the privilege of the writ of habeas corpus." Only because a number of Republicans proved unwilling to endorse such an obvious censure of Thomas Jefferson did the bill fail to pass, and even then it failed by a narrow margin.

This ideological rift between Republicans sorely vexed the president; no doubt it embarrassed him as well. He was not given to theorizing about liberty, and neither was his party, for the roots as well as the aims of the Republican revolution lay elsewhere; and yet the freedom and happiness of the citizenry was assumed to be the end product of their crusade to rid the nation of moneychangers and monocrats, of public debts and foreign entanglements. Now the party was embroiled in a hassle over whether tyrannical means were justified in the cause of liberty, and the president was caught in a squeeze. When out of office, he had most often espoused the position currently taken by the House, but he had not always done so even then;[7] and as president he had drifted steadily if unconsciously toward the intolerant authoritarian position taken now by the Senate. In the two years that remained of his presidency he would move almost completely into the latter camp.

Not, however, without pain. Just after Congress adjourned in March he was seized—as often happened to him during periods of intense stress and inability to cope—with a fierce migraine headache. He had suffered worse, but this one was bad enough: it lasted for three weeks, during which he spent all but an hour or so a day alone in a darkened room.

The Burr-Wilkinson affair, spectacular as it was and would continue to be, was not the only business occupying Congress and the Jefferson administration during the winter session of 1806–1807. Two other important matters, namely the slave trade and the Monroe-Pinkney treaty, also came up for disposition, and both were affected by the ideological split among Republicans.

As to the slave trade, the Constitution had prohibited congressional interference with it for twenty years, but that moratorium was soon to expire. In his annual message, Jefferson reminded Congress of the impending expiration and recommended the abolition of the trade with a law to become effective January 1, 1808. He made the proposal as a part of a broad series of recommendations which, in his judgment, would strengthen the nation in ways that were consistent with Republican principles. Specifically, foreseeing a treasury surplus in a few more years, he proposed a constitutional amendment that would empower Congress to appropriate funds for public education and internal transportation. He also proposed legislation to improve the defenses of the seaports and either to reorganize the militias or create an enlarged volunteer army. The package was humane, reasonable, and remarkably far-sighted, especially considering the semihysterical myopia that was beclouding Washington at just that moment.

The slave trade, however, was the only one of these proposals on which Congress acted. This might be regarded as surprising, since the slave party was in full control of both houses of Congress, but there was more to the matter than was readily apparent. For one thing, despite the fairly rapid spread of cotton plantations on the Carolina piedmont and in Tennessee, there was an excess, not a shortage, of slave labor in the United States: South Carolina was the only state which had allowed the importation of slaves in the thirty years since the Declaration of Independence, and even there importing slaves had been prohibited during twenty-four of the thirty years.[8] For another thing, feeding the surplus slave population was a serious economic problem in the old tobacco belt of the upper South, where the cultivation of cotton was not possible. Many slaveholders in that area foresaw profits as well as the solution of a social problem in supplying the labor needs of an expanding cotton-growing business—a prospect that would be considerably enhanced if the importation of slaves from abroad were outlawed.

The debate on the bill, foreshadowing many another debate in years to come, illustrated that it is easier to denounce something as evil than to rectify it. The first draft of the bill forbade the importation of slaves and imposed a penalty of a fine and forfeiture upon violators. Forfeiture, however, would give the United States government title to the slaves, and under existing law it would sell them at public auction. Northerners balked at making the federal government into a slaveholder and slave trader, and after some rancorous debate the fate of forfeited slaves was left to the individual states. The Senate version of the bill prohibited vessels of less than forty tons from carrying slaves in the domestic coastal trade; this elicited a cry of outrage from several southerners in the House, who declared that any interference in the domestic slave trade would be an unconstitutional infringement of the rights of the states which could later be used as a precedent that would lead to emancipation. One southerner talked of civil war, and John Randolph prophesied that if disunion should ever come, the line of division would be not between eastern and western but between slaveholding and nonslaveholding states. The feature was left in, but by and large, enforcement of the measure was left to the states.

The outburst of states'-rights sentiment in the House was part of the same mood that inspired the rejection of the Senate bill suspending habeas corpus; both reflected, in Henry Adams's words, a "reaction which, at Randolph's bidding, swept the Southern Republicans back to their practices of 1801 and their professions of 1798."[9] In such a mood, the House totally rejected Jefferson's proposals for strengthening the fortifications of the seaports and for shoring up the army and the militias. The president's own son-in-law denounced the doctrine "that to preserve peace we ought to be prepared for war"; other southerners reiterated that view, talking as if cities were public burdens or even public enemies and maintaining that to defend them was to invite attack. While refusing to spend money, the House Republicans also cut taxes: they abolished the salt tax, the last important source of domestic revenue, thus making the treasury's dependence upon import duties virtually total.

Which was an interesting thing to do at that juncture, for commercial relations with Great Britain, the nation's principal source of imports, were just then foundering on the reefs of Republican ideology. The negotiations between Messrs. Pinkney and Monroe and Lords Holland and Auckland had already been moving along fairly well in late November, when news of Napoleon's Berlin Decree arrived in London. The decree announced its paper blockade by declaring that ships of all nations were forbidden to trade with England or carry English goods, on pain of forfeiture when they arrived at any Continental port. Since Napoleon was thus telling Americans they could not trade with England, Monroe and Pinkney assumed that the United States would have no real choice but to side with England in the dispute, and they pushed forward to conclude the best deal with England that was possible in the circumstances.

The treaty was concluded at the end of December, and though it could scarcely be regarded as a diplomatic triumph, it contained some important advantages for the United States. Several minor points concerning relations with Canada were settled, American rights to trade in the British East Indies were confirmed, and—most significantly—the right of Americans to engage as neutrals in the carrying trade between belligerents and their colonies, by way of United States ports, was expressly confirmed. In exchange, the United States made two concessions. First, goods brought into the United States from France and Spain and their colonies were no longer to be given drawbacks of import duties upon being reexported, since such refunds made a mockery of the doctrine of the broken voyage by confirming that the goods were imported only for the purpose of reexportation. Second, the United States pledged not to cut off trade with Britain, through either a nonimportation or a nonexportation act, for a period of ten years. A third provision was tacked on at the end: the British stipulated that the treaty would not be binding unless they were assured that the United States would refuse to submit to the Berlin Decree. Since submission would amount to refusing to trade with Britain, Monroe and Pinkney signed this addendum without hesitation, and forwarded the treaty to the president.

Jefferson received the treaty on March 3, 1807, the last day of the congressional session. He and Madison had declared, upon learning that the negotiations were proceeding without an agreement on impressments, that no treaty without such an agreement would be approved. Now, when Jefferson read the addendum concerning the Berlin Decree, he announced that that amounted to requiring the United States to engage in commercial war against France, and said that the addendum alone made the treaty unacceptable. In rejecting the treaty he took the extraordinary and rather high-handed step of refusing to submit it to the Senate for consideration. Some believed he did so out of fear that the Senate would ratify the treaty despite his misgivings; others believed he was exacting a sort of petty vengeance upon the Senate for having more or less forced him to initiate the Pinkney mission against his will.

In any event, the treaty was dead, and all prospects for the continuation of amicable relations with Britain died with it. Already the British had started getting tougher. In Orders in Council issued on January 7, 1807, Britain had struck back at the Berlin Decree by prohibiting the coasting trade between ports of France and her allies; inasmuch as Americans in the neutral carrying trade normally shopped around in several French or Spanish ports, this regulation was a genuine and costly nuisance. Soon afterward, Jefferson wrote a private letter to Bowdoin in Paris, suggesting that the United States would join France in enforcing Napoleon's Continental System if Napoleon would either force Spain to cede Florida and Mexico to the United States or give his blessings to American conquest of Spanish possessions.[10] The last was doubly ironic, in view of the fact that Aaron Burr was in jail on charges of entertaining just such an aspiration.

As to Burr himself, the aftermath of his arrest was a spectacular trial and some dazzling forensic pyrotechnics, but he had ceased to be a central figure in the ongoing drama of Jefferson's presidency. He was arraigned before a federal circuit court in Richmond, with John Marshall presiding. A grand jury, populated by eminent Virginians and headed by no less a figure than John Randolph, indicted him and various of his associates and failed by a narrow margin to indict the prosecution's principal witness, General Wilkinson. In the legal skirmishing that took place before the trial in August, Chief Justice Marshall and President Jefferson became involved in a celebrated difference of opinion over the question whether the president or documents in his possession could be subpoenaed. Marshall issued a subpoena, but Jefferson refused to comply beyond submitting some documents to the district attorney, not to the court, with instructions that the attorney withhold such parts of the documents as he regarded as not "directly material for the purposes of justice"; and Jefferson's position stood. The trial itself was colorful but anticlimactic, and Burr and his associates were acquitted on all counts.

Burr and his attorneys charged—what some historians have echoed—that Jefferson hounded Burr, violated his civil rights with Wilkinsonian abandon, and conducted what amounted to persecution in his determination to have Burr jailed or executed. Jefferson was not above hounding and persecuting his enemies, and he could be ruthless in suppressing civil rights when it suited his needs, as he had already demonstrated and would soon demonstrate far more vividly. Even as the Burr trial was going on, he was denouncing the press with a vehemence that bordered on paranoia, and was engaged in efforts to throttle opposition publishers in Connecticut with what he called "a few wholesome prosecutions." Nevertheless, his treatment of Burr's case, far from being persecution, was less than half-hearted prosecution. Indictments were sought and obtained for treason, which as a narrowly defined constitutional crime could not be made to stick, and for the misdemeanor of levying war against Spain, which Burr might have done had not Jefferson given him more than fair warning with his conspiracy proclamation. Efforts to find evidence to convict Burr on either charge were slipshod and unenthusiastic. The prosecution was not even conducted by the attorney general, but by an inept and inconsequential lawyer named George Hay, who was hopelessly outclassed by Burr and his assembly of brilliant counsel. Had Jefferson really wanted to persecute Burr, the government's case would have been managed far more carefully; and as a last resort, Jefferson could have seen to Burr's extradition to New Jersey, where the former vice-president was still under indictment for the murder of Alexander Hamilton.

In sum, Jefferson's handling of Burr's case was so moderate as to border on the negligent. The key to the president's course of action may lie in a letter that Jefferson wrote to Senator Giles on April 20. Forecasting that Burr would be acquitted because of Marshall's perversion of "all the principles of law," Jefferson declared that "all this, however, will work well." The public outcry over the acquittal would make it possible to pass a constitutional amendment providing for the popular election of federal judges. If the courts' "protection of Burr produces this amendment, it will do more good than his condemnation would have done," Jefferson said, adding that "if his punishment can be commuted now for a useful amendment of the Constitution, I shall rejoice in it."[11]

But Burr and Marshall, as well as Spanish conquest and the courts, were shunted to secondary roles even before the trial took place; relations with the United Kingdom of Great Britain now occupied center stage, and would do so until long after Jefferson had left the White House. The British, not knowing that Jefferson was secretly proposing to join Napoleon in commercial warfare against them, were nonetheless convinced that for reasons of dogma or temerity he was virtually a puppet of Napoleon's anyway; and they resolved that if the United States persisted in acting like an ally of France, it must be treated as an enemy of Great Britain. A foretoken of what lay ahead came early in the spring, when the king ousted the relatively pro-American ministry and replaced it with a hard-line, anti-American Tory ministry. Less than three months later, on the first day of summer, came an explosion.

Commodore James Barron of the American navy, a mediocre sailor with a gift for ingratiating himself with influential Republican politicians, had been entrusted with command of the Humphreys frigate *Chesapeake*, then being fitted at Norfolk for duty in the Mediterranean. Quite carelessly, the local recruiting officer signed on to *Chesapeake* a considerable number of deserters from the Royal Navy, who were especially insulting to their former officers upon encountering them in the streets of Norfolk. At least three of the deserters were American citizens, but they had volunteered for, not been impressed into, British service. Vice Admiral George C. Berkeley, commanding the American squadron of the British navy from his post in Halifax, was incensed at what he heard of all this, and he authorized his captains to employ extreme means in recovering the deserters. As it happened, several British men-of-war lay off of Norfolk, in pursuit of French vessels that had sailed into Chesapeake Bay for repairs, and the British ships received Berkeley's special instructions.

On June 21, 1807, Barron took *Chesapeake* out of Norfolk in a state that was far from seaworthy: planking, ropes, cannon, and other equipment were stacked randomly about the decks, and Barron had troubled himself to inspect the ship only cursorily. The master of H.M.S. *Leopard* hailed *Chesapeake* and demanded the surrender of various deserters. Barron refused, whereupon *Leopard* fired a quick succession of broadsides, killing three men and wounding eighteen, including Barron himself. Barron struck his colors in surrender; whereupon *Leopard* took four crewmen but disdainfully refused Barron's offer that *Chesapeake* be taken as a prize of war.

Americans in every seaport cried for vengeance, adopted resolutions vowing to prevent British naval vessels from obtaining necessary fresh water and supplies, and looked to the president for stern measures of retribution. Jefferson and his advisors held several emergency meetings, but retribution was not among the courses they seriously considered, for the means for exacting it were nonexistent. Instead, they sent instructions—ironically, aboard U.S.S. *Revenge*—to Monroe in London, ordering him to demand "reparation for the past, and security for the future." Specifically, Monroe was somehow to require the British government to renounce the actions of *Leopard*, chastise her captain, compensate the United States for the losses, send a special envoy to Washington to apologize, and publicly announce the abolition of impressment from American merchant and naval vessels on the high seas. The president and cabinet resolved to call Congress into early session on October 26, by which time the British reply should be in hand. For the interim, Jefferson issued a proclamation ordering British warships out of American waters, forbidding them from getting water and supplies in the United States, and declaring that any Americans who assisted in supplying them would be prosecuted. Finally, the state governors were alerted to be prepared to call out 100,000 militiamen.

But one does not bind one's self hand and foot and then issue ultimatums; and besides, the British were as angry in 1807 as the Americans were. British sea captains patrolling the American coast responded to the popular resolutions and the president's proclamation by threatening alternately to blockade American ports or to level them. They would not, of course, actually open hostilities in the absence of orders from London, but the British government was perilously close to issuing just such orders. For one thing, England was faced with a grave new naval threat. In the summer of 1807 the Emperor Napoleon met with the Emperor Alexander I of Russia on a raft at Tilsit, and as a consequence Russia pulled out of the Third Coalition. Since Napoleon had already crushed Austria and Prussia—the other members of the coalition—Britain now stood alone against the Continent. Fearing a resurgence of Continental naval power if France could combine its own small sea power with that of Russia and that of neutral Denmark, the British moved swiftly to remove Denmark from the play: they virtually destroyed Copenhagen and seized the entire Danish navy, towing it to England. So much for "neutrals" who by design or circumstance comported themselves in accordance with policy that favored Napoleon.

For another thing, a large and growing element of the British population came, in this crisis, to embrace a strongly anti-American attitude. The British prided themselves as being the freest people on earth, American pretensions to the role notwithstanding; and it was a sore spot to them indeed that the Americans had for years been growing rich by supplying Britain's enemies with goods and services, and had the permission of the ministry and Parliament to do so. Had the new Tory ministry responded to Jefferson's ultimatum by declaring war on the United States, the decision would have been greeted with cheers in most parts of England.

Whatever the decision was to be, it was in the hands of those ministers of the Crown of Britain whom Thomas Jefferson had assailed so eloquently thirty-one years earlier. The War for Independence, the making of the Constitution, and the achievements of Hamiltonian Federalism had all been undone; after six and a half years of Jeffersonian Republicanism, the Americans were more dependent upon the whim of George III and the will of his ministers in 1807 than they had been in 1775.

7

★★★★★

SHIPWRECK: 1808

As a system of national policy, Jeffersonian Republicanism was bankrupt by the summer of 1807. By fall, the president himself began to suffer what amounted to a paralysis of will. He had always had a tendency, when faced with difficult or unpleasant decisions, to procrastinate in the hope that changing circumstances would improve his options; but now every change deepened his dilemma, and he simply could not think of anything reasonable to do.

Indecisiveness and self-doubt are scarcely the stuff of presidential leadership in times of national danger. But until December Jefferson could not move, he could only wait—without knowing what he was waiting for and without knowing what he would do when it came. In this vacuum, James Madison emerged with a far-fetched scheme that became administration policy. At first, Jefferson distrusted and failed to understand the policy, and Gallatin flatly disapproved it, but in the course of a few months the president came to embrace it and regard it as his own. He also rationalized it as a noble effort to avoid both war and submission to tyranny, and set out to enforce it with fanatical zeal.

The name of the scheme was embargo. In its name, Thomas Jefferson conducted a fifteen-month reign of oppression and repression that was unprecedented in American history and would not be matched for another hundred and ten years, when Jefferson's ideological heir Woodrow Wilson occupied the presidency.

The administration was unrealistic in its expectation that a re-

reply from Britain regarding the attack on *Chesapeake* would be received by October 26, the day set for the early reconvening of Congress. Madison did receive summaries of informal talks that Monroe had had with George Canning, the British foreign secretary, prior to the arrival of the formal instructions and demands, but these reports were scarcely encouraging. Canning's position was equivocal, disclaiming the right to search naval vessels but saying that apologies and reparations for the *Chesapeake* incident would be forthcoming only if the officers involved "should prove to have been culpable."[1] No such proof seemed likely to appear, since the officers had acted under orders from the admiral at the Halifax station, who in turn was intimately connected with leading political figures in London.

Three other bits of intelligence reinforced a pessimistic view. One was a report that the deserters seized from *Chesapeake* had been court-martialed in Halifax, that several (including three Americans) had been found guilty, and that one of them (not an American, but a man Madison had insisted was an American) had been hanged. The second was the news of the Royal Navy's invasion of neutral Denmark and its seizure of that tiny nation's entire naval fleet. The third was a letter Jefferson received from David Humphreys, a former American minister to Spain who had just returned from London. Humphreys warned Jefferson that widespread hostility toward the United States prevailed in England, and said that a war against the Americans now would be even more popular than the war against the rebellious colonies had been in 1776.

Jefferson agreed with Madison upon "the absolute necessity of a radical cure," and the president's first draft of his message to Congress read like a manifesto calling for war. Gallatin, however, while believing that war was unavoidable, counseled moderation. For a variety of reasons he urged a delay. He wanted to allow several months for American vessels abroad to be able to return safely; he thought that Canada could best be attacked in winter, when ice would prevent the British navy from bringing in men and supplies; and at all events he believed that world opinion would be more favorable toward the justice of the American position if it were Britain who declared war first. The last point was typical of the administration's inability to face reality, for in all the world the only opinions that mattered were those of France and Britain, and neither had the slightest interest in the "justice" of what the United States did. Yet Jefferson was persuaded by Gallatin's arguments, and he toned down his message accordingly. Thus when the congressmen convened, knowing only that a warship of the United States Navy had been attacked and that members of its crew had been forcibly removed, they were greeted with a presidential message that told them little and recommended virtually nothing.[2]

As everyone waited, news from the Continent arrived to compound the administration's difficulties. Napoleon, who had more or less (and unofficially) exempted American vessels from his Berlin Decree until now, announced that there would be no exceptions in the future: thenceforth, the United States, like all other nations, must be for him or against him in his commercial warfare with Britain. Forthwith, American vessels began to be seized in Continental ports. Moreover, Napoleon dispatched an army to invade and crush Portugal, thereby demonstrating what he had in store for all uncooperative neutrals—or, rather, demonstrating that he would no longer tolerate the existence of neutrals.

That development narrowed and clarified the Americans' options. Great Britain would allow American shippers to trade with Britain and its possessions, under moderate and mostly traditional restrictions, but only if the United States government expressly rejected the Berlin Decree and accepted the right of the Royal Navy to search American vessels for deserters and to impress any who were found. If the United States agreed to trade with Britain on those (or any other) terms, however, the French would seize any American vessels that ventured into a Continental port. Alternatively, the French would allow American ships to trade with the Continent, but only if the United States government forbade them to trade with Britain and its colonies. If the United States accepted that option, American vessels would be seized by the British upon attempting to venture into a Continental port. As a practical matter, in other words, Americans could trade with Britain and its possessions and with French and Spanish possessions in America, but they could not trade with the European mainland. Since the trade that was thus available to them constituted perhaps three-quarters of their normal trade and accounted for an even larger portion of the revenues of the federal government, one might have supposed that a decision to abide by the British orders and to reject the French decrees would have come easily.

The Jeffersonians, however, did not see the options in that practical light: to them the choice had to do with ideology and national honor. To submit to the arbitrary commands of either Britain or France was to violate both their ideology and their sense of honor; but the only alternative to submission, as they saw things,

141

was war, and they were neither prepared for war nor willing to become prepared for war. Thus impaled on the horns of a dilemma of their own making, they were immobilized. Congress reorganized itself somewhat—the House deposed Macon as Speaker and Randolph as floor leader—so as to be better prepared to follow any lead the president should offer, but the president offered none.

At the end of November a formal reply to the American demands regarding the *Chesapeake* finally arrived; in Jefferson's words, Canning's answer was "unfriendly, proud, and harsh." The British foreign secretary admitted that British naval officers had committed an unauthorized hostile act, and he said that the United States was entitled to reparations. However, Canning added, since the United States had also committed hostile acts—for instance, the enlistment of deserters—those acts must be considered first. And while other matters relating to the *Chesapeake* affair might be discussed, impressment was not one of them. Since Monroe was explicitly instructed not to separate the question of impressment from that of the *Chesapeake*, he was unable to discuss the matter further. Accordingly, Canning announced that he was sending a special envoy to America to continue the negotiations. Jefferson turned Canning's message, as well as related documents, over to Congress on December 8, again without recommendations. That course of conduct was characteristic of Jefferson during his long crisis of will. Normally he directed foreign relations with a strong hand and was extremely secretive with Congress as well as the public; during the winter of 1807–1808 he lavished diplomatic correspondence upon Congress and repeatedly insisted that the policy being pursued emanated from Congress, not from the president.

In early and mid December, however, there was no policy, only drift. Indeed, through oversight and a flukish combination of circumstances the Non-Importation Act of 1806, which had long been suspended and had virtually been forgotten, went into effect on December 14, 1807. By that time a goodly measure of sentiment for some kind of stronger restriction on commerce was being voiced among the restive congressmen. Some spoke of an embargo—which is to say a law prohibiting all American vessels from leaving home —but embargos were universally regarded as temporary and stopgap measures preparatory to war, and war was not one of the viable options. Others talked about a law that would prohibit Americans from trading with England and France; but given the circumstances, that would have been nearly the same as an embargo and would have amounted to capitulation to both belligerents. In any event, all such talk was idle unless and until someone should take the lead.

Then, suddenly and somewhat mysteriously, the administration moved: on December 18 Jefferson sent Congress two documents and a brief message recommending "the inhibition of the departure of our vessels." One of the documents was Napoleon's official ruling that the Berlin Decree applied to American shipping; the other was a proclamation of George III's, which not only reasserted the right of impressment but also extended it to apply to war vessels. A third document, which was not yet officially in Jefferson's possession but was known from an abridgment of it that had been published in several newspapers on December 17, doubtless also influenced the administration's decision, perhaps more than the two official documents did. This was a British Order in Council that had been adopted on November 11 in retaliation against Napoleon's latest edict. In brief, the order announced that all vessels trading with France or its allies and their colonies would be subject to confiscation unless they first entered a British port and obtained a license for each voyage. What this came down to was a declaration that Americans might trade with and through Britain, or not trade at all.

The administration opted for no trade at all, and Congress moved swiftly to ratify that choice. The Senate suspended its rules and passed the embargo bill on Friday, December 18, 1807, within a few hours of receiving the president's message; the House passed the bill the following Monday; and on Tuesday Jefferson signed it into law. The act was directed against American vessels registered in the foreign trade, and it prohibited them from obtaining clearance for foreign ports unless they were specially authorized to do so by the president. They and smaller coasting vessels could continue to engage in the domestic coasting trade; but to prevent them from heading for foreign ports once they were at sea, they were required to post a bond of double the value of the vessel and its cargo. Foreign vessels that happened to be in an American port at the time the act was passed were permitted to clear with their cargoes, and foreign ships could continue to bring goods into the United States.

The original intention of this first embargo act—several more acts were to come—was clear, though not all the parties to its adoption viewed it in the same way. The terms of the act indicate that it was aimed at protecting American vessels by keeping them off the high seas, not at preventing trade as such. Jefferson made this explicit in a letter explaining the policy to John Taylor of Caroline, the most eminent theoretical spokesman for Republicanism. By "keeping at home our vessels, cargoes & seamen," Jefferson

143

wrote, the embargo "saves us the necessity of making their capture the cause of immediate war." Soon or late, peace would return to Europe, and by the time war came again perhaps "our debt may be paid, our revenues clear, & our strength increased." How the United States could pay its debts and clear its revenues with only minimal revenues from imports Jefferson did not say, but just now he believed that the most prudent course was to run from the fight—or as he put it, to "keep within ourselves." The president did not regard this course with enthusiasm, but as the lesser of evils.[3] Not entirely unjustly, many critics of the embargo regarded it as voluntary capitulation to Napoleon, since he did not have the means of forcing the Americans to curtail their maritime commerce, whereas the British did. Others, with no less justice, maintained that the policy was one of craven capitulation to both offending belligerents.

Gallatin totally disapproved of the policy and foresaw pernicious consequences in the effort to enforce it. He believed its adoption reflected a hasty and unthinking reaction to the news from Europe; he also believed that from every point of view—"privations, sufferings, revenue, effect on the enemy, politics at home"—war was preferable to a "permanent" (or indefinite, as opposed to a three or four months') embargo. "As to the hope that it may . . . induce England to treat us better," Gallatin added, "I think it entirely groundless." Moreover, he treated the president to a sage bit of "Jeffersonian" philosophy, warning that "governmental prohibitions do always more mischief than had been calculated; and it is not without much hesitation that a statesman should hazard to regulate the concerns of individuals as if he could do it better than themselves."[4] Gallatin's objections were to no avail, and once the embargo became law he devoted his customary diligence and his methodical genius to enforcing it.

The true architect of the policy was James Madison, who conceived it as a variant form of the kind of economic warfare he had been advocating for fifteen years. Madison explained and attempted to justify his conception of the embargo in a series of unsigned editorials published in the semiofficial party newspaper, the *National Intelligencer*, immediately after the act was passed. In addition to making war virtually impossible, Madison argued, the embargo would demonstrate to the world that the Americans possessed "a virtue and a patriotism which can take any shape that will best suit the occasion." More to the point and more important, though the policy would impose minor hardships upon Americans it would prove totally disruptive to Europeans, for it would deprive them of goods they could not do without. Faced with severe economic dislocations and the prospect of actual starvation, the tyrants of Europe would rapidly be forced to mend their ways. Thus, the embargo was not a desperate choice of the lesser of evils, but a powerful weapon delivered to America by a "benignant providence."[5] It is to be observed that the idea of starving Europe into submission was more than a little far-fetched, inasmuch as Europeans bought precious little of their foodstuff from the United States; the only people who were dependent upon imported American food were those in the West Indies, and in fact, during the life of the embargo, tens of thousands of black slaves there went hungry. It is also to be observed that Madison viewed the aim of the act as being an interdiction of all trade, not merely a prohibition against shipping as the law actually stipulated.

The law rapidly evolved in the direction of Madison's interpretation of its purpose, and as the law evolved, the president's attitude evolved also. A second embargo act was passed on January 8, 1808, barely two weeks after the enactment of the first. A loophole had been discovered in the first act, namely that coasting vessels and fishing and whaling boats had not been required to post bonds guaranteeing that they would not sail for foreign ports. That oversight was corrected, and extremely harsh penalties were added; in addition to forfeitures and heavy fines, for instance, merchants who violated the law were forever debarred from credit on customs duties, and if a captain did so, his oath was made forever inadmissible before a customs officer. In effect, merchants and masters were to be driven out of their professions for a single violation.

Despite the harshness of the punishments prescribed for violations, the embargo was at first fairly popular and therefore met with little resistance or violation. Many people apparently shared Jefferson's wishful thinking that the policy would stimulate Britain to a quick change of heart and, indeed, that Canning's special envoy would be prepared to offer something satisfactory; and many also shared the president's more hard-nosed belief that war was coming and that the embargo would give the country time to prepare for it. Both expectations ended in frustration.

The special British envoy, George Rose, arrived in mid January. In discussions with Madison he contended that, since Britain had disavowed the attack on *Chesapeake* and had (surprisingly) gone so far as to recall Admiral Berkeley, sufficient atonement had been made. However, Britain was also willing to make reparations; but first, the United States must withdraw Jefferson's proclamation prohibiting ships of the Royal Navy from entering American waters. Madison balked, and the negotiations threatened to break down. Then Madison proposed a scheme whereby the agreement on reparations and the recall of the proclamation would be practically simultaneous, and on that basis, Rose presented his country's offer of reparations. Britain was willing to discharge the men taken from *Chesapeake* and to make monetary compensation to the widows and orphans of the men who were killed in the attack, provided that it could be proved that these men were neither British subjects nor deserters. Madison found that offer acceptable, but he regarded as unacceptable two further stipulations demanded by the British: that the United States disavow the conduct of its agents in recruiting deserters and that it disavow the conduct of Captain Barron in shielding them.[6] Madison refused to admit any such conduct, and thus the negotiations collapsed. To Pinkney, who was alone in London now that Monroe had come home, the diminuitive secretary of state wrote peevishly that until the insult of the *Chesapeake* were atoned, the United States would not relax its restrictions on British commerce even if the objectionable Orders in Council were revoked.

The breakdown of negotiations with Rose came in mid February. For some reason Jefferson did not inform Congress of the situation for more than a month, but on February 25, nine days after Madison and Rose had agreed that they could not reach an agreement, the president asked Congress for a huge increase in the size of the army. He and his advisors had decided earlier that in the event of war with Britain a force of thirty thousand men (as opposed to the existing force of about twenty-five hundred) would be necessary for domestic defense and offensive operations in Canada. Having come to believe, despite what he had said in his first inaugural address, that the militias would be unreliable, and expecting that Congress would balk at creating so large a "standing army," Jefferson asked that the regular force be increased to only six thousand men but that it be supplemented by a twenty-four-thousand-man "volunteer" army, which was to be enlisted for a specific period of years. Congress did balk: it authorized a gradual increase of the regular army to ten thousand, but nothing more.

Negotiations had failed, and Congress had politely refused to satisfy the president's inclination toward war; all that was left was for Jefferson to discover what Madison already knew, namely that the embargo was a heaven-sent magic weapon. Before he came to that discovery, however, he became incapacitated again with another migraine headache, this one lasting a little under two weeks. Meanwhile (on March 12) Congress proceeded to pass still a third embargo measure. This one prohibited, for the first time, the export of any goods, by land or sea, subject to a fine of $10,000 and forfeiture of the goods for each offense; and thus Madison's original conception of the embargo policy became law. The new act also severely increased the penalties for violations of the first two acts, and it vested the president with broad discretionary authority to enforce or grant exceptions to the embargo. As this vast augmentation of presidential power was being enacted, Thomas Jefferson lay silent and immobilized in a darkened room.

Then, late in March, he was stung to action, and he embraced the coercive concept of the embargo with a convert's zeal. What provoked him was something that was always enough to raise his ire: a challenge to his authority combined with a personal attack. In New England, opposition to the embargo had been minimal in December and January, for the law actually had no effects since the ports were frozen anyway; but when the thaws came, between mid February and early March, legal prohibition of shipping became real, and severe economic dislocation and unemployment were immediately felt. Protests were widespread, and many shippers simply ignored the law, secretly taking on cargoes and leaving without clearance papers in the expectation that British officials would not require such documents. In upper New England and in upstate New York the law was quite openly flouted: a brisk trade to Canada by land and rivers had flourished before all exports were prohibited, and when the third embargo act outlawed such trade it was continued despite the law.

In these circumstances the old arch Federalist, Senator Timothy Pickering of Massachusetts, saw opportunity. Pickering held a number of conferences with George Rose, during which he proposed the formation of a pro-British party in New England and (in flagrant violation of the Logan Act of 1799, which forbade individual Americans from attempting to influence the policies of foreign governments toward the United States) urged Rose to urge Canning to continue a hard line against America. Pickering was convinced that under sustained British pressure the Jeffersonian Republicans would grow ever more extreme in efforts to enforce the embargo and that such a course would be political suicide for them.

Moreover, Pickering made a bold move to hasten the Republicans' demise. In an open letter to Republican Governor James Sullivan of Massachusetts—which Sullivan refused even to read, but which Pickering had distributed widely for publication—Pickering blasted the embargo and called for what amounted to nullification of it by the legislatures of the commercial states. More tellingly, he played upon the fact that Jefferson had presented no real arguments for the enactment of the embargo, and he cleverly twisted the evidence to suggest that the president had forced the embargo through Congress on orders from Napoleon. This charge, and the letter in general, had an electric effect in Massachusetts: in the state elections in mid March, Federalists regained control of both houses of the legislature and came within a handful of votes of defeating Sullivan. Too, as a by-product, Pickering's rival John Quincy Adams, who supported the embargo, was in effect forced to resign his seat in the Senate.

Jefferson was particularly sensitive to charges that he was subservient to Napoleon, that he dictated policy to Congress, and that he was excessively secretive. On March 22 he responded to Pickering's letter by dumping on Congress a huge mass of diplomatic documents—every edict and order and dispatch that was even remotely connected with restrictions on international commerce. He also took great pains to declare that the policy had been created by acts of Congress, not by executive fiat. Then, as his headache came to an end during the course of the next week or ten days, he gradually resolved to enforce the embargo and to regard it as an instrument of coercion rather than of withdrawal. Americans, he now believed, must be persuaded to honor the embargo by convincing them "that while the embargo gives us double rations, it is starving our enemies."[7] As for those few unpatriotic Americans who chose not to go along with this enlightened means of avoiding both submission and war—those who failed to appreciate that inflicting death by starvation was more humane than inflicting death by bayonet or musket ball—they would be subjected to enlightenment by force.

The first fruit of the president's new-found determination was a proposal that Congress endow him with broad and patently unconstitutional enforcement powers. On March 30 Jefferson wrote out his proposal and handed it to Gallatin, who had thus far supervised the effort to enforce the embargo; after several of Gallatin's minor suggestions had been incorporated, the recommendations were introduced in Congress. Two of the recommendations were especially important. One was that collectors should be empowered to seize cargoes, without a warrant or the prospect of a trial, upon the mere formation of a suspicion that a shipper or merchant *contemplated* a violation of the embargo. This was in direct opposition to the Fourth and Fifth amendments of the Bill of Rights; it was also a more sweeping power than had been given to the king's agents by the hated writs of assistance, one of the principal forms of "tyranny" that had provoked the American colonists to revolution. The other requested power was simple: Jefferson wanted to be authorized to use the army and the navy to enforce the law.

While Congress debated these proposals, the president made his first effort at repressing resistance by force. In the region of Lake Champlain, considerable numbers of entrepreneurs from Vermont and New York were transporting goods to Canada on gigantic rafts. In an attempt to stop them, Jefferson issued (on April 18, 1808, the thirty-third anniversary of the first battle of the War for American Independence) a proclamation declaring the region to be in a state of insurrection. He ordered all state and federal officials and "all other persons, civil and military, who shall be found within the vicinage" to proceed at once to suppress the alleged rebellion "by all means in their power, by force of arms or otherwise."[8] The governors of New York and Vermont, against their wishes but under strong political pressure from the president, ordered out the militias, though they were too late, in this instance, to stop the smugglers. In vain, local residents protested being subjected, wholesale, to the stigma of insurrection for the law violations of a few.

Six days after the issuance of the proclamation, Jefferson signed into law the Enforcement Act that he had requested. The act was aimed especially at the coasting trade, which afforded greatest opportunity for ocean-borne violations of the embargo. Probably nine-tenths of the trade between states was carried in coasting vessels, and many cities, from Boston to Charleston, were entirely dependent upon imported food for survival. Yet it was easy for a coasting vessel, once cleared, to sail for Nova Scotia or the West Indies, under the pretense of having been blown off course in a storm. The profits of such voyages were so high that they more than compensated for forfeiture of the shipper's bond, should the excuse not be believed. Moreover, almost no shipper felt bound by conscience or patriotism to obey the embargo if he could successfully violate it, for the law deprived him of his property and livelihood in the interest of a policy that he regarded as questionable on grounds of constitutionality, morality, and plain good sense. The

Enforcement Act was aimed at stopping the violators, whatever the cost; as Jefferson had requested, personal penalties were greatly stiffened, use of the armed forces was authorized, and collectors were empowered to seize vessels and cargoes upon the mere suspicion of intent to evade the embargo. In states adjacent to foreign territory, the power of seizure amounted to direct confiscation; elsewhere it amounted only to detention and was to be exercised only by the collectors, but every case was turned over to the president, who was empowered to decide it in his sole discretion.

On April 28 Gallatin got out a circular letter providing guidelines for the collectors in applying their new powers, but the president promptly (May 6) toughened and personalized the rules. In the interest of the embargo, Jefferson was prepared to supervise, with minute and personal attention, not only what his fellow citizens should eat but how much they should eat. All proposals to ship flour or provisions to ports commonly engaged in the export trade were to be denied, no matter how much the inhabitants pleaded hunger. Indeed, no flour was to be moved at all unless the governor of the importing state issued an official certificate of need. The interstate movement of any commodities other than food, being "not of a farthing's benefit to the nation at large," was to be stopped entirely. In conclusion, Jefferson said, "I really think it would be well . . . to consider every shipment of provisions, lumber, flaxseed, tar, cotton, tobacco, &c . . . as sufficiently suspicious for detention and reference here. . . . Where you are doubtful, consider me as voting for detention."[9]

Jefferson also made it clear that he intended to suppress all domestic commerce that was conducted only for profit—which is to say merely for the livelihood of the tens of thousands of sailors, fishermen, whalers, shippers, and merchants who were engaged in it. In a circular letter to the governors (May 6 and 16) he said that the "real" needs of the citizenry, meaning food, could be met, but suppliers must not use that as "a cover for the crimes against their country." To Gallatin, a few weeks later, he reiterated the sentiment: "I do not wish a single citizen in any of the States to be deprived of a meal of bread," he said, "but I set down the exercise of commerce, merely for profit, as nothing when it carries with it the danger of defeating the objects of the embargo."[10]

The new enforcement policy was soon challenged in the courts, and on May 28, to the president's mortification, the policy was overruled by one of his own Republican appointees. The collector at Charleston had refused clearance for a ship with a cargo of cotton and rice consigned to Baltimore, not because he suspected any intention to violate the embargo, but because he was bound by executive order. The owners brought suit for a writ of mandamus ordering the collector to clear the vessel, and Supreme Court Justice William Johnson, presiding over the Circuit Court, issued the writ; the law, he ruled, empowered collectors (not the president) to detain on suspicion, and the president had exceeded his authority in ordering a blanket policy. Jefferson's attorney general, Caesar Rodney, quickly issued and released to the press a contrary opinion, which was thenceforth followed by the administration in disregarding the decision. Rodney's opinion also subjected Johnson to a scathing rebuke for interfering with the executive.

During the course of the summer, Jefferson and Gallatin became convinced that judges and juries were generally untrustworthy, so instead of going to the courts, they evolved a policy of relying increasingly upon martial law and the armed forces. As early as May 28 Gallatin proposed the occupation of the Lake Champlain area by a force of the regular army, but no such steps were immediately taken. Then in June a militia company captured a large raft of lumber on the lake, only to have it recaptured by a band of lumberjacks. Five of the rescuers were subsequently arrested and, at the direction of Attorney General Rodney, were charged with treason; but the charge could not be made to stick. (Had the House approved the treason bill authored three months earlier by Jefferson's intimate friend and Senate floor leader William Giles, the men would all have been hanged along with half the citizenry of New York and New England; the bill passed by the Senate prescribed the death penalty for anyone who resisted "the general execution of any public law." Instead, the constitutional definition of treason remained intact, and in October, Republican Justice Brockholst Livingston acquitted the accused with a ringing denunciation of their very indictment.)

The immediate result of the June "insurrection" of the lumberjacks on Lake Champlain was to provoke Jefferson and Gallatin into generous use of armed force. Gallatin advised the president that "arbitrary powers" which were "equally dangerous and odious" must be exerted if the embargo was to be enforced. Jefferson wholeheartedly agreed, saying that "Congress must legalize all *means* which may be necessary to obtain its *end*" and then proceeding to act as if all possible means had already been legalized. By July the navy, which had recently been somewhat enlarged to protect American shipping, was being regularly deployed instead against American shipping. In August, Jefferson instructed the secretaries of war and navy, "on the first symptom," to "fly to the spot" and "suppress any commotion." Without legal authority and without issuing proclamations, he ordered out the regular army—which had recently been enlarged to defend American citizens—as a normal enforcement agency. By mid September, Gallatin was able to report to the president that all parts of the northern frontier except Vermont (where the militia was in charge) either were or soon would be under control of the army.[11]

Nonetheless, civil disobedience continued to spread. Pitched battles erupted frequently, and scores of people were wounded, some even killed. By November, when Congress was scheduled to reconvene, Jefferson was declaring whole towns to be under the taint of treason, and he was desperately preparing ever more nightmarish remedies, including the penultimate solution to the problem of uncooperative courts: persons accused of violating or intending to violate the embargo would, in effect, be deprived of the right to offer any real defense. The president also suggested to at least one congressman that historically, in times of emergency, "the universal resource is a dictator."[12]

Verily, in its effort to avoid war with Europe, the Republican government of the United States was levying war against its own citizens.

(Interestingly, as the domestic implications of his foreign policy became clear, James Madison suffered a physical and emotional breakdown. He experienced the recurrence of an affliction that had repeatedly plagued him during his young manhood, until he learned how to escape from it by controlling himself and avoiding stress: epileptiform hysteria, which is to say epileptic seizures brought on by emotional tension.)[13]

And it was all for naught: as a result of the embargo, some Nova Scotia fishermen and a good many West Indian slaves went hungry during much of the year, and there was some unemployment in English factory towns, but the general effect upon the international economy was so slight that the French and British could regard the American policy with contemptuous amusement.

There was, however, a change in the state of affairs in Europe, one that would have spelled enormous opportunity for the United States had not the Jefferson administration locked itself and the nation into a policy straightjacket. Just as the embargo was being enacted, Napoleon had committed the first of a set of blunders that began a long process of undoing for him and his Corsican brand of military despotism. In December of 1807 he sent an army of 100,000 men into Spain, ostensibly to protect Spain against the British but actually to enforce his own version of an embargo. Three months later a conspiracy forced Charles IV to abdicate in favor of his son Ferdinand, the idol of the Spanish people, who was expected to pull Spain away from the dominance of the hated French and Napoleon. In May, however, Napoleon forced Ferdinand off the throne, replacing him with his own brother, Joseph Bonaparte. That was a mistake of monumental proportions: the Spanish masses rose to resist, and fought for their king with unremitting ferocity and cunning. Napoleon had at his disposal the most powerful armies the world had ever known, and they could crush the Spanish army at will; but no army can subdue a whole people when it refuses to be subdued, and against the sustained rage of the Spanish nation, Napoleon's troops were all but useless. In August the British moved to take advantage of the tumults, sending 15,000 men to Portugal under Gen. Arthur Wellesley (who later became the duke of Wellington). Wellesley ejected the French from Portugal and then moved into Spain to join forces with the guerrillas. Napoleon personally stormed into Spain with an army of 225,000 men and drove the British back to Portugal; but he could not force Wellesley out of the Iberian Peninsula. During the next six years, one after another of Napoleon's brilliant marshals lost an army and a reputation to what the emperor called "the Spanish cancer."

Had the Republican administration been less adamant in its hostility toward Britain, or even had it been concerned with the interests of the United States rather than with its own ideological fixation, Jefferson could have capitalized upon the opportunities afforded by the Peninsular War and thereby made his last year in office a triumph instead of a tragedy. The long-coveted Floridas could have been seized virtually without a struggle, for war-torn and bankrupt Spain was incapable of sending resistance; and the seizure could have been justified, had a justification been wanted, on the ground that the United States was liberating Florida from the tyranny of the Bonapartes—even as the Spaniards were struggling to liberate Spain—for the territory was the personal property of the Spanish crown that Joseph Bonaparte now wore. Moreover, the Peninsular War created new trade opportunities which, if only the embargo should be repealed, would yield the United States an economic boom of enormous proportions. Spain and Portugal were reopened to American trade, and the presence there of ever-growing

153

numbers of British soldiers generated an expanded market, at inflated prices, for American grain and rice. But Jefferson was having no part of it: upon being thus presented with an opportunity whereby, with a change of policy, the American people could redeem their sense of honor as well as regain and increase their profits, the president held doggedly to the calamitous policy of embargo.

In these circumstances it might have been expected that the Republicans would have been roundly defeated in the presidential and congressional elections of 1808, but so to expect would be to overlook the political revolution that had taken place since 1801. Despite the machinations of Timothy Pickering, despite the Federalist victories in Massachusetts, and despite the growth of anti-administration sentiment that infected a large portion of the population north of the Potomac and probably a large majority east of the Delaware, the Federalists simply were not an organized national political party, and the Republicans were.

The elections therefore reflected the operations of the existing political machinery and had virtually nothing to do with issues, principles, or policies. Congressional Republicans met in formal caucus, as they had been in the habit of doing informally for a dozen years, to determine whom they should back for president; Madison, Monroe, and Vice-President Clinton all had supporters, and in the absence of such a nominating caucus the election would doubtless have gone into the House of Representatives for want of a candidate with a majority of the electoral votes. The supporters of Monroe and Clinton tried to make common cause beforehand, but could not agree, and so most of them boycotted the party caucus, in the realization they could not win. Those who did attend voted for Madison, 83 to 6—meaning that the secretary of state was nominated by a majority of the majority, which worked out to be 47 percent of the members of Congress.

Federalists held a secret convention in New York—the first national nominating convention of an American political party, such as it was—and agreed, as in 1804, to support Charles Cotesworth Pinckney of South Carolina for president and Rufus King of New York for vice-president. In addition to lacking a real organization, however, and to lacking supporters anywhere in the interior south and west of the Delaware River, the Federalists suffered from an internal split. The more conservative Federalists, especially those who had been active during the glory years of Washington and Hamilton, were unreconciled to the idea of popular politicking, and preferred to stand on high Federalist principles; the younger and more desperate ones insisted that that was no way to win elections, and they sought in vain to adapt to the Federalist cause the kind of popular electioneering tactics that had brought about the success of the Republicans. (It was the younger faction that worked into the campaign the matter of Madison's health, with variations of the following editorial: "Unfortunately for his [Madison's] country, he is sickly, valetudinarian, and subject to spasmodic affections, which operate unfavorably on his nervous fluid, considered by philosophers as one of the most powerful agents of our intellectual faculties." At such campaigning, however, the Federalists were generally inept.) [14]

The presidential election was simply no contest, though the results of other elections were mixed. Madison got 122 electoral votes to Pinckney's 47, but Federalists came back to life in every northern state except Pennsylvania: Federalists retained control of the legislatures of Delaware and Connecticut, regained control in New York and in most of the rest of New England, won the lower house in Maryland, and won a whopping 70 percent of the congressional seats in all states north of the Potomac save Pennsylvania. In Pennsylvania and south of the Potomac, however, they won nothing at all. Slaveholders and evangelical Protestants and Scotch-Irishmen—the heart of the Revolution of 1800–1801—were still Jeffersonian Republicans, almost to a man.

Now it was lame-duck time in earnest: the last four months of the Tenth Congress, elected in 1806 and expiring on March 4, 1809, and the last four months of the presidency of Thomas Jefferson. The president, for his part, was determined to continue his personal efforts to enforce the embargo until his last day in office; but as far as policy was concerned, he was equally determined not to make any. He described himself as "but a spectator," and said: "I have thought it right to take no part myself in proposing measures, the execution of which will devolve upon my successor. I am therefore chiefly an unmeddling listener to what others say." [15]

Between President-elect Madison, however, and his unofficial choice for secretary of state, Albert Gallatin, a plan of action was evolved. Actually the plan was, for the most part, one that Gallatin had worked out by mid November; Madison came to embrace it, with modifications, by mid December. They agreed that the embargo had failed as a coercive instrument, but instead of abandoning it, they now proposed that it be turned to the purpose that embargoes traditionally served, namely as a step preliminary to war.

The embargo would be propped up by still another enforcement act, far more stringent even than the existing enforcement acts, but it would also be set to expire on June 1, 1809. Meanwhile the position would be maintained that the French decrees and the British orders amounted to war against the United States, large-scale preparations for war would be commenced, and the president would be empowered to issue letters of marque and reprisal against the shipping of both nations. (Such letters authorized private armed vessels, in time of war, to prey upon enemy merchant ships in what would in peacetime be regarded as piracy.) Meanwhile, too, a novel system of nonintercourse would be adopted, to succeed the embargo when it expired: commerce with both France and England would be prohibited, but if either nation dropped its restrictions regarding American commerce, the United States would open trade with that power and declare war on the other. Finally, the newly elected Eleventh Congress was to convene late in May (instead of November) and declare war on one or both nations. Gallatin and Madison expected that Britain would relent and that Napoleon would not, and thus that by summer the United States would be at war against France and its nominal ally Spain, with Britain as America's official or unofficial ally.

All things considered, the Gallatin-Madison plan was the most reasonable one for which support could be expected, and at first it appeared likely to be adopted. Speaker of the House George Washington Campbell was totally committed to serving the upcoming Madison administration, and he took the lead in pushing its measures through Congress. By the middle of January, laws activating an increased army and navy had been passed, and so had a new enforcement act and a resolution calling for the convening of Congress in May.

But a rebellion was in the works, or rather several rebellions were, and together these not only frustrated the plans of the president-elect but resulted in the humiliation of the outgoing president as well. The first rebellion was in New England, where the popular and political outcry against the new enforcement act nearly reached the proportions of mass hysteria. The new law was, in truth, an extreme measure, even as compared with its predecessors. For coasting vessels, bonds of six times the value of ship and cargo were required even before cargoes could be loaded; shipowners were forbidden to sell their vessels without posting exhorbitant bonds against the possibility of violation of the embargo by the new owners; and virtually all legal defenses for accused violators were abolished.

Furthermore, collectors were empowered to seize, at their discretion, any goods in transit anywhere in the United States, with the support of the army, the navy, and the militias, and they were not liable to lawsuits for their actions. The response to the law in New England and New York was almost as extreme as the act itself. Town meeting after town meeting drew enormous crowds—four thousand adult males in Boston, out of a total population of less than thirty thousand—and adopted resolutions condemning the embargo and the administration, denouncing the president as a lackey of Napoleon, and hinting at dismemberment of the Union. The legislature of Massachusetts adopted resolutions of a similar tenor, as did that of Connecticut, and both talked of "interposing" the authority of states between their citizens and the national government, pointedly adopting the language of the Virginia and Kentucky resolutions of 1798–1799—which Madison and Jefferson had secretly written, and with which the Republicans in opposition had been openly identified. The wily Senator Pickering sought to transform this opposition into a movement for secession and the formation of a New England confederation that would include New York. He had been trying to do so for years, off and on, but now he gained respectable support throughout the region and faced at least a fair prospect of success.

The Republican members of Congress from New York and New England responded to all this by going into a veritable frenzy. They had been among the president's most loyal supporters, and Jefferson now tried to keep them in line by treating them to more lavish doses of wine and food and charm than they had ever known; but they were straining at the leash. One of them, Congressman Ezekiel Bacon of Massachusetts, sought the counsel of the recently ousted Senator John Quincy Adams, and on the strength of that advice, Bacon became convinced that only a repeal of the embargo, forthwith, could save the Union. Assiduously, Bacon spent the month of January persuading northern Republicans to join him in his new-found wisdom.[16]

And that was not the only congressional revolt. In the Senate, Samuel Smith had long opposed Gallatin for his niggardly naval policy, and now he found an unexpected ally in Senator Giles, who was angered to learn that Gallatin was Madison's choice for secretary of state, an office that Giles himself had expected to get. The Smith-Giles coalition, supported by New Englanders, pushed through a bill providing for the immediate activation of every vessel the navy owned, including all the gunboats. This would have been so ex-

157

pensive as to undermine totally Gallatin's carefully calculated plans for financing a war, and Gallatin worked desperately to rally support in the House for a more orderly plan of mobilization. Both houses of Congress were divided, and the naval controversy set them against one another.

The showdown came, or at least began, on January 30, 1809. Wilson Cary Nicholas, a staunch friend of Gallatin's, introduced on that day a House resolution incorporating the Madison-Gallatin plan: it called for the repeal of the embargo on June 1 and for the authorization of letters of marque and reprisal against either Great Britain or France or both, if at that time "their Orders or Edicts violating the lawful commerce and neutral rights of the United States shall be in force." Nicholas agreed to divide the resolution so as to permit a test vote on repeal of the embargo.

After five days of debate in committee of the whole, the House voted to reject June 1 as the expiration date, voting instead to kill it as of March 4—Jefferson's last day in office, which meant that Jefferson's presidency and the embargo would die together. After a few more days the proposal to issue letters of marque and reprisal was voted down, meaning that Madison's approach to the international problem had also been rejected. A Federalist senator, unable to believe what was happening, wrote that "Jefferson is a host; and if the wand of that magician is not broken, he will yet defeat the attempt" to kill the embargo.[17] But the magician's wand was broken, and so was the magician. By February 27 both houses had passed a bill repealing the embargo, and on March 1 the defeated and disheartened president signed it into law.

There was a feeble gesture toward face-saving built into the repealing law: it prohibited trade with either France or Britain or their dependencies, and it provided that trade would be resumed upon repeal of the restrictive orders and edicts. The sponsors of the nonintercourse feature admitted, however, that it was merely a device for nominally avoiding submission. None expected it to be enforced, and Gallatin was not even prepared to try to enforce it.

And there was a last, calculated cruelty aimed at the fallen president. Some months earlier, Jefferson had appointed an old friend, William Short, to a legally nonexistent post as minister to Russia, expecting that the Senate would confirm the appointment and thus support one of his pet projects, the opening of diplomatic relations with Tsar Alexander I. For political reasons, he held back an announcement of the appointment until the last minute; and when the senators received it, they summarily and unanimously rejected it.

Embittered and exhausted, Thomas Jefferson continued to enforce the embargo as vigorously as he could, down to the very last day. On March 4, 1809, he was at Madison's side as Chief Justice John Marshall administered the oath of office to the president-elect. He remained in Washington about a week, packing his belongings, before quitting the place forever. Then the sixty-five-year-old Father of American Liberty mounted a horse, to ride through snow and storm for three days and nights until he regained the sanctuary of his home at Monticello. In the seventeen years that remained of his life, he never again left the foothills of the Blue Ridge Mountains.

8

★★★★★

EPILOGUE: THE CRISIS AND THE FAITH

Jeffersonian Republicanism was an ideology and an idea, a system of values and a way of looking at things; and as the aphorism goes, ideas and ideals have consequences. But it was also a program of action, carefully crafted and methodically executed; and as we are sometimes wont to forget, actions have consequences, too. To appraise Jefferson's presidency, it is therefore necessary to take both sets of criteria into account.

In the realm of ideas and ideology, Jeffersonian Republicanism was a body of thought that had been taken largely from the Oppositionist tradition of eighteenth-century England, principally as incorporated in the writings of Charles Davenant, John Trenchard, Thomas Gordon, James Burgh, and most particularly Henry St. John, Viscount Bolingbroke. This system of thought is explicated rather fully in the text, and it would be pointless to reiterate the effort here. It is useful, however, to remember that we are speaking of *oppositionist* thought: Bolingbroke and his predecessors and followers (whether calling themselves Tories or Commonwealthmen or Real Whigs) were condemning and seeking to undo the Financial Revolution and its attendant political corruption, as epitomized by the ministry of Sir Robert Walpole. In its stead, they proposed to restore a pristine and largely imaginary past in which life was rural, relationships were personal, the gentry ruled as a natural aristocracy, the main corpus of the citizenry was an honest yeomanry, commerce and craft-manufacturing existed only as handmaidens to agriculture, standing armies and privileged monopolies and fictitious paper wealth were all unknown, and government was limited—limited to an essentially passive function as impartial arbiter and defender of the existing social order, and limited by the unwritten but inviolable Constitution, dividing power among three separate, distinct, and coequal branches. In other words, the Jeffersonians' ideological forebears were reactionaries, swimming against the tide of history, for the world aborning was the depersonalized world of money, machines, cities, and big government.

The Jeffersonians, though castigated by their enemies as dangerous innovators and radicals, were likewise resisting the emergence of the modern world. They had seen the Hamiltonian Federalists attempting to transform and corrupt America, even as the Oppositionists had seen Walpole and the new monied classes transform and corrupt England, and they swallowed the Oppositionists' ideas and ideology whole. The Jeffersonians republicanized Bolingbroke, to be sure, developing the doctrine that absolute separation of powers, with a strictly limited presidency, was guaranteed by the written Constitution. In their hearts, however, they did not trust paper constitutions, and their view of Jefferson's mission as president did not differ substantively and significantly from Bolingbroke's idea of a Patriot King: a head of state who would rally the entire nation to his banner, and then, in an act of supreme wisdom and virtue, voluntarily restrain himself and thus give vitality and meaning to the constitutional system. The Republicans also added the doctrine of states' rights, but that was mainly a tactical position which most of them abandoned—except rhetorically—once they came into control of the national government. The only genuine changes they brought to the ideology were two. One was to relocate its social base, from that of an Anglican gentry to that of southern slaveholders, Celtic-American back-country men, and evangelical Protestants. The other was to put the ideology into practice.

If who they were and what they were seeking are thus understood, it is evident that they remained remarkably true to their principles throughout Jefferson's presidency—despite charges to the contrary by a host of critics, ranging from Alexander Hamilton to Henry Adams to Leonard Levy. Moreover, they were remarkably successful in accomplishing what they set out to do. They set out to destroy the complex financial mechanism that Hamilton had built around the public debt, and they went a long way toward that goal —so close that if war could have been avoided for another eight years, their success might have been total. They also set out to secure the frontiers of the United States by expanding the country's territorial domain into the vast wilderness, and they succeeded so well that it became possible to dream that the United States could remain a nation of uncorrupted farmers for a thousand years to come.

And yet on the broader scale they failed, and failed calamitously—not because of their own shortcomings, but because their system was incompatible with the immediate current of events, with the broad sweep of history, and with the nature of man and society. As an abstract idea, Bolingbrokism *cum* Jeffersonian Republicanism may have been flawless, and it was certainly appealing. In the real world, it contradicted and destroyed itself.

At the core of the Republicans' thinking lay the assumption, almost Marxian in its naïveté, that only two things must be done to remake America as an ideal society and a beacon unto mankind. First, the public debt must be extinguished, for with it would die stockjobbing, paper-shuffling, "monopoly" banking, excisemen, placemen, and all the other instrumentalities of corruption that the Walpole/Hamilton system "artificially" created. Second, governmental power must be confined to its constitutional limits, which implied reduction of the functions of government but also, and more importantly, meant adherence to the rules of the separation of powers—that being the only legitimate method, in their view, whereby a free government could exercise its authority. If ancient ways were thus restored, the Jeffersonians believed, liberty and independence would inevitably follow. In turn, liberty and independence—by which they meant the absence of governmental restraint or favor and the absence of effective interference from foreign powers—would make it possible for every man, equal in rights but not in talents, to pursue happiness in his own way and to find his own "natural" level in the natural order.

Things did not work out that way, especially in regard to relations with foreign powers: far from freeing the country from foreign interference, Republican policy sorely impaired the nation's ability to determine its own destiny. In their eagerness to retire the public debt, the Jeffersonians tried diligently to economize. Toward that end they slashed military and naval appropriations so much as to render the United States incapable of defending itself—at a time when the entire Western world was at war. Simultaneously, in their haste to destroy all vestiges of the Hamiltonian system, the Jeffersonians abolished virtually all internal taxes. This relieved the

farmers and planters of an onerous tax burden and arrested the pro-
liferation of hated excisemen, but it also made national revenues
almost totally dependent upon duties on imports—which meant
dependent upon the uninterrupted flow of international commerce,
which in turn depended upon the will of Napoleon Bonaparte and
the ministers of King George III.

For two or three years the Jeffersonians were extremely lucky.
That is to say, during that period the kaleidoscope of events in
Europe turned briefly and flukishly in their favor. They obtained
Louisiana as a result of a concatenation of circumstances that was
wildly improbable and was never to be repeated. They were able
to pay off much of the public debt and to accumulate sizable
treasury surpluses because Great Britain, out of consideration for
its own interests, allowed the Americans to engage in a trade of de-
batable legality, thus swelling the volume of American imports and,
concomitantly, the revenues flowing into the United States Treasury.

From 1803 onward, however, each turn of the international
wheel was less favorable to the United States. By 1805 it was apparent that West Florida—for which the Jeffersonians hungered
almost obsessively, since its strategic and economic value was considerably greater than that of all Louisiana excepting New Orleans
—would not become American in the way that Louisiana had. In
the same year it began to be clear that the British would not long
continue to allow the United States to grow wealthy by trading
with Britain's mortal enemies.

But for their ideology, the Jeffersonians could have reversed
their earlier policy stance, embraced Britain, and become hostile
toward France and Spain, thus enabling the nation to continue to
prosper and expand. Given their ideological commitment, they
could not do so. Moreover, given the consequences of their actions
so far, they lacked the strength to make even a token show of force
against Great Britain. Thus in 1807, when both Britain and France
forbade the United States to engage in international commerce
except as tributaries to themselves, the embargo—a policy of pusil-
lanimity and bungling, billed as a noble experiment in peaceful
coercion—was the only course open to them.

At home, as they became ever more deeply impaled upon the
horns of their self-created international dilemma, the Jeffersonians
became progressively less tolerant of opposition or criticism. From
the beginning they had shown considerable disdain for the federal
courts; as Jefferson's second term wore on, this disdain degenerated
into contempt for due process of law and for law itself. Thus the

embargo became a program of domestic tyranny in inverse ratio to its ineffectiveness as an instrument of international policy: the more the policy was found wanting, the more rigorously was it enforced.

The embargo, then, both as a bankrupt foreign policy and as a reign of domestic oppression, was not a sudden aberration but the logical and virtually certain outcome of the Jeffersonian ideology put into practice: the ideology's yield was dependence rather than independence, oppression rather than liberty.

One other aspect of the Jeffersonian experience wants notice, and that concerns the Republicans' conception of the presidency as a limited branch of government, absolutely separate from the legislative branch. In practice, adherence to that ideal was impossible because of the very nature of the presidential office. For one thing, though some presidential powers are relatively independent, others are intermeshed with those of Congress. For another, the American executive branch is "republicanized," or kept from being monarchical, by being made elective for a fixed term of years. To be sure, the Republicans' political machinery was so effective that Jefferson could doubtless have been elected to a third and even a fourth term, had he so chosen. But Washington's two-term precedent was strong, and, what was more telling, the psychic cost of the presidential office was and is frightful; by the seventh or eighth year Jefferson, like Washington before him and like most two-term presidents who followed him, was physically, emotionally, and spiritually exhausted. The second term was therefore a lame-duck term, and that fact subtly but significantly altered the relationship between the president and Congress. Pure though Jefferson's motives and the motives of many Republican congressmen were, it was important to them that his popularity would cease to be of use to them in seeking reelection, and it was important to him that he would not need their political support in 1808. In the circumstances, Jefferson did what lame-duck presidents normally do—that is, he gravitated toward the arena in which he had less to do with Congress, the area of foreign relations; and Congress, and especially the Senate, also followed the norm by rising at the end to regain powers that it believed had been more or less usurped from it.

Still another crucial aspect of the American presidency, one with which the Republicans were not at all prepared to cope, is that the Constitution vests in one office and one person two distinct and nearly incompatible roles which under the British system had come to be divided between the king and his ministers. One is the truly monarchical function, that of serving as the ritualistic symbol of the nation. The other is the purely executive function, that of fashioning policy and directing its implementation. Success in the one hinges upon the president's charisma, his leadership, and his abstract appeal to the whole people; success in the other hinges upon the president's skill in tangible dealings with small groups and individual human beings. The Republicans' conception of the presidency was, in these terms, entirely unrealistic: they disavowed the first role and wanted the president to fill the second by standing as aloof from Congress as a proper king stands from his subjects.

Jefferson was superbly gifted at playing both roles, and he was able to play them without offending Republican sensibilities or prejudices. He ostentatiously disdained the pomp and pageantry that had marked the presidencies of Washington and Adams, but all the while he assiduously and effectively courted popularity. Foreign ministers and Federalist critics alike commented upon his inordinate love of popularity, and marked it as a weakness of character; perhaps it was, but it was also true wisdom, for reverence toward the Crown was a deep-rooted habit in the English-speaking world, and love of the president as king-surrogate was a crucial social adhesive for the diffuse and pluralistic infant United States. Indeed, in this respect Jefferson made a profound contribution toward the perdurance of the republic. Washington had been a veritable demigod and a symbol of the nation, and thus provided a sort of half-way house between monarchy and republicanism; Jefferson humanized the presidency and served as a symbol, not of the nation, but of the people, and thus made the transition complete.

In the role of policy-maker and administrator, Jefferson was even more skilled. After his inaugural he abandoned the monarchical practice of appearing in person before Congress; he never held court or levees, but invited congressmen in small groups for dinner, where he wore homespun and hosted them in the manner of a country squire; he never openly initiated legislation, and only deferentially suggested that Congress might look into one subject or another; he never vetoed a bill on policy grounds, and would not have dreamed of doing so. In sum, he allowed Congress to function with no overt presidential direction and with only the gentlest of presidential guidance. As to cabinet meetings, he conducted them as a democracy of equals. And yet, almost until the end, he ran Congress more successfully and more thoroughly than did any preceding president and precious few succeeding presidents, and the cabinet always reflected his will except when he had no firm opinions on a matter. Moreover, he did so without the use of bribery, patronage, corruption, or coercion: it all flowed from the force of his intellect, his character, and his personality.

But, perversely, that too was a weakness of the Jeffersonian scheme of things: the system could be made to work only with a Thomas Jefferson at the helm. When Jefferson himself faltered, as he did on several occasions during his presidency, the government almost stopped functioning except in the routine operations of Gallatin's Treasury machinery. When Jefferson left the office, all the shortcomings of his method of administration became manifest. The cabinet became a center of petty bickering and continuous cabalizing, and Congress split into irreconcilable factions and repeatedly asserted its will against the president.[1]

For all these reasons, Jefferson's legacy to his successor was a can of serpents. Jefferson's second term was merely a calamity; Madison's first would be a disaster.

There is more to a presidency than the tangible events that happen during and in consequence of it: there are also the myths it inspires. For a time, of course, memories were too fresh, feelings were too strong, and events were too unpleasant to admit of the kind of romanticization that is a necessary prelude to myth-making. By 1826, however—when Jefferson along with John Adams died on the fiftieth anniversary of the Declaration of Independence—memories had mellowed, new rivalries had replaced the old, and artful and designing men were looking to the past for heroes whose lives could be used or misused to justify their own doings. Jefferson was admirably suited for such use and misuse, for he had written and acted in a greater variety of ways on a greater variety of subjects than any of the other Founding Fathers, and he was more quotable than any of them save possibly Adams alone.

But the Jefferson legend developed along curiously divided lines. In the realm of formal historical writing, he fared poorly until well into the twentieth century. Most of the early historians were New Englanders, who made heroes of Washington, Hamilton, and other Federalists and who excoriated, when they did not ignore, Jefferson and his followers. Jefferson's first biography, that by Henry Randall, did not appear until 1857, and Randall's work was a virtual apology for secession and Civil War. Thirty years later, Henry Adams, a great-grandson of Jefferson's Federalist predecessor, published his massive *History of the United States during the Presidencies of Thomas Jefferson and James Madison*. Adams's work was thorough and was actually a great deal less biased than is commonly supposed by those who cite but do not read it; but even so, it was hardly a favorable treatment. Still another generation later, in a powerful and influential book called *The Promise of American Life*, Herbert Croly lumped Jefferson with Andrew Jackson, Jefferson's heir as carrier of the Bolingbrokean tradition, and denounced both for equating democracy with state or local autonomy and for equating tyranny with centralized government, thus making "faith in the people equivalent to a profound suspicion of responsible official leadership" on the national level. Croly's work was a favorite of Theodore Roosevelt's; it became required reading for nationally oriented Progressives.

Meanwhile, in the realm of folklore and political rhetoric, which ordinary Americans heard and heeded more frequently and more trustingly than they did the staid pronouncements of historians, Jefferson was exalted as the patron saint of all good things.[2] The range of causes for which his name was invoked is staggering: democracy and partisanship, states' rights and nationalism, slavery and abolitionism, egalitarianism and racism, imperialism and isolationism, populism and laissez-faire capitalism, the planned and the decentralized society. In the nineteenth century, so long as rural values continued to prevail in America despite the relentless march of industrialization, Jefferson continued to be identified with the agrarian tradition; in the twentieth, when the center of American life and values became the city, his connection with that ideal was all but forgotten, and instead he came to be regarded as the champion of the "have-nots" against the "haves," of the "common man" (or the "forgotten man" or the "little fellow") against aristocrats and plutocrats.

In the 1920s and 1930s the two strands of the legend began to come together. The Democratic politician-historian Claude G. Bowers and the more scholarly Gilbert Chinard began the process of beatification through the written word, and though the Jefferson they described was one he would scarcely have recognized, the process has continued. Franklin Roosevelt's New Deal depicted itself as thoroughly Jeffersonian, though given to the use of "Hamiltonian means to accomplish Jeffersonian ends"—and while building a federal bureaucracy almost as large as the population of the entire country had been during Jefferson's time and while extending its regulatory power apace, it built Jefferson a monument which declared his true mission to have been as a libertarian. In time, and in our own time, "Jefferson" and "Jeffersonian" came to mean merely "good," or "that which the nation aspires to be."

The real Jefferson—the one who once lived in Virginia and once worked in the President's House—was lost in the shuffle. So, too, was the America he wanted his country to become; and in a nation of crime-ridden cities and poisoned air, of credit cards and gigantic corporations, of welfare rolls and massive bureaucracies, of staggering military budgets and astronomical public debts, of corruption and alienation, that loss is the more poignant. He and his followers set out to deflect the course of History, and History ended up devouring them and turning even their memory to its own purposes. History has a way of doing that.

Notes

CHAPTER 1

1. My analysis of urban conditions is drawn, in considerable measure, from Gary L. Browne's brilliant doctoral dissertation, "Baltimore in the Nation, 1776–1860" (Wayne State University, 1972). This provocative and perceptive work is currently being revised for publication.

   The influence of immigrants during this period has not been thoroughly explored. Except for the years 1798 to 1800, arrivals of alien immigrants were not required to be reported until 1819, and so there are no official records on the subject. The total number arriving between 1776 and 1819 has been estimated at 250,000, or only about 5,000 a year. See United States Bureau of the Census, *Historical Statistics of the United States, Colonial Times to 1957* (Washington, D.C.: Government Printing Office, 1960), p. 48. Judging from newspapers and correspondence in the 1790s, Irish immigrants were numerous and disruptive in New York and Philadelphia, French émigrés from Haiti had a considerable impact in those cities and Baltimore, and most non-Irish immigrants from the British Isles were absorbed on the southwestern frontier.

2. John Eacott Manahan, "The Cavalier Remounted: A Study of the Origins of Virginia's Population, 1607–1700" (Ph.D. diss., University of Virginia, 1947).

3. See Forrest McDonald and Grady McWhiney, "The Antebellum Southern Herdsman: A Reinterpretation," *Journal of Southern History* 41:2 (May 1975).

4. This account is based largely upon John B. Boles, *The Great Revival, 1787–1805* (Lexington: University Press of Kentucky, 1972), with corrections suggested by Professor William G. McLoughlin. See also Sydney E. Ahlstrom, *A Religious History of the American People* (New Haven, Conn.: Yale University Press, 1972), and Whitney R. Cross, *The Burned-over District: The Social and Intellectual History of Enthusiastic Religion in Western New York, 1800–1850* (New York: Harper & Row, 1965).

5. Boles, *Great Revival*, pp. 12–19.

6. Ibid., p. 21.

7. Ibid., p. 56.

8. This analysis is drawn largely from the extremely rich and thorough study of Opposition writings in Rodger D. Parker, "The Gospel of Opposition: A Study in Eighteenth Century Anglo-American Ideology" (Ph.D. diss., Wayne State University, 1975). There is, however, a considerable body of literature on the subject; see the Note on the Sources, below.

CHAPTER 2

1. This analysis of Jefferson's thinking is based upon Harold Trevor Colbourn, *The Lamp of Experience: Whig History and the Intellectual Origins of the American Revolution* (Chapel Hill: Univer-

sity of North Carolina Press, for the Institute of Early American History and Culture at Williamsburg, Va., 1965).

2. Noble E. Cunningham, Jr., *The Jeffersonian Republicans in Power: Party Operations, 1801–1809* (Chapel Hill: University of North Carolina Press, for the Institute of Early American History and Culture at Williamsburg, Va., 1963).

3. Jefferson to Walter Jones, March 31, 1801, in Andrew A. Lipscomb and Albert E. Bergh, eds., *The Writings of Thomas Jefferson*, 20 vols. (Washington, D.C.: Thomas Jefferson Memorial Association, 1903–1904), 10:256.

4. Sidney H. Aronson, *Status and Kinship in the Higher Civil Service: Standards of Selection in the Administrations of John Adams, Thomas Jefferson, and Andrew Jackson* (Cambridge, Mass.: Harvard University Press, 1964).

5. Alexander Balinky's *Albert Gallatin: Fiscal Theories and Policies* (New Brunswick, N.J.: Rutgers University Press, 1958) is the crucial work on Gallatin as secretary of the treasury.

6. January 26, 1811, in Paul Leicester Ford, ed., *The Works of Thomas Jefferson*, 12 vols. (New York: G. P. Putnam's Sons, 1904–1905), 11:185, as quoted in Leonard D. White, *The Jeffersonians: A Study in Administrative History, 1801–1829* (New York: Macmillan, 1951), pp. 79–80.

7. White, *The Jeffersonians*, pp. 47–48, quoting Adams's *Memoirs*, 5:281.

8. Samuel P. Huntington, in *The Soldier and the State: The Theory and Politics of Civil-Military Relations* (Cambridge, Mass.: Harvard University Press, 1957), argues that Jefferson's influence was long felt at West Point through an emphasis on "technicism" that retarded the development of military professionalism.

9. If the expenditures during the quasi war with France are included, the Federalists spent considerably more than the Republicans; otherwise, Federalist military spending was less.

10. In the Land Act of 1804, Republicans did reduce the minimum cash price of public lands from $2 to $1.64 an acre, as well as reducing the minimum purchase from 320 to 160 acres. Too, in the Ohio Enabling Act of 1802, they established the policy of reserving one section in each township to be used for educational purposes. None of these changes, however, made much difference to buyers: most land was still sold in large quantities at auctions in which actual prices were far higher than the legally established minimum.

11. Kathryn Turner, "Federalist Policy and the Judiciary Act of 1801," *William and Mary Quarterly*, 3d ser., 22:27 (January 1965).

12. February 3, 1807, and September 20, 1810, in Ford, *Works*, 10:347 n and 11:146, as quoted by White in *The Jeffersonians*, p. 6.

CHAPTER 3

1. Charles Callan Tansill, *The United States and Santo Domingo, 1798–1873: A Chapter in Caribbean Diplomacy* (Gloucester, Mass.: Peter Smith, 1967), pp. 80–81.

2. Jefferson to Livingston, April 18, 1802, in *The Writings of Thomas Jefferson*, ed. Paul Leicester Ford, 10 vols. (New York: G. P. Put-

nam's Sons, 1892–1899), 8:143–147; see also Jefferson to Du Pont, April 25, 1802, in *The Correspondence of Jefferson and Du Pont de Nemours*, ed. Gilbert Chinard (Baltimore, Md.: The Johns Hopkins Press, 1931), pp. 46–49.

3. *The Works of Alexander Hamilton*, ed. Henry Cabot Lodge (New York: G. P. Putnam's Sons, 1885), 5:465 ("Pericles" to *New York Evening Post*, February 8, 1803).

4. Elijah Wilson Lyon, *Louisiana in French Diplomacy, 1759–1804* (Norman: University of Oklahoma Press, 1934), p. 194; Henry Adams, *History of the United States of America during the First Administration of Thomas Jefferson*, 2 vols. (New York: Charles Scribner's Sons, 1921), 2:27,

quoting Barbé-Marbois's *The History of Louisiana.*

5. *Life and Letters of George Cabot*, ed. Henry Cabot Lodge (Boston: Little, Brown, 1877), p. 331.

6. Much later (in 1828) the Supreme Court upheld this constitutional position in *American Insurance Company* v. *Canter* (1 Peters 511).

7. Paine to Jefferson, September 23, 1803, in *The Complete Writings of Thomas Paine*, ed. Philip S. Foner, 2 vols. (New York: Citadel Press, 1945), 2:1447–1448.

CHAPTER 4

1. On Jefferson's indifference to the possibility that the West might ultimately secede, see Dumas Malone, *Jefferson the President: First Term, 1801–1805* (Boston: Little, Brown, 1970), p. 317. Canada was also a part of Jefferson's vision, but he believed that there "the pear will fall when it is ripe."

2. Balinky, *Gallatin*, p. 121.

3. September 13, 1803, in Lipscomb and Bergh, *Writings*, 10:390.

4. Adams, *History: First Administration*, 2:122.

5. Cunningham, *Jeffersonian Republicans in Power*, pp. 288–290.

6. Malone, *First Term*, p. 451; William Plumer, *William Plumer's Memorandum of Proceedings in the United States Senate, 1803–1807*, ed. Everett S. Brown (New York: Macmillan, 1923), p. 269.

7. Malone, *First Term*, p. 454; Adams, *History: First Administration*, 2:216.

8. Federalist Justice Alfred Moore of North Carolina resigned in 1804 and was replaced by Jefferson's appointee, William Johnson of

South Carolina. All the other justices were Federalists.

9. John Quincy Adams, diary entry of December 21, 1804, quoted in Charles Warren, *The Supreme Court in United States History*, 2 vols. (Boston: Little, Brown, 1923), 1:294.

10. Albert J. Beveridge, *The Life of John Marshall*, 4 vols. (Boston: Houghton Mifflin, 1916—1919), 3:200–204.

11. *New York Evening Post*, February 6, 1805.

12. The appointees were J. B. Prevost, Burr's stepson, who became a territorial judge; Joseph Browne, Burr's brother-in-law, who became secretary of the territory; and Gen. James Wilkinson, who became territorial governor. It should be pointed out that the Louisiana Territory was upper Louisiana—all the purchase area except the present state of Louisiana, which was called Orleans Territory.

13. Beveridge, *Marshall*, 3:217–220.

CHAPTER 5

1. Clifford L. Egan, "The United States, France, and West Florida, 1803–1807," *Florida Historical Quarterly* 47:229–230 (1968–1969).

2. Ibid., p. 233.

3. Ibid., p. 234.

4. Ibid., p. 236.

5. Ibid., p. 237.

6. Alfred L. Burt, *The United States,*

Great Britain, and British North America: From the Revolution to the Establishment of Peace after the War of 1812 (New Haven, Conn.: Yale University Press, 1940), p. 230. Burt's work is supplemented, but not rendered obsolete, by the fuller treatment in Bradford Perkins, *Prologue to War: England and the United States, 1805-1812* (Berkeley: University of California Press, 1961).

7. Egan, "The United States, France, and West Florida," 47:239 n.

8. Ibid., p. 239.

9. Henry Adams, *History of the United States of America during the Second Administration of Thomas Jefferson*, 2 vols. (New York: Charles Scribner's Sons, 1921), 1:134-137.

10. Extension of the Mediterranean Fund, which Jefferson had requested in his secret message, was a way of ensuring adequate funds in the treasury against the expected cost of the purchase. The fund was already being used more or less fraudulently, and it was perpetuated by means that scarcely were to the administration's honor. A year earlier, Preble had forced the pasha of Tripoli and the pasha's Algerian and Moroccan counterparts to offer terms of surrender; the administration, instead of authorizing

Preble to accept the terms and then bringing him back as a hero, replaced him with Commodore James Barron and sent Tobias Lear to negotiate. Dragging out the negotiations kept the war nominally alive, and thus kept alive the pretext for the Mediterranean Fund.

11. Tansill, *United States and Santo Domingo*, pp. 108-109; Adams, *History: Second Administration*, 1:141-143.

12. Adams, *History: Second Administration*, 1:155-157.

13. Whether Jefferson had anything to do with engineering Nicholson's withdrawal from the House is problematical. Adams, *History: Second Administration*, 1:166-167, erroneously says that the judicial post was a federal appointment, a statement that Dumas Malone refutes in *Jefferson the President: Second Term, 1805-1809* (Boston: Little, Brown, 1974). Jefferson did, however, offer Nicholson a collectorship some months later. In any event, whether it was fortuitous or otherwise, Nicholson's unexpected resignation was advantageous to the administration, for despite proposing the nonimportation bill that bore his name, he joined Randolph in seeking to delay or block its passage.

CHAPTER 6

1. Adams, *History: Second Administration*, 1:252.

2. In Adams, 1:253-254, there is a decoded version of this famous letter. For comments on the original and upon various bogus versions, see the Note on the Sources, below.

3. Burt, *The United States, Great Britain, and British North America*, pp. 235-236.

4. Malone, *Second Term*, pp. 247-248.

5. Beveridge, *Life of Marshall*, 3:328-329; Walter F. McCaleb, *The*

Aaron Burr Conspiracy (originally published 1903; republished with an additional volume, New York: Argosy-Antiquarian, 1966), p. 169; Leonard Levy, *Jefferson and Civil Liberties: The Darker Side* (New York: Quadrangle/New York Times Book Co., 1973), p. 81.

6. Malone, *Second Term*, pp. 264-266.

7. In 1794 Jefferson had endorsed the French Revolution's Reign of Terror—wherein twenty thousand accused enemies of the Revolu-

tion were beheaded—and went so far as to suggest that the beheading of virtually the entire population of Europe would be justified if the result were "freedom."

8. South Carolina had permitted the importation of slaves between 1783 and 1786, during which time about seventy-five hundred slaves were brought into the state from Africa. The legislature then banned the trade in a succession of acts until 1804. In that year, anticipating a congressional act in 1808, it reopened the trade, and in the next four years some thirty-nine thousand more slaves were imported.

9. Adams, *History: Second Administration*, 1:350.

10. Ibid., 1:436–437.

11. Ibid., 1:447.

CHAPTER 7

1. Malone, *Second Term*, p. 452.
2. Ibid., p. 455.
3. Ibid., p. 483.
4. Gallatin to Jefferson, December 18, 1807, in *The Writings of Albert Gallatin*, ed. Henry Adams, 3 vols. (Philadelphia: Lippincott, 1879), 1:368.
5. Irving Brant, *James Madison*, 6 vols. (Indianapolis, Ind.: Bobbs-Merrill, 1941–1961), 4:402–403; *National Intelligencer* (Washington, D.C.), December 23, 25, and 28, 1807.
6. In fact, Barron had been court-martialed and suspended for five years—not, however, for shielding deserters, but for his ineptness in handling the encounter with H.M.S. *Leopard*.
7. Malone, *Second Term*, p. 585. It should be added that, given Jefferson's unreserved commitment to enforce the embargo, the administration had little option but to resort to armed force; for treasury agents and marshals of the federal courts, the only regular law-enforcement personnel of the federal government, were quite inadequate to the task. President Washington had established a precedent for using troops, both in enforcing the neutrality proclamation of 1793 and in suppressing the Whiskey Rebellion of 1794. There was, however, a crucial difference between those cases and the enforcement of the embargo: Washington had called upon the state governors for voluntary assistance, and they had complied by supplying militia troops. This course of action was justified by the Fugitive Slave Act of 1793, which required state officials to help enforce the national law; and essentially the same course was endorsed in the 1808 act outlawing the slave trade. Use of federal troops in the routine enforcement of an act of Congress, however, was without precedent, and was in spirit and substance drastically different from the use of militiamen with the authorization of state governors.

8. Levy, *Jefferson and Civil Liberties*, p. 107.
9. Jefferson to Gallatin, May 6, 1808, in *Writings of Gallatin*, 1:385–386.
10. Malone, *Second Term*, pp. 590–591.
11. Levy, *Jefferson and Civil Liberties*, pp. 116 and 119.
12. Ibid., pp. 114–125.
13. Ralph L. Ketcham, *James Madison: A Biography* (New York: Macmillan, 1971), p. 51; Brant, *Madison*, 1:105–107; 4:412, 439–440, 470.
14. *American Citizen*, August 15, 1808, as quoted in Brant, *Madison*, p. 439.
15. Malone, *Second Term*, p. 622.
16. Jefferson was entirely convinced that Bacon's "conversion" was the work of Joseph Story, who served a brief time in Congress as the successor to Jacob Crowninshield; but all the evidence indicates that

he was mistaken. See Malone, *Second Term*, pp. 645-646. Madison obviously did not share Jefferson's belief that Story was a "pseudo-Republican," for in 1811 he appointed Story to the Supreme Court. Adams, in *History:*

Second Administration, 2:437 and 437 n, almost inadvertently makes it clear that Bacon took his stand on advice from John Quincy Adams.

17. Adams, *History: Second Administration*, 2:440.

CHAPTER 8

1. On the shortcomings of Jefferson's methods as a basis for a regular system of administration, see White, *Jeffersonian Republicans*, passim.

2. The history of the use and misuse of Jefferson's "image" is superbly treated in Merrill D. Peterson, *The Jeffersonian Image in the American Mind* (New York: Oxford University Press, 1960).

A Note on the Sources

Of the enormous mass of materials on Jefferson and his contemporaries, certain published primary materials are indispensable, as are a handful of secondary works. Unfortunately, the definitive edition of Jefferson's writings, *The Papers of Thomas Jefferson*, ed, Julian P. Boyd, 21 vols. to date (Princeton, N.J.: Princeton University Press, 1950—), extends only to 1791. These volumes are valuable for understanding the man, but for the presidential years one must rely on two older collections that are far from complete. One is *The Writings of Thomas Jefferson*, ed. Paul Leicester Ford, 10 vols. (New York: G. P. Putnam's Sons, 1892–1899). The other is *The Writings of Thomas Jefferson*, ed. Andrew A. Lipscomb and Albert E. Bergh, 20 vols. (Washington, D.C.: Thomas Jefferson Memorial Association, 1903–1904). For a fuller description of other published Jefferson papers, and of the extant manuscript collections as well, see Dumas Malone, *Jefferson the President: First Term, 1801–1805* (Boston: Little, Brown, 1970), pp. 509–513, and the same author's *Jefferson the President: Second Term, 1805–1809* (Boston: Little, Brown, 1974), pp. 675-678. These volumes also list all the important collections, published and in manuscript, of the papers of Madison, Gallatin, Randolph, Burr, and various lesser figures. Two other bibliographies are extremely valuable. One is in John S. Pancake's provocative interpretive work *Thomas Jefferson & Alexander Hamilton* (Woodbury, N.Y.: Barron's Educational Series, 1974); the other is in Marshall Smelser's survey, *The Democratic Republic, 1801–1815* (New York: Harper & Row, 1968). Finally, four additional sets of documents, two public and two private, are indispensable to the student of the period. The public documents are *Annals of the Congress of the United States*, Seventh through Tenth Congresses (Washington, D.C.: Gales & Seaton, 1851), and *American State Papers: Foreign Relations*, ed. Walter Lowrie and Matthew St. Clair Clarke, 38 vols. (Washington, D.C.: Gales & Seaton, 1832–1861); vols. 2 and 3 relate to the Jeffersonian period. The private documents are vol. 1 of John Quincy Adams's *Memoirs*, ed. Charles Francis Adams (Philadelphia: Lippincott, 1874), and William Plumer, *William Plumer's Memorandum of Proceedings in the*

United States Senate, 1803–1807, ed. Everett S. Brown (New York: Macmillan, 1923).

As to secondary works, the appropriate place to begin is with Henry Adams, *History of the United States during the Presidencies of Thomas Jefferson and James Madison,* 9 vols. (New York: Charles Scribner's Sons, 1889–1891), the first four volumes of which are devoted to Jefferson's presidency. Adams's work is biased in various ways, but it still contains information as well as perceptive insights that are not generally available elsewhere, and it is superb reading. Second in importance as a general work is Leonard D. White, *The Jeffersonians: A Study in Administrative History, 1801–1829* (New York: Macmillan, 1951). Of the many biographies of Jefferson, most are worthless and only two are genuinely necessary for an understanding of the presidency—Malone's two volumes and Merrill D. Peterson's *Thomas Jefferson and the New Nation: A Biography* (New York: Oxford University Press, 1970). Both works are marked by a Jeffersonian bias, but both are rich in meticulously accurate detail. Malone's volumes, especially that on the second term, are often tediously argumentative, and in his efforts to justify Jefferson's conduct—to defend him against various charges made by contemporaries and by modern historians—Malone sometimes proves more than he intends to prove. For instance, in attempting to show that Jefferson did not persecute Burr, contrary to the charge made by Leonard Levy in *Jefferson and Civil Liberties: The Darker Side* (New York: Quadrangle/New York Times Book Company, 1973), Malone supplies so much evidence to the contrary as to justify the assertion that Jefferson was actually lax in handling Burr's prosecution—thereby causing one to wonder why he was so lax. In regard to this and several other matters, my own interpretation is derived from careful study of Malone's data without concern for how he interprets them, which has resulted in my reading the episodes differently from either Jefferson's critics or his leading defender.

The same general observation is true of Irving Brant's *James Madison,* 6 vols. (Indianapolis, Ind: Bobbs-Merrill, 1941–1961), the fourth volume of which covers Jefferson's presidency. Brant argues convincingly that Madison was responsible for many of the policies that were long thought to have originated with Jefferson. But Brant assigns credit where I would assign blame: most of Madison's policies, in my judgment, were wrong-headed and had predictably calamitous results.

Which brings us to the principal point of difference between my interpretation of Jefferson's presidency and the interpretations of scholars whose knowledge of the detailed history of the period is sometimes much wider than my own. Twentieth-century students of Jefferson and his followers have been "Jeffersonians," in an idealized and, in my opinion, unsound sense of that term; they entirely disregard the Oppositionist tradition which lay at the very heart of Jeffersonian Republicanism. (For a discussion of materials bearing on that tradition, see the sources cited for chapter 1, below.) The one significant exception is Alexander Balinky's *Albert Gallatin: Fiscal Theories and Policies* (New Brunswick, N.J.: Rutgers University Press, 1958). Though Balinky is unaware of the Oppositionist tradition as such, his analysis of Gallatin's thinking is sound, and it accurately captures the Oppositionist spirit. Balinky appraises Gallatin's policies in their own terms and finds them inherently self-defeating. I have followed his interpretation in the present volume.

Two other recent works, outside the mainstream of writing on Jefferson, should also be noticed. One is Levy's *Jefferson and Civil Liberties*—a devastating critique, put together like a lawyer's brief, whose argument is that Jefferson was not a civil libertarian in practice. Levy's book contains much interesting and valuable information; it certainly does not deserve the high-handed treatment it received at the hands of various "Jeffersonian" scholars (see the preface to the paperback edition), but in actuality the work is most unhistorical. It sets up a straw-man Jefferson and then knocks him down; had Levy understood the Oppositionist tradition, he would have found nothing surprising or inconsistent in Jefferson's conduct as president, and he might have been more sympathetic and less prone to semihysterical overstatement.

The other recent work is Fawn Brodie's popular effort at psychoanalyzing Jefferson, *Thomas Jefferson: An Intimate History* (New York: W. W. Norton, 1974). Unlike many scholars who idolize Jefferson, I am not offended by Ms. Brodie's insistence that Jefferson did, as some contemporaries charged, sire a number of children by a slave mistress, Sally Hemings. Rather, I regard that part of his private life as irrelevant to his qualities as a public man. To be sure, the inner man is quite relevant to the public man, but Ms. Brodie's description of the inner Jefferson bears little resemblance to the Jefferson I have come to know. Moreover, her account is woefully inadequate and often inaccurate as history.

Finally, at the risk of eliciting cries of outrage from nearly every academic historian alive, I would recommend that anyone interested in obtaining a further understanding of the period might treat himself to Gore Vidal's delightful novel *Burr* (New York:

Random House, 1973). Vidal's work is not flawless as an account of events, but as a characterization of Burr and of Burr's perception of his contemporaries, it is masterful.

The references that follow are to works which, in addition to the foregoing, were most useful in the writing of each chapter.

CHAPTER 1

The classic description of the United States at the time of Jefferson's election is that in the first six chapters of Adams's *History*, which are conveniently republished as *The United States in 1800* (Ithaca, N.Y.: Great Seal Books, 1955). To go beyond Adams and attempt the kind of pluralistic analysis essayed here, one must resort to a host of sources. Of most immediate value are contemporary works of description and travel, among the more useful of which are François A. Michaux, *Travels to the West of the Alleghany Mountains* . . . (Paris, 1804); David B. Warden, *A Statistical, Political, and Historical Account of the United States of North America* . . . , 3 vols. (Edinburgh: A. Constable, 1819); Charles W. Janson, *The Stranger in America, 1793–1806* (London, 1807; republished, New York: Press of the Pioneers, 1935); William Faux, *Memorable Days in America: Being a Journal of a Tour to the United States* (London: Simpkin & Marshall, 1823); John Davis, *Travels of Four Years and a Half in the United States of America* . . . (London and New York, 1803); Isaac Weld, Jr., *Travels through the States of North America* . . . , 2 vols. (London: J. Stockdale, 1800); and Timothy Dwight, *Travels: In New-England and New York* (New Haven, Conn.: T. Dwight, 1821–1822).

Studies of states during the period are devoted mainly to politics, but most of them include some descriptions and analysis of society and the economy. Among these are Richard J. Purcell, *Connecticut in Transition, 1775–1818* (new ed.; Middletown, Conn.: Wesleyan University Press, 1963); John A. Munroe, *Federalist Delaware, 1775–1815* (New Brunswick, N.J.: Rutgers University Press, 1954); Carl E. Prince, *New Jersey's Jeffersonian Republicans: The Genesis of an Early Party Machine, 1789–1817* (Chapel Hill: University of North Carolina Press, for the Institute of Early American History and Culture at Williamsburg, Va., 1967); John H. Wolfe, *Jeffersonian Democracy in South Carolina* (Chapel Hill: University of North Carolina Press, 1940); Chilton Williamson, *Vermont in Quandary, 1763–1825* (Montpelier: Vermont Historical Society, 1949); Paul Goodman, *The Democratic-Republicans of Massachusetts* (Cambridge, Mass.: Harvard University Press, 1964); James

M. Banner, Jr., *To the Hartford Convention: The Federalists and the Origins of Party Politics in Massachusetts, 1789–1815* (New York: Alfred A. Knopf, 1970); Alvin Kass, *Politics in New York State, 1800–1830* (Syracuse, N.Y.: Syracuse University Press, 1965); and Sanford W. Higginbotham, *The Keystone in the Democratic Arch: Pennsylvania Politics, 1800–1816* (Harrisburg: Pennsylvania Historical and Museum Commission, 1952). An excellent general work on a state that was devoutly Jeffersonian and was central to the triumph of Republicanism is Hugh Talmage Lefler and Albert Ray Newsome, *North Carolina: The History of a Southern State* (Chapel Hill: University of North Carolina Press, 1954). The crucial state, of course, is Virginia, and works on it are numerous. Still indispensable for understanding the Virginian is Charles S. Sydnor, *Gentlemen Freeholders* (Chapel Hill: University of North Carolina Press, for the Institute of Early American History and Culture at Williamsburg, Va., 1952). Other works include J. R. Pole, "Representation and Authority in Virginia from the Revolution to Reform," *Journal of Southern History* 24:16–50 (1958); Norman K. Risjord, "The Virginia Federalists," *Journal of Southern History* 33:486–517 (1967); Richard Beale Davis, *Intellectual Life in Jefferson's Virginia, 1790–1830* (Chapel Hill: University of North Carolina Press, 1964); Dumas Malone, "Mr. Jefferson and the Traditions of Virginia," *Virginia Magazine of History and Biography* 75:131–142 (1967); C. Ray Keim, "Primogeniture and Entail in Colonial Virginia," *William and Mary Quarterly*, 3d ser., 25:545–586 (1968); Harry Ammon, "The Republican Party in Virginia, 1789 to 1824" (Ph.D. dissertation, University of Virginia, 1948); and Jack P. Greene, *Landon Carter: An Inquiry into the Personal Values and Social Imperatives of the Eighteenth-Century Virginia Gentry* (Charlottesville, Va.: Dominion Books, 1967).

On the economy, urban life, and related matters, valuable works include Curtis P. Nettels, *The Emergence of a National Economy, 1775–1815* (New York: Holt, Rinehart & Winston, 1962); Bray Hammond, *Banks and Politics in America: From the Revolution to the Civil War* (Princeton, N.J.: Princeton University Press, 1957); John H. Coatsworth, "American Trade with European Colonies in the Caribbean and South America, 1790–1812," *William and Mary Quarterly*, 3d ser., 24:243–266 (1967); William T. Whitney, Jr., "The Crowninshields of Salem, 1800–1808: A Study in the Politics of Commercial Growth," *Essex Institute Historical Collections* 94:1–36 (January 1958) and 79–118 (April 1958); and Benjamin W. Labaree, *Patriots and Partisans: the Merchants of Newbury-*

port, 1764–1815 (Cambridge, Mass.: Harvard University Press, 1962). The most perceptive work on both the economy and urban life during the period is Gary L. Browne, "Baltimore in the Nation, 1776–1860" (Ph.D. dissertation, Wayne State University, 1972).

Ethnic diversity in early-nineteenth-century America is a subject that has not been adequately explored. On the diversity of the Americans' British ancestors, a most useful article is J. G. A. Pocock, "British History: A Plea for a New Subject," *New Zealand Journal of History* 8:3–21 (1974). On the ethnic origins of the Virginians, the most valuable study is John Eacott Manahan, "The Cavalier Remounted: A Study of the Origins of Virginia's Population, 1607–1700" (Ph.D. dissertation, University of Virginia, 1947). Two good works on the Scots are Wallace Notestein, *The Scot in History* (New Haven, Conn.: Yale University Press, 1946), and T. Christopher Smout, *A History of the Scottish People, 1560–1830* (New York: Charles Scribner's Sons, 1969). Informative works on Celtic peoples in America are James G. Leyburn, *The Scotch-Irish: A Social History* (Chapel Hill: University of North Carolina Press, 1962); Ian C. C. Graham, *Colonists from Scotland: Emigration to North America, 1707–1783* (Ithaca, N.Y.: Cornell University Press, for the American Historical Association, 1956); and Duane G. Meyer, *The Highland Scots of North Carolina, 1732–1776* (Chapel Hill: University of North Carolina Press, 1961). On many matters relating to Celts and Celtic-Americans, I have drawn on the researches of Michael Enright of Wayne State University.

On matters of religion and the Second Great Awakening, I have followed John B. Boles, *The Great Revival, 1787–1805* (Lexington: University Press of Kentucky, 1972), with corrections suggested by Professor William G. McLoughlin of Brown University. Also useful are Sydney E. Ahlstrom, *A Religious History of the American People* (New Haven: Conn.: Yale University Press, 1972); Whitney R. Cross, *The Burned-over District: The Social and Intellectual History of Enthusiastic Religion in Western New York, 1800–1850* (New York: Harper & Row, 1965); William G. McLoughlin, *Isaac Backus and the American Pietistic Tradition* (Boston: Little, Brown, 1967); and William Gribbin, "Republican Religion and the American Churches in the Early National Period," *Historian* 35:61–74 (1972).

The literature on the ideology of Jeffersonian Republicanism requires some comment. I have read a large number of conventional older works on the subject, and I have found most of them wanting. Representative of these are Adrienne Koch, *The Philos-*

ophy of Thomas Jefferson (New York: Columbia University Press, 1943); Caleb Perry Patterson, *The Constitutional Principles of Thomas Jefferson* (Austin: University of Texas Press, 1953); and Stuart Gerry Brown, *The First Republicans: Political Philosophy and Public Policy in the Party of Jefferson and Madison* (Syracuse, N.Y.: Syracuse University Press, 1954). Far better is the best modern study of the subject, Richard Buel, *Securing the Revolution: Ideology in American Politics, 1789–1815* (Ithaca, N.Y.: Cornell University Press, 1972). To understand the Jeffersonians, I believe, one must first become thoroughly familiar with the eighteenth-century English Oppositionists. Among the works that facilitate that undertaking, the most important are Isaac Kramnick, *Bolingbroke and His Circle* (Cambridge, Mass.: Harvard University Press, 1968); *Lord Bolingbroke: Historical Writings*, ed. Isaac Kramnick (Chicago and London: University of Chicago Press, 1972); Caroline Robbins, *The Eighteenth-Century Commonwealthman: Studies in the Transmission, Development, and Circumstance of English Liberal Thought from the Restoration of Charles II until the War with the Thirteen Colonies* (Cambridge, Mass.: Harvard University Press, 1959); Harold Trevor Colbourn, *The Lamp of Experience: Whig History and the Intellectual Origins of the American Revolution* (Chapel Hill: University of North Carolina Press, for the Institute of Early American History and Culture at Williamsburg, Va., 1965); and David L. Jacobson, ed., *The English Libertarian Heritage: From the Writings of John Trenchard and Thomas Gordon in The Independent Whig and Cato's Letters* (Indianapolis, Ind.: Bobbs-Merrill, 1965). None of these, however, is nearly so thorough or sound in perspective as Rodger D. Parker, "The Gospel of Opposition: A Study in Eighteenth Century Anglo-American Ideology" (Ph.D. dissertation, Wayne State University, 1975), on which I have relied quite heavily. Few scholars have attempted to establish the connections between the Oppositionists and the American Republicans; Parker does so, as does Bernard Bailyn, in *The Ideological Origins of the American Revolution* (Cambridge, Mass.: Harvard University Press, 1967), to some extent, and as Buel does to a considerably greater extent in *Securing the Revolution*. If, however, one steeps one's self in Opposition ideology and rhetoric, and then studies the arguments of Republicans against the Hamiltonian system, the connection becomes palpably evident. For a quick way to see the connections, one may consult Charles A. Beard, *Economic Origins of Jeffersonian Democracy* (New York: Macmillan, 1915), chapter 7 and the sources cited therein. Though Beard himself was unaware of the English origins of Republican thinking, virtually every word he quoted in that chapter could have been lifted directly from Bolingbroke's Oppositionist journal of the 1730s, *The Craftsman.*

Finally, there is the matter of slaveholding and Jeffersonianism. Most Jeffersonian scholars have treated this subject as if it were only tangential to Republicanism, or have ignored it or tried to explain it away; but there is no escaping the fact that most of the Jeffersonian leaders, excepting those in New York and Pennsylvania, were slaveholders. Moreover, though a great deal has been published on the subject of slavery in recent years, little of the literature offers much in the way of factual analysis of the effects of the institution upon slaveholders—who, after all, were rather more important in shaping American history than were the slaves. A few works do shed some light on the subject, among them being Winthrop D. Jordan, *White over Black: American Attitudes toward the Negro, 1550–1812* (Chapel Hill: University of North Carolina Press, for the Institute of Early American History and Culture at Williamsburg, Va., 1968); James Hugo Johnston, *Race Relations in Virginia & Miscegenation in the South, 1776–1860* (Amherst: University of Massachusetts Press, 1970); Donald L. Robinson, *Slavery in the Structure of American Politics, 1765–1820* (New York: Harcourt, Brace, Jovanovich, 1971); Robert McColley, *Slavery and Jeffersonian Virginia* (Urbana: University of Illinois Press, 1964); Patrick S. Brady, "The Slave Trade and Sectionalism in South Carolina, 1787–1808," *Journal of Southern History* 38:601-620 (1972); and Keith M. Bailor, "John Taylor of Caroline: Continuity, Change, and Discontinuity in Virginia's Sentiments toward Slavery, 1790–1820," *Virginia Magazine of History and Biography* 75:290–304 (1967). Until the subject has been more thoroughly explored from the slaveholder's point of view, one will do well to consult the old classic, Lewis C. Gray's *History of Agriculture in the Southern United States to 1860,* 2 vols. (originally published 1932; republished, Gloucester, Mass.: Peter Smith, 1958).

CHAPTER 2

In addition to the sources cited for chapter 1—especially the studies of states and of ideology—a number of works were valuable in putting together this chapter. The standard work on the Jeffersonians as politicians is Noble E. Cunningham, Jr., *The Jeffersonian Republicans in Power: Party Operations, 1801–1809* (Chapel Hill: University of North Carolina Press, for the Institute of Early American History and Culture at Williamsburg, Va., 1963). I have tempered my reading of the subject by a study of Robert Schweitzer, "A Computer Analysis of Roll Call Votes in the Seventh through Twelfth Congresses" (M.A. thesis, Wayne State University, 1974). Other useful studies include Norman K. Risjord, *The Old Republicans: Southern Conservatism in the Age of Jefferson* (New York: Columbia University Press, 1965); Sydney H. Aronson, *Status and Kinship in the Higher Civil Service: Standards of Selection in the Administrations of John Adams, Thomas Jefferson, and Andrew Jackson* (Cambridge, Mass.: Harvard University Press, 1964); Paul Goodman, "Social Status of Party Leadership: The House of Representatives, 1797–1804," *William and Mary Quarterly*, 3d ser., 5:465–474 (1968); Carl E. Prince, "The Passing of the Aristocracy: Jefferson's Removal of the Federalists, 1801–1805," *Journal of American History* 57:563–575 (1970); and James Sterling Young, *The Washington Community, 1800–1828* (New York: Columbia University Press, 1966).

Among the more useful biographies of Republicans are Dice Robins Anderson, *William Branch Giles: A Study in the Politics of Virginia and the Nation from 1790 to 1830* (originally published 1914; republished, Gloucester, Mass.: Peter Smith, 1965); Frank A. Cassell, *Merchant Congressman in the Young Republic: Samuel Smith of Maryland, 1752–1839* (Madison: University of Wisconsin Press, 1971); Henry Adams, *John Randolph* (originally published 1882; republished, Greenwich, Conn.: Fawcett Publications, 1961); Raymond Walters, Jr., *Albert Gallatin: Jeffersonian Financier and Diplomat* (New York: Macmillan, 1957); Ralph L. Ketcham, *James Madison: A Biography* (New York: Macmillan, 1971), a more balanced and more readable work than Brant's; William H. Gaines, Jr., *Thomas Mann Randolph: Jefferson's Son-in-Law* (Baton Rouge: Louisiana State University Press, 1966); Lowell Hayes Harrison, *John Breckenridge: Jeffersonian Republican* (Louisville, Ky.: Filson Club, 1969); Nathan Schachner, *Aaron Burr: A Biography* (New York: F. A. Stokes, 1937); George Dangerfield, *Chancellor Robert Livingston of New York, 1746–1813* (New York: Harcourt, Brace, 1960); Henry H. Simms, *Life of John Taylor* (Richmond, Va.: William Byrd Press, 1932); and Harry Ammon, *James Monroe: The Quest for National Identity* (New York: McGraw-Hill, 1971).

On administrative policy, the key works are White's *The Jeffersonians* and Balinky's *Albert Gallatin*. On Republicanism and land speculation, a few works are excellent, including C. Peter Magrath, *Yazoo: Law and Politics in the New Republic; the Case of Fletcher v. Peck* (Providence, R.I.: Brown University Press, 1966); Kathryn Turner, "Federalist Policy and the Judiciary Act of 1801," *William and Mary Quarterly*, 3d ser., 22:3–32 (1965); Paul Demund Evans, *The Holland Land Company* (Buffalo, N.Y.: Buffalo Historical Society, 1924); Shaw Livermore, *Early American Land Companies: Their Influence on Corporate Development* (New York: Commonwealth Fund, 1939); Thomas Perkins Abernethy, *From Frontier to Plantation in Tennessee: A Study in Frontier Democracy* (Chapel Hill: University of North Carolina Press, 1932). In a class by itself is Arthur P. Whitaker, *The Mississippi Question, 1795–1803: A Study in Trade, Politics, and Diplomacy* (New York: D. Appleton-Century, 1934).

On the Jeffersonians and the courts, the proper place to begin is with two older works that are highly critical of the Republicans: Albert J. Beveridge, *The Life of John Marshall*, 4 vols. (Boston, Mass.: Houghton, Mifflin, 1916–1919); and Charles Warren, *The Supreme Court in United States History*, 2 vols. (Boston: Little, Brown, 1926). See also Kathryn Turner, "The Midnight Judges," *University of Pennsylvania Law Review* 109:494–523 (1960–1961); Patterson, *The Constitutional Principles of Thomas Jefferson*; and Jerry W. Knudson, "The Jeffersonian Assault on the Federalist Judiciary, 1802–1805," *American Journal of Legal History* 14:55–75 (1970).

CHAPTER 3

Of the works previously cited, those most useful for this chapter are Dangerfield, *Livingston*; Ammon, *Monroe*; Brant, *Madison*, vol. 4; Ketcham, *Madison*; Malone, *First Term*; Adams, *History*; Whitaker, *Mississippi Question*; Balinky, *Gallatin*; Nettels, *Emergence of a National Economy*; Banner, *To the Hartford Convention*; Abernethy, *Frontier to Plantation in Tennessee*; and Coatsworth, "American Trade with European Colonies." On relations with Britain, see Alfred L. Burt, *The United States, Great Britain, and British North America: From the Revolution to the Establishment of Peace after the War of 1812* (New Haven, Conn.: Yale University Press, 1940); Bradford Perkins, *The First Rapprochement: England and the United States, 1795–1805* (Philadelphia: University of Pennsylvania Press, 1955); and Robert Ernst, *Rufus King: American Federalist* (Chapel Hill: University of North Carolina Press, 1968). In regard to France and its American possessions, see Stuart Sprague, "Jefferson, Kentucky and the Closing of the Port of New Orleans, 1802–03," *Register of the Kentucky Historical Society* (1972); Elijah

Wilson Lyon, *Louisiana in French Diplomacy, 1759–1804* (Norman: University of Oklahoma Press, 1934); Rayford W. Logan, *The Diplomatic Relations of the United States with Haiti, 1776–1891* (Chapel Hill: University of North Carolina Press, 1941); Charles Callan Tansill, *The United States and Santo Domingo, 1798–1873: A Chapter in Caribbean Diplomacy* (originally published 1938; republished, Gloucester, Mass.: Peter Smith, 1967); Cyril L. R. James, *The Black Jacobins* (2d ed., rev.; New York: Vintage Books, 1963). For Federalist reaction to the Louisiana Purchase, see Henry Adams, ed., *Documents Relating to New England Federalism, 1800–1815* (Boston: Little, Brown, 1877). On the navy and Tripoli, see Louis B. Wright and Julia H. Macleod, *The First Americans in North Africa: William Eaton's Struggle for a Vigorous Policy against the Barbary Pirates, 1799–1805* (Princeton, N.J.: Princeton University Press, 1945); Gardner W. Allen, *Our Navy and the Barbary Corsairs* (Boston: Houghton Mifflin, 1905); Harold H. Sprout and Margaret Sprout, *The Rise of American Naval Power* (Princeton, N.J.: Princeton University Press, 1967); Fletcher Pratt, *The Compact History of the United States Navy* (New York: Hawthorn Books, 1957); and Forrest McDonald, *The Boys Were Men: The American Navy in the Age of Fighting Sail* (New York: G. P. Putnam's Sons, 1971). For West Florida, the indispensable tool is James A. Servies, "A Bibliography of West Florida," 3 vols., typescript copy in the library of the University of West Florida, Pensacola, which has a large collection of the relevant materials. The classic work on the subject is Isaac J. Cox, *The West Florida Controversy, 1798–1813* (Baltimore, Md.: The Johns Hopkins Press, 1918).

CHAPTER 4

Christopher McKee, *Edward Preble: A Naval Biography, 1761–1807* (Annapolis, Md.: Naval Institute Press, 1972); Fletcher Pratt, *Preble's Boys* (New York: Sloane, 1950); McDonald, *Boys Were Men*; Balinky, *Gallatin*; Plumer, *Memorandum*; Schachner, *Burr*; Lynn W. Turner, "The Impeachment of John Pickering," *American Historical Review* 54:485–507 (1949), and *William Plumer of New Hampshire, 1759–1850* (Chapel Hill: University of North Carolina Press, for the Institute of Early American History and Culture at Williamsburg, Va., 1962); Warren, *Supreme Court*; Beveridge, *Marshall*; David Hackett Fischer, *The Revolution of American Conservatism: The Federalist Party in the Era of Jeffersonian Democracy* (New York: Harper & Row, 1965); Linda K. Kerber, *Federalists in Dissent: Imagery and Ideology in Jeffersonian*

America (Ithaca, N.Y.: Cornell University Press, 1970); Banner, *To the Hartford Convention*; Malone, *First Term*; Adams, *First Administration*, vol. 2; Adams, *New England Federalism*; Adams, *Randolph*; William Cabell Bruce, *John Randolph of Roanoke, 1773–1833*, 2 vols. (New York: G. P. Putnam's Sons, 1922); Ernest Wilder Spaulding, *His Excellency, George Clinton* (New York: Macmillan, 1938); Matthew L. Davis, *Memoirs of Aaron Burr, with Miscellaneous Selections from His Correspondence*, vol. 2 (New York: Harper & Brothers, 1858); Samuel H. Wandell and Meade Minnigerode, *Aaron Burr*, 2 vols. (New York: G. P. Putnam's Sons, 1925); Richard B. Lillich, "The Chase Impeachment," *American Journal of Legal History* 4:49–72 (1960); Richard E. Ellis, *The Jeffersonian Crisis: Courts and Politics in the Young Republic* (New York: Oxford University Press, 1971); *Interview in Weehawken: The Burr-Hamilton Duel, as Told in the Original Documents*, ed. Harold C. Syrett and Jean G. Cooke, with an Introduction and Conclusion by Willard M. Wallace (Middleton, Conn.: Wesleyan University Press, 1960); Cunningham, *Jeffersonians in Power*; Anderson, *Giles*; Magrath, *Yazoo*; Charles H. Haskins, "The Yazoo Land Companies," vol. 5, pt. 4, pp. 393–437, of *Papers of the American Historical Association*, 1891 (New York: G. P. Putnam's Sons, 1891); James Fairfax McLaughlin, *Matthew Lyon: The Hampden of Congress* (New York: Wynkoop, Hallenbach, Crawford Co., 1900).

CHAPTER 5

Clifford L. Egan, "The United States, France, and West Florida, 1803–1807," *Florida Historical Quarterly* 47:227–252 (1968–1969); Ammon, *Monroe*; Dangerfield, *Livingston*; Burt, *United States, Great Britain, and British North America*; Bradford Perkins, *Prologue to War: England and the United States, 1805–1812* (Berkeley and Los Angeles: University of California Press, 1961); Herbert Heaton, "Non-Importation, 1806–1812," *Journal of Economic History* 1:178–198 (1941); Drew R. McCoy, "Republicanism and American Foreign Policy: James Madison and the Political Economy of Commercial Discrimination, 1789 to 1794," *William and Mary Quarterly* 31:633–646 (1974); Brant, *Madison*; Ernst, *King*; Arthur P. Whitaker, *The United States and the Independence of Latin America, 1800–1830* (Baltimore, Md.: The Johns Hopkins Press, 1941); Adams, *Second Administration*, vol. 1; Malone, *Second Term*; Cox, *West Florida Controversy*; Adams, *Randolph*; Bruce, *Randolph*; Helen R. Pinkney, *Christopher Gore: Federalist of Massachusetts, 1758–1827* (Waltham, Mass.: Gore Place Society, 1969);

Plumer, *Memorandum*; Tansill, *Santo Domingo*; Cassell, *Smith*; James F. Zimmerman, *Impressment of American Seamen* (New York: Columbia University Press, 1925); John S. Pancake, "The 'Invisibles': A Chapter in the Opposition to President Madison," *Journal of Southern History* 21:17–37 (1955); William S. Robertson, *The Life of Miranda*, 2 vols. (Chapel Hill: University of North Carolina Press, 1929); James R. Jacobs, *Tarnished Warrior: Major-General James Wilkinson* (New York: Macmillan, 1938).

The Burr conspiracy requires considerable comment. In addition to the various biographies already cited and the most recent biography—Herbert S. Parmet and Marie B. Hecht, *Aaron Burr: Portrait of an Ambitious Man* (New York: Macmillan, 1967), which adds little that is new—there are two principal works on the subject. One is Walter F. McCaleb, *The Aaron Burr Conspiracy; and, A New Light on Aaron Burr*, which combines two books, the first originally published in 1903 and revised in 1936, the other originally published in 1963 (New York: Argosy-Antiquarian, 1966). The second work is Thomas P. Abernethy, *The Burr Conspiracy* (New York: Oxford University Press, 1954). McCaleb's argument is that Burr was entirely innocent of intent to do anything except attack Spain in the event of war, and that the charges against him reflected Jefferson's vindictiveness and Wilkinson's duplicity; Abernethy's argument is that Burr was a man of boundless ambition and treachery who intended to separate the West from the United States and that he was essentially guilty as charged in the indictments against him. Most historians have accepted Abernethy's version, but I have long been unconvinced. My suspicions were heightened in the 1960s, when a student of mine at Brown University, Thomas Dunne, spent most of his spare time for four years as an undergraduate in examining all the manuscript source materials on Burr that he could find—in the New York Historical Society, Princeton University Library, the Library of Congress, the University of Virginia Library, the Newberry Library, and various other places. Mr. Dunne reported to me that in his researches he had never encountered a shred of *direct* evidence that Burr was ever guilty of any public wrongdoing. Since then I have gone over most of the same material and reached the same conclusion.

That, however, left the "conspiracy" entirely unexplained. After poring over all the published works—original and secondary—that bear upon the subject, I assigned another student the tasks of reexamining those works and compiling an outline chronology of every event that could even remotely be viewed as bearing on the conspiracy. The result was a lengthy paper by the Reverend Robert Miller, "A Calendar of the Aaron Burr Conspiracy" (Wayne State University, 1971, manuscript in my possession), which revealed discrepancies and unexplained facts in both McCaleb's and Abernethy's accounts. The version that I have presented here and in chapter 6 represents an effort to reconcile what is known about the subject; I may be wrong, but this explanation satisfies me, whereas no other explanation does.

CHAPTER 6

In regard to Burr, see the note for chapter 5, plus Levy, *Jefferson and Civil Liberties*, and William Coker, "Peter Bryan Bruin: Soldier, Frontiersman, and Judge" (unpublished manuscript, lent to me by the author). One other matter should be mentioned. Various decoded versions of Burr's famous letter to Wilkinson of July 29, 1806, have appeared in print; Adams, McCaleb, Abernethy, and Parmet and Hecht, for instance, reproduce it in whole or in part. The manuscripts department of the Alderman Library, University of Virginia, Charlottesville, has a number of manuscript versions— for example, in the McGregor Collection, Accession Number 5726. None of these, however, is the letter that Burr wrote: that letter, or rather one of the two original copies, is in the Graf Collection, numbers 502 and 503, at the Newberry Library, Chicago, and it is of course in code. The key to the cipher that Burr used is in the Burr Papers in the Princeton University Library.

As to other subjects treated in this chapter, most of the relevant works have already been cited. The more important of these are Malone, *Second Term*; Adams, *Second Administration*; Egan, "United States, France, and West Florida"; Ammon, *Monroe*; Whitaker, *United States and Latin American Independence*; Burt, *United States, Great Britain, and British North America*; Perkins, *Prologue to War*; Heaton, "Non-Importation"; Brant, *Madison*; Anderson, *Giles*; Beveridge, *Marshall*; Adams, *Randolph*; Bruce, *Randolph*; McColley, *Slavery in Jeffersonian Virginia*; Cassell, *Samuel Smith*; and Brady, "Slave Trade and Sectionalism in South Carolina."

There are, however, some other important works, including Samuel W. Bryant, *The Sea and the States: A Maritime History of the American People* (New York: Thomas Y. Crowell, 1947); William Cohen, "Thomas Jefferson and the Problem of Slavery," *Journal of American History* 56:503–526 (1969); Robert K. Faulkner, "John Marshall and the Burr Trial," *Journal of American History* 53:247–258 (1966); Anthony Steel, "Impressment in the Monroe-Pinkney Negotiation, 1806–1807," *American Historical Review* 57:352–369

(1952), and "More Light on the *Chesapeake*," *Mariner's Mirror* 39:243–265 (1953); and William E. B. Du Bois, *The Suppression of the African Slave-Trade to the United States of America, 1638– 1870* (originally published 1896; republished, with a new introduction by A. Norman Klein, New York: Schocken Books, 1969).

CHAPTER 7

Works previously cited that are most useful for the present chapter are Adams, *Second Administration*; Malone, *Second Term*; Brant, *Madison*; Levy, *Jefferson and Civil Liberties*; Burt, *United States, Great Britain, and British North America*; Perkins, *Prologue to War*; Ammon, *Monroe*; Williamson, *Vermont*; Cunningham, *Jeffersonians in Power*; and White, *The Jeffersonians*. The last-named work contains an excellent concise summary of all the embargo legislation.

There are two full-length studies of the embargo: Walter W. Jennings, *The American Embargo, 1807–1809* (Iowa City: University of Iowa Studies, 1921), and Louis M. Sears, *Jefferson and the Embargo* (Durham, N.C.: Duke University Press, 1927). The latter work contains useful information, but interpretively it is palpable nonsense: it attempts to make Jefferson out as a pacifist, but contains abundant evidence refuting its own thesis. Useful in understanding Jefferson's military policy are Richard A. Erney, "The Public Life of Henry Dearborn" (Ph.D. dissertation, Columbia University, 1957); Samuel P. Huntington, *The Soldier and the State: The Theory and Politics of Civil-Military Relations* (Cambridge, Mass.: Harvard University Press, 1957); and James R. Jacobs, *The Beginning of the U.S. Army, 1783–1812* (Princeton, N.J.: Princeton University Press, 1947). Some light on the legal aspects of the embargo is shed in Donald G. Morgan, *Justice William Johnson: The First Dissenter* (Columbia: University of South Carolina Press, 1954). The Federalists' reaction to the embargo and/or accounts of their electioneering in 1808 are covered in Fischer, *Revolution of American Conservatism*; Kerber, *Federalists in Dissent*; Banner, *To the Hartford Convention*; Pinkney, *Christopher Gore*; Samuel Eliot Morison, *Harrison Gray Otis, 1765–1848: The Urbane Federalist* (originally published in 2 vols., 1913; rewritten and republished in 1 vol., Boston: Houghton Mifflin, 1969); Adams, *Documents Relating to New England Federalism*; Morton Borden, *The Federalism of James A. Bayard* (New York: Columbia University Press, 1955); and Robin D. S. Higham, "The Port of Boston and the Embargo of 1807–1809," *American Neptune* 16:189–210 (1956).

Index